Education and the Family

D0081926

Why it is that success, deprivation or disadvantage are so often passed down intergenerationally? What part does education play?

The educational achievement of parents is often reflected in that of their children and there are many underlying causes for such a relationship. *Education and the Family* argues that government policy has an important role to play in addressing this inequality even though many of the causes lie within the home. Although each child should be supported to achieve his or her objectives, differences in the willingness or capabilities of families to take advantage of educational opportunities exacerbate social class differences and limit actual equality of opportunity for many. Understanding the causes of this transmission is key to both tackling social class inequality and expanding the skill base of the economy.

By providing an overview of academic and policy thinking in relation to the role of the family, this book explores the educational success of children. It focuses on the education of the parents but also considers how the family – compared to wider, external influences such as schools – is a driver of differences in educational outcomes. It concludes with a consideration of what policy-makers are attempting to do about this key issue and why, and how this will impact on schools and teachers.

This book will interest researchers and academics in education and social policy, as well as teachers and other education and social policy practitioners.

Leon Feinstein is Professor of Education and Social Policy and Director, **Kathryn Duckworth** is Research Officer and **Ricardo Sabates** is Senior Research Officer, all at the Centre for Research on the Wider Benefits of Learning, Institute of Education, University of London, UK.

Foundations and Futures of Education

Series Editors:
Peter Aggleton *University of London, UK*
David Halpin *University of London, UK*
Sally Power *Cardiff University, UK*

Education and the Family

Passing success across the generations

Leon Feinstein,
Kathryn Duckworth and
Ricardo Sabates

Routledge
Taylor & Francis Group

LONDON AND NEW YORK

MT

First published 2008
by Routledge
2 Park Square, Milton Park, Abingdon, Oxon OX14 4RN

Simultaneously published in the USA and Canada
by Routledge
270 Madison Avenue, New York, NY 10016

*Routledge is an imprint of the Taylor & Francis Group, an
informa business*

© 2008 Leon Feinstein, Kathryn Duckworth and Ricardo Sabates

Typeset in Galliard by
Florence Production Ltd, Stoodleigh, Devon
Printed and bound in Great Britain by
TJ International, Padstow, Cornwall

British Library Cataloguing in Publication Data
A catalogue record for this book is available from the British Library

Library of Congress Cataloging in Publication Data
Feinstein, L.
    Education and the family : passing success across the
    generations/Leon Feinstein, Kathryn Duckworth and
    Ricardo Sabates.
        p. cm.
    1. Home and school – Great Britain.   2. Parents – Education
    – Great Britain.   3. Parental influences – Great Britain.
    4. Success – Great Britain.   5. Educational sociology – Great
    Britain.   I. Duckworth, Kathryn.   II. Sabates, Ricardo.
    III. Title.
    LC225.33.G7F45 2008
    371.19′2–dc22   2007051680

ISBN10: 0–415–39636–0 (hbk)
ISBN10: 0–415–39637–9 (pbk)
ISBN10: 0–203–89492–8 (ebk)

ISBN13: 978–0–415–39636–3 (hbk)
ISBN13: 978–0–415–39637–0 (pbk)
ISBN13: 978–0–203–89492–7 (ebk)

11/9/09

Contents

Illustrations

Figures

Tables

Series editors' foreword

One of the most remarkable transformations over the last 200 years has been the universal development of mass education. With each successive decade, provision has expanded to encompass more learners at more stages in their lives. The ambitions for education systems have also expanded to encompass objectives as diverse as personal fulfilment and well-being, cultural transmission, active citizenship, social cohesion and, increasingly, international economic competitiveness.

The broad range of ambitions and the sheer pace of change have created a climate in which it is sometimes difficult to stand back and make sense of what education is for and where it should be going. *Foundations and Futures of Education* provides an opportunity to engage with these fundamental issues in new and exciting ways. The series adopts a broad and interdisciplinary stance, including historical, philosophical, sociological, psychological and comparative approaches as well as those from within the fields of media and cultural studies. The series also reflects wider conceptions of education embedded in concepts such as 'the knowledge economy', 'the learning society' and 'lifelong learning'.

In each volume, the academic rigour of the arguments is balanced with accessible writing, which we hope will engage the interest of those working in and for education, as well as a wide range of undergraduate and postgraduate students. Although it will be clear that there are few 'easy answers' to many of the questions currently being asked, we hope that you will find the debates and dialogues exciting and thought-provoking.

In this book, Leon Feinstein, Kathryn Duckworth and Ricardo Sabates take a close look at the relationship between the family and education. Within educational research it is often assumed that we understand this relationship. To some extent this is true, inasmuch as we know that children from particular kinds of families are likely to do better or worse at school than children from other kinds of families. However, while we may be able to identify broad patterns, we are often unable to identify which factors are really important. How much does the level of parental education actually matter? And if it is important, which aspects of that education appear most significant? To what extent do other factors have a bearing? Does parental education matter more or less than family size, structure or income? And what about other contextual factors, such as pre-schooling, schooling and the neighbourhood?

Feinstein, Duckworth and Sabates attempt to answer these, and other, vital questions through a detailed look at the available evidence. Meticulous in its examination of the subtle interrelationships between different factors, the book provides an unparalleled synthesis of research in this area. The questions it asks and answers are not only important for researchers, they are also of the utmost relevance for all those who are interested in addressing the intergenerational transmission of educational inequalities. The authors conclude their scholarly account by drawing out its implications for policy and practice in education.

Preface

This book has been written by a group of colleagues at the Centre for Research on the Wider Benefits of Learning, a research centre funded since 1999 by the UK government's Department of Education to investigate the importance of education for the wider well-being of individuals, families and societies. This has been a time of rapid change in policy, made evident by the changes in the name of the government department that in 1999 was called the Department for Education and Employment, changed to the Department for Education and Skills and in 2007 split into the Department for Children, Schools and Families (DCSF) and a separate Department for Innovation, Universities and Skills.

These changes show the increasing emphasis on children and families as a focus of policy in the UK, captured in the important Every Child Matters legislation, which made the wider well-being of children an important responsibility of schools and related agencies. Alongside this has been a concern for equality of opportunity that has been expressed in terms of concerns about child poverty, social immobility, the achievement gap and debates about meritocracy. Yet, throughout the ten years of Blair's government, these concerns were always secondary to a focus on rising standards in schools and on economic growth and productivity.

We will see what the next decade holds for trends in policy but, as this book makes apparent, inequality of opportunity is very closely related to inequality of outcomes as the outcomes of one generation create or block opportunity for the next. We focus on education as an important driver of opportunity but also as a driver of social inequality. It stands alongside income and occupation as a key marker of opportunity or risk and, although we can be optimistic about the exciting possibilities that good experiences of learning and education can provide, we must also be concerned about the impact of negative experiences of learning and particularly of inequality in access.

This book focuses on the family and, as we write, this has once again become a contested site of political debate. We caution against this politicisation of family structure. We present evidence that family relationships are of great importance for child development, achievement and well-being, but so are a great many other factors. The book argues against the notion that there are 'magic bullets' in policy that politicians can point to for easy quick wins. It is regrettable when politicians attempt to do this as it betrays a deep lack of understanding about the true complexities and difficulties of family life, particularly for those experiencing the highest levels of poverty, family conflict and/or social exclusion.

The book concludes with an analysis of how preventive social and education policy may draw on the skill and local knowledge of practitioners and information about child development and family context to provide support to those in need so as to reduce the long-term consequences of risk and disadvantage. We show that it is not ignorance about who needs help that limits our capacity to deliver it. The education system could evolve rapidly in the next few years to meet the challenges set out here and elsewhere or it could continue in its traditionalist form, focusing on school standards within a limited set of structures. We hope for the former and for a time of innovation, collaboration and broadening of opportunity.

Leon Feinstein
Institute of Education, University of London
24 October 2007

Acknowledgements

This book was written while the authors were working for the Centre for Research on the Wider Benefits of Learning (WBL). This research would not have been possible without the essential contributions from the Centre's core funders, the Department for Children, Schools and Families (DCSF). We would also like to thank the Number 10 Strategy Unit and HM Treasury for their funding of, and interest in, the research in Chapter 8 on preventive policy action.

A great many academics, policy-makers and practitioners have discussed this work with us and made telling contributions that have shaped the content and direction of this book. We are indebted to contributions from colleagues in the WBL who worked with us on elements of the book, in particular John Bynner, Tom Schuller and Cathie Hammond. Rachel Barker and Sue Stone (now retired) from the DCSF also made helpful comments on earlier drafts of this work. We are grateful to members of the WBL Family Advisory Panel who commented on this research, as well as to colleagues at the Center for the Analysis of Pathways from Childhood to Adulthood (CAPCA), University of Michigan, in particular Pamela Davis-Kean, Katherine Magnuson, Jacquelynne Eccles and Steve Peck, with whom we discussed our conceptual framework a great deal. Helpful conversations were held with Nick Pierce (Institute for Public Policy Research), Will Paxton (previously at the DCSF), Barbara Hearne (National Children's Bureau), Caroline Abrahams (Local Government Agency) and Vidhya Alekson (previously at Social Market Foundation and HM Treasury). David Budge (Institute of Education) also made helpful comments on the text. We would like to thank the series editors for inviting us to be part of this series and, in particular, for their patience, persistence and judicious editing.

We would like to thank the Department for Education and Skills (DfES) and HM Treasury for permission to reproduce material developed in research programmes funded by them. The views that are expressed in this work are those of the authors and do not necessarily reflect the views of these government departments. All errors and omissions are our own.

Finally, we would like to thank our friends and families for their under-standing while we were busy with this task. This book is dedicated to Max Feinstein-Henry, Mike and Sheena Duckworth, and Rachel, Oliver and Asher Sabates.

Abbreviations

ADD	attention deficit disorder
ADHD	attention deficit hyperactivity disorder
BCS 70	1970 British Cohort Study
BHPS	British Household Panel Survey
BMI	body mass index
CAPCA	Centre for the Analysis of Pathways from Childhood to Adulthood
CQO	Childcare Qualities and Outcomes
DCSF	Department for Children, Schools and Families
DfES	Department for Education and Skills
ECM	Every Child Matters
EPPE	Effective Provision of Pre-school Education
HLE	home learning environment
HOME	Home Observation for Measurement of the Environmental Scale
HOME-SF	Home Observation for Measurement of the Environmental Scale – Short Form
IV	instrumental variable
LEA	local education authority
NBER-TH	US National Bureau of Economic Research – Thorndike-Hagen sample
NCDS	National Child Development Study
NEET	not in employment, education or training
NIACE	National Institute of Adult Continuing Education
NICHD	National Institute of Child Health and Development
NLSY	National Longitudinal Survey of Youth
NVQ	National Vocational Qualification
OECD	Organisation for Economic Cooperation and Development
PIRLS	Progress in International Reading Literacy Study

PSID	US Panel Study of Income Dynamics
PSID-CDS	US Panel Study of Income Dynamics-Child Development Study
RCTs	randomised control trials
SES	socio-economic status
SEI	Socio-Economic Index
SEN	special educational needs
WBL	Wider Benefits of Learning

1 Introduction

With its prioritisation of 'education, education, and education', the incoming UK Labour government of 1997 emphasised the potentially crucial role that the education system might play in the service of meeting wide-ranging government objectives. However, these objectives have varied widely from concerns about economic productivity to health, citizenship and social mobility, and it has never been entirely clear in policy, theory or practice whether the education system is the answer to the problem of social immobility and entrenched disadvantage, or part of the problem. Perhaps much depends on what we mean by 'education', how we view the role of education in the lives of individuals, what objectives we set the education system and how we set out to implement these objectives.

This book is concerned with the question of social mobility and the deep and abiding connection between the wealth and resources of parents and that of their children. Why it is that success, deprivation or disadvantage are so often passed down intergenerationally? How do the mechanisms that drive inequalities of opportunity work and what are the pathways for intergenerational effects? Understanding the nature and causes of this transmission is important for tackling social class inequality, expanding the skill base of the UK economy and developing a more sustainable future.

Our emphasis in this book is on the particular role that education plays in passing down success and failure across generations. Considering theory and evidence, we put forward a model to understand the pervading influence of parents' education in the intergenerational transmission of educational advantage. The focus is on the education of the parents but this requires a consideration of all other key features of the family environment. Therefore, we also lay out the evidence to ascertain which factors are most important, how such factors are in part pathways for the effect of education and how the different factors interact.

The focus of the book is very much on the family, but we contextualise the family within wider, external influences, primarily those at the community level, and consider the question of how important the family is relative to schools and neighbourhoods as a driver of national-level differences in educational outcomes. The focus on analysis of the family enables clarification of some of the processes at work there and of how they play out, constrained and provided for by micro-level (individual), meso-level (community) and macro-level (national) factors.

Background

It is well established that there is a strong relationship between the educational achievement of parents and that of their children. There are many underlying influences behind such a relationship. Some, such as genes, are beyond immediate policy intervention. Others, such as income and parenting, are more appropriate as sites of policy intervention, but are nonetheless strongly contested both in terms of the extent to which they play a causal role and the extent to which they should be thought of as fundamental policy mechanisms.

Despite these controversies, this book takes the view that policy interventions are required. The intergenerational transmission of educational success is a key driver of the persistence of social class differences in advanced societies such as the UK, and a barrier to equality of opportunity. Although each child should be supported to achieve their full potential, differences in the capabilities and resources of families to take advantage of educational opportunities exacerbate social class differences and limit actual equality of opportunity for many.

This book is about education and the family in two senses, then. In the first sense, it is about the role of the educational attainments of parents in the development of educational success for their children. In the second sense, it is concerned with how education can be a site for policy now, with the role of schools and other educational institutions in the development of children's achievement, and with the complex interactions between home and school in the formation of positive outcomes for children.

The context

Defining success

People differ in how they define success and have political and ethical debates about it, although there are also some widely accepted elements in our culture. It may be that, for most people, access to wealth, power and control over resources is a crucial element in their judgement of success. Others may chase more abstract aims such as fame, compassion, artistic endeavour and so on, but we need have no single notion of what is meant by success.

If we define success as an individual's achievement of their own aims, then it may become clear that, when we talk about passing success across the generations, we are referring not just to access to material resources (important though this always is), but also to access to wider features of human potential and to social networks, or identity and social capital, as they are sometimes termed. However, aims are not exogenous to this system; they are formed within the particular social and economic contexts of individuals, and so one cannot take their achievement to be an objective or value-free indicator of success. Furthermore, one cannot say that someone has experienced success in their life and development solely on the basis of achieving their own objectives, if their life and its context have already led to them diminishing those objectives. Therefore, the democratic perspective, which says that success is whatever people mean by it, is not without problems for an analysis seeking to understand the role of education in impacting on intergenerational patterns of access to resources and advantage.

For these reasons, we primarily associate success in this book with school achievement, such as scores in tests of ability in reading and maths, and educational attainment, such as gaining qualifications and continuing into further and/or higher education. We do not mean to suggest that achieving academically should be the benchmark of personal value or of success generally. In fact, for many children and young people succeeding in school is *not* a good yardstick of success in those terms, and this conflict over the values and objectives of young people is an important element of the dynamics at play in the intergenerational transmission of resources and of education policy failure. Moreover, there is growing recognition of the importance of broader sets of capabilities that support and interact with more traditional notions of academic success, such as attention-related skills, social and communication skills, and behavioural self-regulation. Nonetheless, educational success does appear to lead to, or be widely associated with, access to most other resources that are important in life and are broadly sought after.

A framework for analysis

The topic of the intergenerational transmission of educational success and advantage is broad and diverse and has been approached in different disciplines, with different methodologies, addressing subtly different research questions. Even within disciplines, authors adopt different empirical strategies. Researchers have used a great many different models to explore the influence of different features of family background on children's development. These different models control and test for different factors, in different combinations, in cross-sectional as well as longitudinal datasets.

Parents' education is a major influence on children's educational success, both directly and through indirect pathways such as income. As such, in quantitative analysis parental education is sometimes modelled as a key causal variable, sometimes as an explanatory or mediating factor and sometimes as a background characteristic (a control). Guo and Harris (2000) model the effect of income on attainment, entering parental education as a control. In many of their specifications, however, the effect of parental education actually proves bigger than the effect of income, but since parental education is not their focus, its actual effect, role and size are rather underplayed. Furthermore, much of the relevant literature here has focused not on understanding the mechanisms through which the intergenerational transmission of educational success occurs, but on exploring only one link in the possible pathways of transmission. Thus, clarifying the role and importance of education and its effects is not easy.

Understanding the possible relationships and the conceptual premises that follow quickly leads to a considerable amount of complexity. In order to understand, model and quantify the role of education in the intergenerational transmission of advantage, it is helpful to use a framework that can place these different strands of research in a common context that can cope with a large degree of interaction between key features of the individual, their family and the wider society. Doing so also enables assessment of the mechanisms involved and their relative importance. Therefore, to structure our presentation of theory and evidence here, we draw on a model of human development influenced by work in the field of developmental psychology, most notably the work of Uri Bronfenbrenner (1979, 1986; Bronfenbrenner and Crouter, 1983). The great advantage of this framework is that it allows for a focus on relationships between the many important factors, rather than a simple list of influences.

This perspective also provides a framework within which to combine economic perspectives with those from other disciplines. One objective has been to present the valuable perspectives described in the developmental literature to those more versed in sociological and economic literature and vice versa. This framework, its origins and how we conceptualise the influence of parents' education in transmitting success across the generations is described in detail in Chapter 3.

An overview

Our starting point, then, is the strong – but by no means necessary or deterministic – correlation between the educational success of parents and that of children. The book fits within three wider concerns: first, the processes and pathways involved in the intergenerational transmission of opportunity generally; second, the effects and importance of education; and third, the implications for education and wider policy. To this end, the book is set out in three separate parts.

PART I *Understanding and conceptualising the importance of parents' education*

In Chapter 2, we begin by setting out some of the issues around defining and measuring education. We go on to summarise evidence on the role of parents' education in passing down educational success and advantage across the generations. The evidence suggests that this role is substantial. Finally, we review some of the most recent empirical evidence aimed at establishing whether the education of parents has a causal impact on the development and life chances of their children and discuss some of the methodological issues around isolating education effects.

In Chapter 3, we outline the general theoretical framework that we use to explain the role of education and describe our conceptual model for understanding the ways in which parents' education influences children's school achievement. We highlight the advantages of this model and discuss its complementarities with other models of intergenerational transfer and social mobility. We also point to potential weaknesses of our approach and set out necessary caveats.

PART II *The influence of parents' education: a review of the evidence*

The centrepiece of the book is a review of the role of the educational achievement of parents in the school achievement of their children. Parents' education is a major influence both directly and via other channels. Our ecologically framed model for understanding the role of parents' education in their children's own educational success attempts to capture this complexity. It has at its centre interactions between parents and children; dynamic processes that support, sustain or hinder successful development. These processes are termed 'proximal' in the ecological model because they are closest to the day-to-day lived experience of the child and impact directly on developmental outcomes. These processes are constrained and influenced by the key features or particular characteristics of the family. Factors such as mental health, parents' beliefs and attitudes and the availability of resources influence the more proximal interactions between parents and children. The family unit is itself influenced by wider social, economic and demographic features, such as parental income, family structure and the education of parents. These factors are termed 'distal' in the ecological model because they are more descriptive factors of a family's socio-economic situation, typically exerting their influence through pathways of mediating factors rather than shaping outcomes directly.

In Part II, we take each of these three main categories of influence and evaluate the empirical evidence on the importance of the main factors in each of these categories. Chapter 4 presents evidence on the influences of proximal processes, Chapter 5 on the influences pertaining to the key features of the family and Chapter 6 on distal family factors. In this way we lay out the evidence to ascertain which factors are most important, how such factors are in part a channel for the effect of education and how the different factors interact. Other contexts besides the family are also important. Pre-schools, schools, peer groups and neighbourhoods provide pathways for effects of family background and so contribute to the intergenerational transmission of educational success. The importance of these other contexts and their relations with the family unit are reviewed in Chapter 7.

PART III *Policy and the wider responsibilities of education: early preventive action*

In the UK, the relationship between home and school has become increasingly a focus of policy, both through the recognition of the importance of home factors in the formation of school achievement and through the recognition of the school as a site for engagement in wider aspects of personal and social development. With the reforms of Every Child Matters (ECM) in England and related legislation in other UK nations, the education system is increasingly seen as a site for wider aspects of social policy that go beyond a narrow focus on educational achievement. Thus educational and social policy have become, and may continue to become, increasingly intertwined. Therefore, this book also considers the implications of this ecological perspective for education and wider social policy.

In Part III, we report findings from a quantitative study of whether it is possible for policy intervention to identify children at risk of adult deprivation from early signals. Chapter 8 presents this new evidence to support debate on this new direction for education and social policy. The starting point for the analysis is the objective of assessing the practicality of early preventive intervention to reduce childhood risk, adult deprivation and the intergenerational persistence of inequality and disadvantage. The policy framework for the analysis is that of progressive universalism, that is, the objective of providing support and intervention on the basis of need within a universal system recognising the entitlement of all to such support. We summarise findings from our own recent research using large-sample UK data about the extent to which information about children and their family environments is predictive of later outcomes. The outcomes of special interest here are those that tend to be associated with personal difficulty and risk for young people and adults, and the social cost for those in their environment and wider society. We also provide an assessment of the extent of persistence and change in childhood risk of adult outcomes as children pass through into adolescence. We go on to assess the levels of change in risk status through childhood, and model the implications of this for the assessment of the value and cost of different intervention scenarios.

It is important to emphasise that, although it is possible to identify childhood risk and to predict likely outcomes for groups at risk on average, it is never possible to predict with certainty the outcome for any individual child. One can make a forecast of likely outcomes and use it, for example, to assess the cost-effectiveness and social value of a set of possible interventions, but this is not the same as suggesting that the future of any child is predetermined. That would not only deny the possibility of intervention, but would also lead to stigmatising effects that would undermine the primary purpose of the intervention. The longitudinal design of these data enables us to assess the level of accuracy in the extent to which we can identify those at risk using early childhood information about family context and child development.

In our view, these findings offer a challenge to which current central and local government should respond with appropriate and measured policy in the interests of social inclusion, personal welfare and the wider economic and social development of the UK. The relationship between childhood risk and high cost or high harm outcomes in adolescence or adulthood is not deterministic, mechanistic or inevitable. There are many steps on the pathway from risk to outcome. There are children at risk who do not experience harmful outcomes and there are children with low apparent or observable risk who do. Therefore, policy responses must allow for flexibility and change. Administrative data should always be augmented by local-level practitioner knowledge and appropriate interventions should also be selected by local practitioners, who should work closely alongside communities and agencies to avoid rigid tracking or excessive and unnecessary stigmatisation of vulnerable young people and their families.

There are challenges from the political left, right and centre to the view that it is the role of the Government to intervene or engage heavily in the domestic sphere. The book concludes in Chapter 9 with a consideration of these debates, and gives a view of what policy-makers are attempting to do and why.

Part I

Understanding and conceptualising the importance of education

2 Understanding the importance of parents' education

The introductory chapter outlined our interest in understanding the role of parents' education in the intergenerational transmission of educational success. But 'education' is a wide-ranging and very general term used to refer in very different ways to the experience and/or results of learning undertaken primarily in institutional settings, such as schools and colleges. The very breadth of this term often conceals or glosses over a number of important distinctions of meaning that are important for a consideration of the impacts of education. For example, there is an important distinction between participation in a learning opportunity, such as doing a degree or taking an evening class, on the one hand, and actual learning on the other. As such, there are some very different channels for the effects of education depending on what is meant by it. Similarly, the different ways in which education can be measured have implications for understanding the effects it can have. We therefore begin this chapter with a discussion of some of the ways in which education can be conceptualised, defined and measured.

The focus throughout this book is on the influence of prior parental education assessed in terms of qualifications and years of schooling. This reflects the approach adopted in the vast majority of the studies that we review in Part II. In the second part of this chapter, we outline in greater detail the background for our consideration of the role that education plays in the passing down of success and failure from one generation to another. We review research that suggests a particular role for parents' education in driving intergenerational inequalities and look at some of the research that explores whether parents' education plays a causal role in the school achievement and life chances of their children. Much of the research that attempts to isolate such causal effects is, however, quite complex, involving particular statistical techniques and methodological issues. In the final section of this chapter we describe these methods, giving examples, and outline their importance for understanding the role of parents' education for children's school outcomes.

Defining education

Education as context

When defined institutionally, education can be thought of as a context. In this way, schools, colleges and other learning institutions can be considered as contexts or developmental settings like those of the family or neighbourhood. In educational contexts, as in other contexts, there are important social relations that impact on the experience and development of the individual. There are interactions with teachers, other adults and peers that may be of vital importance in the formation of cultural and personal identities for individuals, social groups and society as a whole. These features of the educational context may result from explicit and deliberate learning experiences that are part of the explicit curricula or from aspects of social interaction that occur outside it, either within or outside the classroom. An experience of being bullied, for example, or of developing a good relationship with another person can each radically transform an individual's self-concept, their image of themselves as a learner and the nature of their engagement in learning then, as well as in the future.

Education as process

As well as referring to contexts of learning, development and experience, education can also refer to the explicit experience of curricula-led learning. By this we mean the experience of being in an interaction with a teacher and being taken through the stages of educational practices intended to develop key skills, capabilities, knowledge and values. These learning processes are not only explicit and deliberate but also implicit and non-deterministic. Higher-level authorities can set curricula and establish the structural boundaries or objectives of institutional learning and in so doing can create challenges and opportunities for learning, but the central experience is a complex interaction of learner, teacher and other learners in a specific form of social exchanges. These dynamic relationships also involve many individual-level, within-person experiences of cognitive, affective and behavioural development as learners engage in cognitive processes that arise from the self-regulation and attention required by the task of learning, as well as from reflection about what has and has not been learnt.

We make this distinction between education as experience of contexts for learning and education as a process within such contexts because the two elements of education have different types of implication for the subsequent development of students. Some of the benefits and/or risks of education result from the membership of or participation in a learning institution, others from the explicit experience of the process of learning. These are distinct, though related.

Education as learning

It is also important to emphasise that there are important experiences of learning that do not take place within educational settings, key examples of which are learning in the workplace and home learning as in parent–child interaction. We discuss the importance of parent–child interactions as contexts for learning in Chapter 4.

Measuring education

The majority of the quantitative studies of the effects of parents' education on children's attainment have focused on the effects of measures of either the number of years of schooling or the educational qualifications gained. However, there are fundamental distinctions between these constructs that matter for how we think about and evaluate the mechanism for the effects of education. It must also be emphasised that each is distinct from a third category, namely the quality of education.

Quantity and qualifications

A particular concern in relation to the use of the number of years of schooling as a measure of educational participation is that it takes no account of the *quality* of that schooling, or of the extent to which learning or other important features of development occurred. Years of schooling is a useful proxy measure of progression within the school system, but the quantity proxy conflates individual progression with learning and gives no guide as to the features of the learning experience in educational settings that may be important for later life outcomes.

As a measure, qualifications gained tend to be highly correlated with the length of educational participation, in that it is generally necessary to attain entry-level qualifications to proceed to the next stage of learning, so those with greater quantity of education (years of schooling) will therefore also tend to have higher levels of qualification. Thus it is difficult to tease out the separate effects of participation and qualification, although consideration of effects for those who fail to qualify at the end of a learning experience can give some guide to the difference in effect of duration and qualification (see, for example, Hungerford and Solon, 1987).

As with the different ways of defining education, however, we emphasise the distinction between years of schooling and qualifications gained as important because some of the benefits may follow from a good experience of learning, while others follow from the socio-economic structural benefits gained from the signalling effect of qualifications. These are different mechanisms for lifetime and intergenerational effects and have very different policy implications. Studies that highlight the importance of the learning process as the mechanism for effects of education on subsequent outcomes suggest the existence of a general mechanism that may bring absolute benefits for all if educational participation were widened. On the other hand, studies that focus on qualifications achieved as the mechanism for education benefits lead to different conclusions, namely that the qualifications support a signalling mechanism according to which education effects follow from the relative positional advantage gained over others through the possession of qualifications. Because it is positional, this advantage would not follow in the same way if there were a widening of participation. The more appropriate policy if the signalling or positional advantage story is the more accurate one may be to reduce the effect of educational differences rather than to expand participation.

Therefore, whether education is conceptualised and measured by qualifications gained or by quantity of participation is an important distinction with strong implications for analysis and inference. However, both measures are at best proxy indicators of education inputs, and so conflate a number of related impacts.

Quality

The previous discussion focused on output measures of learning, but the nature of education effects is likely to depend heavily on the nature of the learning experience. Key features of this are conceptualised by educationalists in terms of constructs such as learning ethos, pedagogy, curricula and assessment, as well as in terms of the broader social relations experienced in a learning context. In conceptual terms, all of these features of learning may have important implications for life chances and for the next generation, either positively or negatively. It would be very useful for policy-makers to know more about the distribution of these different aspects of quality within and between education systems. It is unfortunate, therefore, that although qualitative and conceptual research indicates that these features of learning are vital, there is very little quantitative research that enables evaluation of the magnitude or external validity of these potential effects. It is also important to recognise that an emphasis on qualifications gained neglects the potentially vital role of non-accredited learning.

Learning through the lifecourse

Another feature of the focus on the years of schooling or of qualifications as measures of education is that the lifecourse benefits of learning tend to be omitted from consideration. For some, the personal and social benefits of learning in adulthood and later life may be particularly substantial. Until we know more about the causal mechanisms for education effects, it is not possible to hypothesise with any conviction about the relative size of effects of different stages of learning or at different ages. If the benefits are driven by income, then earlier education may be more influential than if the benefits are to do with features of identity and resilience. Little is known about these relative trade-offs.

It is also worth emphasising the importance of complementarities in learning (Cunha *et al.*, 2006), that is, the notion that learning begets more learning. This tends to be associated with the view that early learning is particularly important, but in relation to family life (and other benefits) it may be that learning through the lifecourse provides vital complementarities and support for individuals and communities that greatly enhance the benefit of earlier experiences of learning.

Parental education and the attainment gap

It has been estimated that at least half of the variance in cognitive development as measured by IQ tests is predictable from levels of functioning in the first three years of life (Bloom, 1964). Although there is strong evidence to suggest that a proportion of this is due to genetic differences, it is also clear that environment plays a substantial and relevant role (Collins *et al.*, 2000; Rutter, 1997). The relation between family social class and children's academic development is now widely established and fairly universal, although with varying degrees of gradient across countries (UNICEF, 2002). Evidence for the UK indicates that the social class gradient kicks in significantly before children enter school (Feinstein, 2003), suggesting that family contexts are particularly important in explaining educational disadvantage.

Social class is about much more than just education, but if one stratifies children's achievement by parental education rather than traditional occupational measures of social class, the gradient is every bit as steep. This is shown for children born in 1970 in Figures 2.1 and 2.2, reproduced from Feinstein (2003).

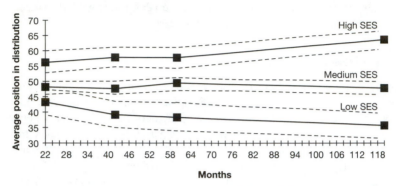

Dotted lines represent intervals of two standard errors. 'High SES' denotes father in professional/managerial occupation and mother similar or registered housewife (307 observations). 'Low SES' denotes father in semi-skilled or unskilled manual occupation and mother similar or housewife (171 observations). 'Medium SES' denotes those omitted from the high and low SES categories (814 observations). Thus, children whose mothers were housewives were categorised by the SES of fathers.

Figure 2.1 Average rank of test scores at 22, 42, 60 and 120 months, by socio-economic status (SES) of parents
Source: Feinstein (2003).

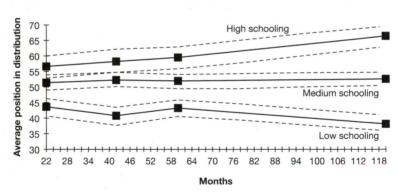

Dotted lines represent intervals of two standard errors. 'High schooling' denotes families where both parents have A-levels or higher (474 observations) 'Low schooling' denotes families where neither parent has qualifications (226 observations). 'Medium schooling' denotes those omitted from the high and low categories (592 observations).

Figure 2.2 Average rank of test scores at 22, 42, 60 and 120 months, by schooling of parents
Source: Feinstein (2003).

This suggests that the same common features underlie the attainment gap however one stratifies parental background, and there is substantial evidence that children's education level and cognitive development are positively related to the education of their parents (see, for example, Wolfe and Haveman, 2002). For example, whether parents left school before the age of fifteen has a strong, negative correlation with the probability that the young person will stay on at school themselves beyond the minimum age required (Bynner and Joshi, 2002; Feinstein *et al.*, 1999; Gregg and Machin, 2000). Other evidence shows that mothers' educational qualifications are positively related to children's school readiness (Christian *et al.*, 1998; Seefeldt *et al.*, 1999), their mathematics and reading test scores (Gayle *et al.*, 2002; Hanson *et al.*, 1997; Hill *et al.*, 2001; Joshi and Verropoulou, 2000; Smith *et al.*, 1997) and their achievement of grades (Smith, 1989).

Important associations also exist in terms of other aspects of family background such as family structure, income, neighbourhood and age of mother (Haveman and Wolfe, 1995; Hobcraft, 1998, 2003). Yet because the education of parents is also thought to impact on all these features of family life, there is reason to suppose that education plays an important and particular role in the intergenerational transmission of school achievement and academic attainment.

Correlation does not imply causation!

In our opening chapter, we argued that the intergenerational transmission of educational success is a key driver of the persistence of social class differences in westernised societies such as the UK. In order to try to understand the role education plays in social mobility, we begin by asking whether the effect of education is causal. The problem of causality is deeply contested, however, and will arise many times in this book, as it does in much of the literature on the economics of education and on wider social science. It therefore requires further discussion here.

The raw statistical association of two variables does not indicate cause, that is, that one influences or determines the other. Both may be driven by other factors. This is known as 'confounding bias'. For example, if children with good relationships with their teachers tend on average to do well in school it does not prove that good teacher relations cause school achievement – both factors may be driven by underlying, confounding factors such as mental health, well-being, cognitive capability and family support. Alternatively, it may be that the two variables influence each other. The correlation of good teacher relations and high school achievement may result in part from the reverse causality that children with high achievement find it easier to form good relationships with teachers than do children who struggle with tests of achievement. Either way, a causal relationship is unclear from the correlation and we can never assume that one exists.

Other issues include the fact that what may be causal in one time or context is not necessarily causal in another. For example, there may be stronger negative consequences for children of being born into a family without educational qualifications in a time of high educational participation than in earlier epochs in which not having qualifications was more usual and normative. Similarly, what is causal from one individual or group of individuals may not be for another. The impact of a programme to provide books for children may be particularly marked for children from disadvantaged families.

Analyses attempting to establish robust, causal effects of education tend to have been undertaken in individual level data in particular social and historical contexts and so the general, universal relevance of the conclusions cannot be stated as beyond reasonable doubt. Moreover, much of the analysis in economics has been of the 'black box' kind, which attempts to quantify the scale of causal relations and to identify true causality rather than association but is not always so concerned with understanding the nature of the mechanism or set of relationships that explain the causation. It is common to find papers in economics journals that test for the causality of the education effect without testing the nature of the mechanism. This is important, as without understanding of the mechanism one cannot be very sure about the likely effects of policy.

Why is it important to consider both the causal relationship and the mechanisms for its effects? In its early stages, brain science observed from cases of brain damage (the famous case of Phineas Gage[1]) that an injury to the frontal lobes of the cerebral cortex can reduce the social agitation and conflict suffered by some individuals with serious mental health problems and psychosis (the frontal lobes are generally important in planning, initiating and inhibiting behaviour). This led to the development of the pre-frontal lobotomy, a form of planned injury to the brain that was found to be effective in reducing aggression but also had considerable permanent side effects and was imposed on a great many individuals without concern for their human rights.

Apart from the ethics of that particular case, part of the problem was that the treatment was provided without understanding the mechanism or the reasons why the operation was effective in its narrow terms. This made it difficult to accurately target those who might benefit from it or appreciate the role of the treatment within the wider context of the life of the individual. Thus, appreciation of causality requires understanding not just of the magnitude of the one-way effect, but also of the context in which it operates and the process by which it occurs.

But is the effect of education causal?

With these issues in mind, an increasing body of literature (largely from economics) has tried to counter such methodological concerns and isolate robust, causal estimates of education effects, such that increases in education, if distributed more widely, would also lead to benefits for those with lower levels of education. There are a number of different statistical techniques available to researchers attempting to establish causality, for example through the use of randomised control trials (RCTs) or using research designs that make use of natural experiments. Other authors address this problem by modelling trajectories in relation to changes in education or use instrumental variable (IV) estimation to identify exogenous variation in the variables of interest and so assess causality more robustly. In the final section of this chapter, we review some of the studies that attempt to isolate a direct, causal effect of parents' education on children's school outcomes and describe their methodologies for doing so. Readers wishing to study these statistical techniques in more detail should refer to econometric texts such as Wooldridge (2002).

Magnuson (2003), for example, draws on the randomly assigned treatment design of a mandatory welfare-to-work programme in the USA to estimate models of changes in maternal education. Under this initiative, welfare recipients with young children were randomly assigned to a group that received an education- or work-focused programme or to a control group that received no additional assistance. The fact that parents are chosen randomly to receive this intervention provides variation to their schooling levels not influenced by unobserved features of the individual, their background or social context. This is referred to as 'exogenous' variation. This type of variation means that the differences observed in the subsequent outcomes between the intervention and control groups can, under a number of additional assumptions, be ascribed to the effect of the programme and can be used to quantify the impact of increases in education on the attainment of their children. Magnuson finds evidence of associations between increases in maternal education and increases in children's school readiness and academic achievement. She also showed that increases in mothers' educational participation were associated with improvements in the quality of home learning environments as assessed by mothers' reports of how often they engaged in different stimulating activities with their child, such as playing guessing games, playing with puzzles or going to the library.

However, randomised controlled interventions are extremely rare in the social sciences. Investigators have therefore used other sources of exogenous variation. A good example of this comes from government policies that attempt to increase participation in post-compulsory schooling. Over the past fifty years, several countries including England, Sweden, Norway and the USA have raised the compulsory school-leaving age. Although this increase affects the whole population in that everyone from a particular cohort has to stay in school for an additional year, its impact on school attainment largely depends on the individual. The increase in post-compulsory schooling is likely to most affect those individuals who were planning to leave the school system at the first opportunity; those individuals who were likely to continue until further education will do so regardless of the shift in policy. The resulting estimate of effects is called the 'local average treatment effect'. It does not reflect effects across the whole population but is biased towards effects for those individuals most likely to be affected (Imbens and Angrist, 1994).

Oreopoulos *et al.* (2003) find that parental education has an independent and significant effect on children's educational attainment. Their estimates indicate that a one-year increase in the education of either parent reduced the probability that their child had to repeat a grade by 2 to 7 percentage points. They also found evidence that having parents with higher levels of education reduced the probability of children aged 15–16 living at home dropping out of school. Similarly, Maurin and McNally (2005) find that additional years of higher education increased the educational attainment of children of the next generation. They estimate that an additional year of higher education by both parents leads to an increase of about 0.38 standard deviations in their child's educational advancement at age 15. For the UK, Chevalier (2004) estimates that, for each extra year of education by parents, the probability of their child staying on after post-compulsory education is increased by 3 to 4 percentage points.

While the majority of studies using this method find effects of parental education, there is some ambiguity about whether the effect of maternal or paternal education is larger. For example, Black *et al.* (2004) find effects of maternal education but not of paternal education, whereas Galindo-Rueda (2003) finds evidence of a positive effect of fathers' schooling on the schooling of their sons, but no effects for maternal schooling.

Behavioural genetic study designs use information on twins and children not living with their biological parents, either adopted or living in care, to condition out the role that 'nature' plays in the intergenerational transmission of educational success; that is, the possibility that children inherit ability from their parents and therefore children of more able parents are likely to be more able themselves and to achieve high levels of education. By using information on non-biological children these studies isolate this problem, unless one thinks that the allocation of adopted children to their adoptive parents is done in such a way that more educated parents adopt more able children.

In general, evidence on the effects of parents' education from these types of studies is more mixed. Sacerdote (2004), for example, finds that having a college-educated adoptive mother increased an adoptee's likelihood of graduating from college by 7 percentage points, and raises a biological child's likelihood of graduating from college by 26 percentage points. Conversely, Behrman and Rosenzweig (2002) and Antonovics and Goldberger (2003), who use within-twin variation to identify education effects, both find while that mother's education does not have an effect on the education of her child, paternal education shows positive and statistically significant effects on children's school attainment (see also Plug, 2004; Plug and Vijverberg, 2005).

Overall, there is robust empirical evidence to suggest that parental education has a causal impact on several measures of children's educational attainment and drop-out rates. What is not clear is whether the effect of parental education is driven by the education of fathers or mothers. In some contexts, evidence suggests that the education of the father is the primary input for the intergenerational transmission of educational success. In other contexts, mothers' education is the key factor.

Similar conclusions were reached by Holmlund *et al.* (2006), based on a recent review of studies that have attempted to isolate these kinds of robust estimates of education effects. They concluded that parents' education does have a causal impact on the education of their children, but emphasise that the size of this impact is substantially smaller than correlational evidence suggests. This highlights the point that the raw association of parental education and child attainment is not a good guide to the effect of the education of parents. Nonetheless, the evidence is fairly strong that a substantial element of the effect is causal and that the causal effect is substantial.

There is also a growing body of evidence that parents' education impacts on the health development of children. For example, several studies suggest that parents' education impacts on the child's birthweight and body mass index (BMI). Grossman and Joyce (1990) obtained a direct estimate of schooling on birthweight for black children in New York City in 1984. They found that black women who completed at least one year of college gave birth to infants who weighed 69 grams more than the newborn babies of women who completed between eight and eleven years of schooling. Currie and Moretti (2002) estimate the effect of maternal education on birthweight and pre-term birth using data from the US Vital Statistics Natality files for 1970–99. Results indicate that an increase in education of one year would reduce the probability of low birthweight by about 0.5 percentage points.

The effect on the probability of a pre-term birth is smaller: 0.4 percentage points. Furthermore, mothers who increased their education between the first and second births reduced the probability of low birthweight and prematurity. Other evidence highlights the strong association between parents' schooling and child mortality, which remains after controlling for parental income or other socio-economic variables (Blakely *et al.*, 2003; Corman and Grossman, 1985; Edwards and Grossman, 1982; Majumder *et al.*, 1997; O'Toole and Wright, 1991).

Summary

There is considerable evidence that parents' education provides protective and sustaining benefits that enable them to support the health and development of their children. However, it is always important to remember that education is strongly influenced by wider economic and social factors that influence the allocation of education. There are also vital social and historical differences in the meaning, significance and measurement of education. Studies have used different estimation strategies in different historical epochs and in different national contexts. Therefore, results are likely to differ and it is not yet always clear why. Indeed, we would argue that, until we have a clear conceptual model as to why education should impact on children's attainments, it is not possible to understand and interpret this range of findings.

Nonetheless, it is clear that children of parents with more education do better in school. This is likely in part to be an effect of education, but the question remains as to why the effect is there. Is it to do with income, values, expectations, parenting or neighbourhood contexts? What other factors may be responsible or relevant? What theories exist to account for the relationship and what is the evidence? What are the implications of all of this for education and social policy? These are the questions that we hope to address in this book in attempting to provide a structural theory to clarify the possible roles of the many factors just mentioned. Although the theory is structural, it is neither deterministic nor a closed system. The fact that it is structural does not, in our view, mean that it should be ignored; but it does mean that it should not be taken too literally. We find it a useful heuristic.

Therefore, in order to understand, model and quantify the role of education in intergenerational transmission it is helpful to use a framework that can place different strands of research in a common context and so enable some assessment of the pathways involved and the relative importance of the different features. We introduce this framework in the next chapter.

3 Conceptualising the influence of parents' education

A framework for analysis

In the previous chapter we put forward our argument for a focus on the particular role that parents' education plays in the achievement of their children and paid particular attention to issues of defining and measuring education and establishing causal effects. These discussions highlight some of the difficulties in understanding and conceptualising education effects. In this chapter, to clarify this hypothesis further and to structure the summary of the diverse literature reviewed, we describe in detail our model for understanding these intergenerational effects and the theoretical framework underpinning it. Recognising the importance of different strands of research across different disciplines, this presentation is followed by a discussion of the complementarities and tensions between alternative models and approaches and sets out some of the resulting caveats of our approach.

The ecological model of human development

The general framework we use to structure and conceptualise the role of education in the intergenerational transmission of educational success draws on contemporary theories of human development (see, for example, Cairns and Hood, 1983; Gottlieb, 1983; Lerner, 1986, 1998; Magnusson and Stattin, 1998; Sameroff, 1983). These theories view behaviour and development as processes that are inextricably linked to the multiple, interrelated contexts or systems within which individuals live. Individuals do not grow up in isolation; nor do they make uniform transitions between childhood, adolescence and adulthood. Rather, human character and competence are shaped by the continuity and change in families, schools, peer groups and neighbourhoods. In order to fully understand the complex and dynamic influences on development it is therefore important to study individuals in context.

One of the most prominent contemporary developmental theorists was Uri Bronfenbrenner. His ecological model of human development (1979,

1986; Bronfenbrenner and Crouter, 1983) is built on the premise that, throughout the lifecourse, development takes place through processes of sustained, progressively more complex, reciprocal interactions between an individual and the dynamic persons, objects and symbols in their immediate environments. This framework of development highlights an important distinction between *proximal* and *distal* processes. This distinction reflects the concentric levels of organisation within which humans exist.

At its centre, the model is based around the interactions between individuals, most often between parents and children, in which dynamic processes support, sustain or hinder successful development. These processes are termed *proximal* in the ecological model and are the primary mechanism for producing development, referring to the day-to-day life of the child. Examples of proximal process variables in the context of the family include aspects of parent–child relationships such as warmth and affection, the use of discipline, control and punishment, as well as the educational content and structure of language used in the home. These processes change and adapt as children develop and mature and are constrained and influenced by the characteristics of both the immediate context, for example the family or school, as well as the more distant social, economic and demographic environment – that is, the *distal* environment.

This distinction between proximal and distal is generic in that it can be applied to any topic, but its precise meaning depends on the context in which it is being applied. For example, in assessing the link between indices of parental occupation and children's attainments in school, occupation is a distal factor if one hypothesises that there are other, important factors that mediate this relationship. These mediating factors can be thought of as pathways explaining why the distal factor exerts an influence on the outcome. Proximal factors are those mediating elements. These are factors closer to the lived experience of the child that have a direct impact on individual development. In the example of the relationship between parental occupation and children's attainment, these factors might include being read to at home from an early age, parental emphasis on the importance of learning, the instruction provided by a teacher and so on. What is proximal and what is distal is entirely dependent on the context under consideration.

Context can be defined in the ecological model as the location and/or institutional grouping within which particular sets of processes occur. This is a particular and rather limiting definition of context but is a useful simplification here. In childhood, key contexts typically include family, pre-school settings, schools, peer-groups and neighbourhoods. The focus in this book on the intergenerational transmission of educational success, particularly in terms of children's school achievement, places an emphasis on the family context as a fundamental locus of interactions relevant to the developing child. However, the family is not independent of these other contexts and there are vital interactions between contexts that are fundamental to the ecological model. We review the importance of other contexts and their relationships with the family context in Chapter 7.

A conceptual model of the intergenerational transmission of educational success

Bronfenbrenner's ecological model underpins our own framework for conceptualising how educational advantage is passed down intergenerationally. We now spell out in more detail our model for structuring and understanding the ways in which parents' education influences children's own development.

Based on his model, our reading of the literature and for the purposes of structuring this book, we make distinctions between three categories of family level influences on children's development: distal family factors, internal characteristics of the family environment, and proximal processes within the family (see also Gottfried and Gottfried, 1984; Gottfried *et al.*, 1994, for similar family-level distinctions). These categories and examples of specific influences in the context of the family are shown in Figure 3.1.

As in Bronfenbrenner's ecological model, distal family factors refer to the more global or descriptive factors that characterise the wider environment of the child and provide an index of a family's demographic or socio-economic situation. Examples of distal family factors include income and parents' occupation. Internal features of the family context are more closely related to the proximal factors that impact on children, mediating the impact of wider contextual factors on the experience of the child. Important internal characteristics of the family environment include the availability of resources, such as cognitively enriching and stimulating materials and activities, parental cognitions (an umbrella term to refer to

Distal family factors	Internal features of the family environment	Proximal family processes
Education Family structure Family size Teenage motherhood Income and poverty Maternal employment	Parental cognitions Mental health and well-being Material resources	Parenting style Educational behaviours Language use Activities outside the home Nutrition

Figure 3.1 Three categories of family-level influences on child development

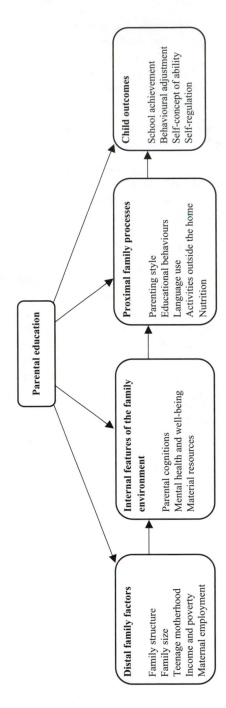

Figure 3.2 Conceptual model for the effects of parents' education on children's school achievement

attitudes, aspirations, expectations, values and beliefs and so on), parents' mental health, well-being and network supports, as well as the physical infrastructure of the home.

These features of the family differ from those of distal factors in that they provide a more substantive measure of the child's immediate environment. Internal family characteristics are more directly related to the day-to-day experiences of the child than are the socio-economic and demographic distal factors, but are distinct from the actual dynamic interactions between parents and children. A factor such as maternal depression, for example, will impact on the child partly through shaping observable, measurable parenting factors, such as maternal warmth and responsiveness, but also indirectly as a feature of the phenomenological world of the child. Conversely, a more distal factor such as mothers' age, for example, is not in any meaningful sense a part of most children's direct, daily life. Mothers' age will tend to mean that certain features of the mother–child relationship will be a certain way – younger mothers tending to give less consistent care, for example – but that is not necessarily so and certainly will not be true in every case. Thus the connection is not a feature of the child's world in the same way as is mothers' mental health; it is more distal. Age matters because of what it may tend to mean for the proximal zone of interaction, but it is not the age of the mother that matters in and of itself.

In Figure 3.1, parents' education is grouped with distal family factors such as income, family size and structure and teenage motherhood. However, as we show throughout this book, the particular importance of education is that it influences each of these distal factors themselves. Our model attempts to clarify the importance of education as a specific distal factor, as well as to provide a structure for the analysis of how these factors interrelate.

The model shown in Figure 3.2 lays out a number of ways in which parents' education may impact on a number of different measures of children's development both directly and indirectly through other mediating features of the distal and proximal environment outlined in the ecological model. These pathways can be summarised by two central hypotheses. Parents' education may matter because:

1   it impacts on (that is, it is mediated by) other important factors, which in turn influence children's development; and
2   it moderates the effects of these other factors, that is, it changes the way in which they operate.

This double impact may operate at every level of the model – for distal factors, key internal characteristics of the family environment and proximal process. To clarify the discussion of these relationships we start with some examples of what we mean by 'mediation' and 'moderation'. The discussion is at this point entirely conjectural. In Part II we assess the nature of the pathways proposed, in terms of both their theoretical foundations and the empirical evidence, in order to build up a comprehensive picture of the ways in which the intergenerational transfer of education occurs. Here, the focus is on clarifying hypotheses rather than evaluating them.

First, let us consider the mediated effect of parents' education via income, an example of a distal factor. Parents' education has a direct effect on family income and, in turn, income has an effect on children's school achievement. Therefore, some of the effect of income on children's achievement is, in a sense, an effect of prior parental education. This is a mediated effect. We can take this example of mediation one step further. Family income influences child achievement through its impact on the more immediate characteristics of the family environment experienced by the child, such as good housing, a more enriched home environment, better schools and so on. These resources are bought with income and thus mediate the income effect, which is itself in part mediating an education effect. In economic terms, this distinction can be thought about in terms of effects of education in changing the level of financial resources available to the household.

Our second hypothesised type of channel for education effects states that the nature of, for example, the income effect described above may itself depend on the parents' level of education. Parents with higher levels of education may spend a given amount of income differently from those with lower education and so be better able to protect children against the effects of poverty or derive greater developmental advantages from high income. Thus education also has a moderating effect (Figure 3.3). Similar relationships are proposed for education and each of the other distal factors. Statistically, a moderating effect is equivalent to an interaction effect. In economic terms, this distinction can be thought about in terms of effects

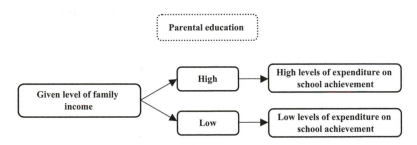

Figure 3.3 Conceptual model for the moderating influences of parental education on income

of education in changing the efficiency and effectiveness of the way those resources are used.

Turning to the key internal features of the family environment, the same double effect of parents' education may apply. First, education may influence mental health and well-being, resulting in mediated effects on children's developmental outcomes. Second, education may also help parents protect children against the impacts of ill health or low levels of parental well-being: parents with higher levels of education are less likely to be depressed, and when they are depressed they are better able to use social networks and access healthcare in order to diminish any possible adverse effects. Education thus moderates the effects of those features of the family on children and their outcomes.

Similarly, in relation to proximal processes, there are again sound foundations for the view that education will have the same double effect. First, parents with greater levels of education are more likely to read to their children, for example. It may also be that education moderates the effects of proximal processes impacting, in the same example, on the ways in which parents read to children (using different voices, asking lots of open-ended questions, alternating between who reads and so on) or on their choice of book (using different books, across a wide range of subjects, as well as reading more challenging characters and stories), and thus moderating the nature of the developmental benefit for the child.

In summary, we hypothesise that parental education may be transmitted intergenerationally through six pathways:

1 by impacting on proximal processes such as teaching practices and educational behaviours in the home;
2 by moderating the effects of proximal processes, changing the nature of their influence;
3 by impacting on the internal features of contexts and, in turn, on proximal processes;
4 by supporting individuals and families in managing a set of charac-teristics and hence moderating the effect of characteristics;
5 by impacting on key distal factors such as income; and/or
6 by moderating the effect of each distal factor, that is, by acting protectively and providing resilience in the family.

In Part II, we describe these processes in more detail and discuss the evidence on the interconnecting links. We note, however, that the lack of focus in the literature on the particular role of parents' education in the intergenerational transfer of educational advantage has meant that the moderating role has not been explored very much. We therefore focus primarily on the pathways for the influence of parents' education that operate via the other factors at the different levels of our model. Chapters 4, 5 and 6 work outwards from the child's immediate environment and consider the family proximal processes, internal features within the family environment and distal factors, respectively. Chapter 7 outlines the importance of other contexts and their possible interactions with one another. For each chapter, we lay out the key factors identified in the literature and focus particularly on the indirect effect hypotheses 1, 3 and 5, assessing the extent to which theory and evidence suggests that each factor is:

- influenced by prior parental education; and
- an important determinant of child development.

For each key factor identified, we provide a summary that indicates the strength of the effect from a theoretical perspective and from the evidence, as well as an assessment of the extent to which the evidence has been able to identify the relevant causal link.

Interdisciplinary perspectives, complementarities and alternative approaches

As we discussed in Chapter 1, one of the advantages of the framework that we adopt here is that it enables us to integrate studies from a number of disciplines. Most notably, studies that explore the impact of distal factors come particularly from economics, sociology and demography, alongside studies that focus more on the nature and influence of proximal processes, which typically come from within developmental and social psychology. Although quantitative, these different strands of research tend to have quite distinct theoretical and methodological foundations. Combining them strengthens our understanding of the how and why parents' education matters for children's educational success.

Integration of approaches from economics and developmental psychology

The application of economic models to the question of children's school achievement commonly derives from Becker (1973) and a neo-classical economic tradition, which considers how children's attainments can be modelled on the basis of an analogy between 'the family' and 'the firm'. In these economic models, the family can be figured as a production unit or 'little factory', producing the basic goods of family well-being such as health, consumption goods and the successful development of children, on the basis of the allocation of time of the productive members of the family in the relevant production processes. Inputs are allocated in such a way as to produce sets of outputs that maximise the utility of the decision-making family members subject to the constraints of the family, such as time, wealth and ability to produce the desired outputs. In this sense parents can choose to influence children's attainment by spending resources of time and money on those activities that produce attainment. The limit to this investment is the limit of time and money available and the ability of the attainment production process to actually produce attainment.

The strength of Becker's economic model is that it makes explicit the substitutions involved in parental decision-making. Money spent on books and computers for children cannot simultaneously be spent on holidays and restaurant meals for parents. Similarly, time spent in the labour market earning income to buy consumer goods cannot be spent on leisure and so on. The decisions about the relative allocation of a family's time and resources depend on the valuations that parents make about the different outputs obtainable by them. These are referred to as 'preferences' and are expressed mathematically in economic modelling as utility functions.

In Becker's model, there are two main channels through which parental education may impact on children's attainment:

1 it may improve the effectiveness of household production and so increase the academic attainment of children through the attainment production function;
2 it may also change the utility function, increasing the weight given to the educational attainment of children and so increasing investments in their schooling, hence increasing their attainments. Equivalently, if education increases patience (enhancing concerns for the long-run), it may also change the nature of household production decisions, giving more weight to increased attainments of children.

The first of these theoretical pathways can also be stated in the terms of our conceptual model for the intergenerational transmission of educational success: the improvement in productivity can be reformulated as an effect of education on the family and proximal processes within it, holding distal factors constant, particularly income. Education enhances productivity for a given level of resource and so moderates the effects of income. Integrating both economic and psychological approaches in our ecologically framed model has the benefit of making explicit the processes by which parents can enhance development or, in the Becker formulation, produce attainment.

The second of Becker's channels through which parents' education has its impact is on the utility function of the household. This can also be re-articulated as an effect of education on parental cognitions: their attitudes, expectations, beliefs and values. These also lead to changes in the allocation of household resources as child development (or educational success) becomes prioritised.

The thrust of this discussion is that, although the theory of the neo-classical economic approach is based on utility-maximising, rational agents, it is not unrelated to developmentally grounded models of human development. The assumption of rationality implies a level of determinism and self-knowledge in Becker's economic model that is absent in develop-mental models. The mechanics of this determinism enables a mathematical clarity with respect to the predictions of the model. This clarity, however, is bought at the cost of a strong and simple specification of the context of individuals' development, consciousness and temperaments. Developmental approaches, on the other hand, offer insights into the processes of household production of children's attainment and development that are left as parts of a 'black box' in the economic approach.

In our ecological formulation, economic and developmental approaches are not empirically separable but offer usefully different perspectives. The economic evidence demonstrates the importance of the distal factors in understanding differences in school achievement and the attainment gap, but we attempt here to place that evidence in a slightly different theoretical and empirical context. In subsequent chapters, we draw on the develop-mental literature to unpack the elements of the household production process. This helps us to clarify the role of parental education as a particularly important distal factor – as one that moderates the whole process of household production.

A 'capitals' model

An alternative approach to the problem of what resources matter could be offered by a focus on 'capitals'. Rather than defining social class as group-level access to resources, with access determined by occupation, itself determined by ownership (or non-ownership) of capital, the ecological approach adopted here recognises that there are a number of important resources (or capitals) and capabilities available to families and that families differ in their access to and/or ownership of these resources and capabilities. Some of this ownership varies in important systematic ways with occupation, access to financial wealth and identification with social class norms and values. However, it is not reducible to these things.

This approach would consider that families differ in their access to or ownership of a number of assets that are productive in the formation of children's attainment. A number of such capital assets have been put forward and/or tested as supportive of the development of attainment, such as social capital (Coleman, 1988), cultural capital (Bourdieu, 1984), identity capital (Côté and Levine, 2002) and financial capital (Bynner and Paxton, 2001), alongside human capital (Becker, 1975; Schultz, 1961), the original extension in economics of the metaphor of capital.

There are many strengths of the capitals model but it is not one that we adopt here. There are problems with this formulation of resources or assets as capitals, particularly for economists, who have a long history of experience with particular notions of capital that do not translate well into psychological and sociological domains of resources. The advantage of the ecological perspective used is that it explicitly focuses on the relationships between elements and, since an essential aspect of the role of education is the way it mediates and moderates other factors, we see a great advantage to an approach that makes these processes explicit. Moreover, many aspects of a capitals approach can be modelled within this multi-level developmental approach.

Nonetheless, the capitals framework highlights the broad range of resources and capabilities that may be important for children's development. Children of more educated parents will tend *on average* to benefit from warmer, more supportive parenting, to live in safer neighbourhoods with better institutional resources and more positive role models, to be placed in higher-quality pre-schools and to attend more successful schools. Thus, exactly like social class or income, education acts as an indicator of differential access to the resources that matter.

A meaning of social class and the role of culture

Any broad-based consideration of the role of education in family dynamics or of the intergenerational transmission of advantage and disadvantage has to address the issues of class and culture. Yet, the analytical framework set out in this book has not been developed within a tradition that emphasises these terms and to a certain extent the terms are unrelated to the framework. In other words, although we recognise the importance and weight of class and culture as themes in discourse and analysis of intergenerational patterns – indeed, it may seem odd to many to think of undertaking such an investigation without using these terms – we have attempted in this book to set out a framework that does not depend on their use.

We are not sociologists or anthropologists and we recognise substantial limitations in our knowledge and understanding of these domains of thought. Nonetheless, we think it is important for transparency and clarity to attempt to specify what we mean by those terms in the context of the analysis presented here. Another way of thinking about this is that we are seeking to use the framework to sketch a structural model of what social class and culture mean in terms of the themes of the book: the relations within the family between parents and children, how these relations are influenced by wider contexts, and how these relations explain within the wider context the cross-generational association of educational achievement. We do not, however, attempt a comprehensive definition or discussion of the terms 'culture' and 'social class', both of which have been the themes of major literatures in social science and wider politics, philosophy, science, art and history.

Social class is a complex notion. It is not equal to education or to income or occupational status. Elements of social class may include income, education, occupation and cultural capital, but even together these factors do not sum to social class. Social class is in some ways a relational and positional measure. It exists in the distribution of assets and advantages across society and not at the level of the individual. It varies in different societies in its rigidity and effect and in the extent to which it is mediated by income or the other factors mentioned.

Class as occupation

Traditional models of class have strongly emphasised the link to occupation. Marxist models, for example, defined class in terms of relationship to ownership of specific means of production, primarily in the capitalist mode of production, of capital or labour. The key distinction was made between capitalists who, in owning physical capital, could exploit a profit and maintain their ownership of resources and elite status; and workers, who were forced to sell their labour power in exchange for a basic wage, suffering alienation and poverty as a result. Thus in the simplest forms of this framework, education, income and occupation were all necessarily linked – determined by ownership of the means of production, reified in notions of social class.

However, models of class developed through the nineteenth and twentieth centuries to provide more sophisticated and sociological notions of class, emphasising shared values and experiences. Therefore, it is unsurprising that statistical analyses routinely find that the occupation of parents is not the only variable that explains the variation in children's school attainment, and that within occupation groups there is substantial variation in achievement. Nonetheless, occupation is a particularly important distal factor, at least in terms of its raw association with children's outcomes.

Some empirical results suggest that the association between parental occupation and child attainment remains significant after controlling for education and income. Replication of results has been consistent in measuring the positive relationship between occupation and children's educational attainments. The mediating factors in the relationship between occupational class and developmental outcomes over the lifecourse are still subject to analysis. Feinstein and Symons (1999) found that parental interest in their children's education explains the variance on attainment otherwise explained by social class, parental education or family size. Sacker *et al.* (2002) found that at ages seven and eleven parental social class as proxied by occupation is mediated by material deprivation, but by age sixteen the effect of occupation is mainly mediated by the school context. Sullivan (2001) found independent effects of occupation on children's GCSE attainment even when cultural capital of parents and the child is included in the analysis.

Class as group membership

Because of the complexity in the notion of class we choose not to reduce it to a single factor such as occupation. The factors such as income, education and occupation that we do address might be seen in combination to create or underpin social class in a wider sense; of social class as group ownership of resources that matter; and of identification with a wider social network of people with similar contexts, structural conditions and, to a certain extent, values. In this sense, the analysis presented in this book provides a breakdown of the factors and processes and their inter-relationships that bring about the attainment gap between children born into different circumstances. However, there is a big and difficult question as to whether this gap is best described as a 'social class gap', an 'income gap' or in other terms, such as a 'family background gap'.

Much important recent UK research on social mobility (Blanden *et al.*, 2002; Blanden *et al.*, 2005) has emphasised the importance of income as the source of the differences in opportunity between children. In part this is useful because of the ease of measurement of income, which unlike social class has a cardinal metric and a simple meaning. However, it may be that this apparent simplicity just pushes the wider complexities into the background, leaving unanswered the questions of why there are differences in income, what features of individuals and families are influenced by income and why these are transmitted across generations. Social class is a useful construct because it responds to these questions.

However, in this book social class is not considered as a distal factor amongst the others investigated in later chapters. This is because we see class as a feature of structure that may moderate the effect of all of the other elements in the model. People differ in the extent to which they identify with particular social class groups, identification that is confused by other features of identity such as gender, race, ethnicity, sexuality, religion, age and place. Yet there are continuing and crucial impacts of the access of parents to resources on the educational success of children. These resources are not exclusively economic in our view, although economic forces are particularly powerful, but it is difficult to understand class without knowing what these resources are. We focus on the latter issue: the specification of the key resources.

The wider context

In Chapter 2, we reviewed evidence on the causal links between parents' education and the health and development of their children. The studies tend to treat education as a distal factor like others. The objective of this book, however, is to explore and model the more complex relationships underlying this distal connection. While the model we have put forward here to understand these relationships and the important role of education does its best to resolve to these issues, it is not without problems. We recognise, therefore, that it is important to place our model and the subsequent analysis within a wider context and to indicate some of the caveats of our approach.

The multi-dimensionality of development

This book aims to bring together theory and evidence on the effects of the diverse sets of family level factors that are associated with education and hence with the success of children. Much of the economic evidence, which centres more on what we term in our model 'distal factors', has focused on school attainment, but there is also considerable research on other domains of children's development. For example, the wide recognition in recent years that what are sometimes called 'non-cognitive' or 'soft' skills – such as attention-related, social and communication skills – are also of value in the labour market has led to the inclusion of them in some definitions of human capital (Bowles *et al.*, 2001; Goldsmith *et al.*, 1997; Healy and Côté, 2001; Heckman and Rubinstein, 2001). Wider skill sets are strongly linked to adult life opportunities (Feinstein and Bynner, 2003), recognised both as sources of productivity benefit (Department for Education and Skills (DfES), 2003) and of social exclusion (Margo and Dixon, 2006). Thus, there is a broad range of other outcomes that may be of interest for different theoretical and policy concerns. These include social competence, behavioural and emotional self-regulation, well-being, life skills, engagement and motivation, and so on (see Eccles and Gootman, 2002; Gottfried *et al.*, 2003).

Moreover, there are also likely to be important differences in the ways in which family factors influence these different domains of development and one cannot at all assume that if, for example, parental income impacts on school test scores it will also impact on behaviour or temperament. Unfortunately, there is a large evidence gap in regard to the relative differences in the nature of effects on different domains. Our ecological model is sufficiently general that it can be applied to all aspects of development, but we do not have detailed evidence on how the model works for all possible outcomes. In this book, therefore, there is discussion at times of development generally and at times of outcomes defined more specifically. The important distinctions in the relevant processes are left to subsequent work.

Dynamic modelling: the agency and resiliency of children

Children are themselves important determinants of their own academic and psychological development and play a key part in the process of educational success and its intergenerational transfer. In economic terminology, the educational achievement that may be considered to be an outcome at age six, say, becomes an input when one is investigating the determinants of achievement at age ten. This dynamic element to understanding development is important in understanding the mechanisms through which intergenerational educational immobility asserts itself.

Moreover, children are not passive recipients of parenting or of their wider environment. Rather, children shape and direct the proximal processes that they experience. As children get older, autonomy strengthens and individuals increasingly choose their own contexts and influence interactions accordingly. These transactional dynamics are essential to the processes of maturation and socialisation (see Dodge, 2006; Sameroff and Chandler, 1975, for further reading here).

In a similar vein, it is well established that children react differently to the same biological or environmental risks. Early experiences, whether good or bad, do not determine an invariant life path. For example, in Werner and Smith's (1992) longitudinal study of high-risk children, one-third had made satisfactory life adjustments by adulthood, despite being born into highly disadvantaged circumstances. Why is it that some individuals succeed despite the odds, breaking cycles of poverty and deprivation (Clarke and Clarke, 2000; Elder *et al.*, 1991), while others from privileged backgrounds struggle to do so?

Theories of risk and resiliency consider why children are likely to show diminished well-being in the face of certain negative biological and environmental conditions (Bynner, 2001; Garmezy, 1985, 1993; Werner, 1989). Fundamental to the notion of risk is the predictability of life chances from prior experience and circumstances. This is expressed through the concept of a 'risk trajectory', wherein one risk factor reinforces another, leading to increasingly restricted outcomes in later life (Rutter, 1990; Schoon *et al.*, 2002). For example, Sameroff and his colleagues (Gutman *et al.*, 2002; Sameroff *et al.*, 1998) have investigated the impact of cumulative risk factors on children's development and have shown that, while there are significant effects of single risk factors, most children with only one risk factor would not end up with a major developmental problem. It is when risk is compounded that it is most damaging, in the sense that the presence of more risk factors is related to a higher probability of negative outcomes. In a comprehensive review of the effects of biological, psychological and social influences on development, Wachs (2000) concluded that no single factor was sufficient to explain developmental outcomes and that only the study of multiple influences simultaneously would produce reasonable explanatory power.

Protective factors, however, may impede or halt risk and risk trajectory processes, promoting resiliency and enabling the child's life to move in positive directions (Garmezy, 1985, 1993). Protective factors work on the more malleable components of development, such as emotional, educational, social and economic influences. These operate alone as well as (more commonly) interacting with each other. They reflect the different kinds of resources that may help the child to resist adversity. Thus, for example, strong parental attitudes and aspirations, as well as sustained encouragement and commitment to children by the schools they attend, may override some of the worst effects of poverty and disadvantage. And in the same ways in which risk factors reinforce other risk factors, protective factors can also have a cumulative effect. Individuals from more privileged homes, for example, often have more educational opportunities, greater access to financial resources when they are needed (for example, to pay for higher education), more positive role models, greater occupational knowledge and better-established informal/kinship networks (Schulenberg *et al.*, 1984).

The conceptual model used in this book is a relatively static one, however, and so largely ignores these dynamic elements of individual development and therefore underrepresents both the agency and resiliency of children somewhat. It nevertheless provides a starting point to understanding cross-generational advantage and will usefully inform subsequent work in exploring the transactional nature of human development. We attempt to operationalise our model of development and integrate the themes of risk and resiliency in Chapter 8. Here we report findings from our own quantitative study of whether it is possible to identify children at risk of adult deprivation from early signals.

The importance of forces operating at other levels of social complexity

The focus on parents' education and its role in intergenerational immobility in this book necessarily places an emphasis on the family as the focal point of interest. The family context itself operates within a wider context comprising agencies and structures that are at similar levels of social complexity (such as other families), at higher levels of local complexity (communities, neighbourhoods, schools, firms, local labour markets and so on) and at the national level of still greater social complexity (education policy, the media and national labour markets). As well as spending time in these different institutional or environmental contexts, children also live within specific historical or social contexts, which also moderate the nature of their experiences and the effects of these experiences on their development.

There are important relations between the elements within each of these levels and there are important interactions between elements at different levels. These agencies and structures and the relationships between them change over time. A number of recent studies (for example, Changing Britain, Changing Lives, 2003; Schoon *et al.*, 2002) have strongly highlighted the important influences of social and historical context on development, and have aided understanding of the changing impact of family circumstance and historical epoch on child development for the UK.

Although we recognise the importance of these wider definitions of context, detailing its importance in the way that we do at the level of the family is beyond the scope of this book. Therefore, much of the analysis described in subsequent chapters ignores this social and historical contingency. This is a problem not only in relation to the conceptual framework but also in regard to the evidence presented. Although the ecological framework that guides the analyses presented here could be applied to any type of social grouping in which children live, at any historical era, the precise estimates of effects or pathways are contingent on time, place and social context. That is why social explanation and science are so complex.

In places we have been regrettably dependent on US evidence, which is particularly strong in methodological and measurement terms, but again context-dependent. There are reasons to view this evidence as relevant to the UK context. However, owing to recent and ongoing investments in large-sample UK longitudinal data collection and analysis (such as the

Millennium Cohort, the survey of the children of the 1970 Birth Cohort, the Effective Provision of Pre-School Project and the Avon Longitudinal Study of Parents and Children), future reviews such as this will have more UK-specific evidence to draw on. Future work will then be better placed to highlight, for example, differences according to educational policy across the four countries of the UK, comparisons across national curricula, changes in the minimum school leaving age and so on.

Education is not the only thing that matters

Education does not act on intergenerational transmission in isolation from other factors. Moreover, we are not claiming that education is the only important factor or the only factor with such wide-ranging influences. This book lays out the mechanisms for the effects of a host of distal and proximal factors on child development and focuses on them in part as channels for the effects of education. This is not to suggest that these other factors do not have importance independently of education. Education may impact on income and so some of the effect of income may be thought of as the channelling of the effect of education, but that is not to subsume the whole income effect under the heading of 'education'. A large component of family income is independent of parents' education, and even to the extent that income mediates the effect of education this can still be conceptualised as an income effect. In policy terms, it may be that an increment to income is a more effective policy tool than attempted increments to education, even if income mediates education effects.

However, even if we control for income, empirical investigations tend to find that the effect of parental education on children's attainments is at least as great as the effect of income. Our aim is not to denigrate the significance of income but to support a more balanced view, which recognises that many factors are important in the development of ability. Therefore, we have highlighted in this chapter the value of the ecological framework as a structure for assessing the interactions between the different factors and assessing the relative importance of each.

We have also hypothesised that education may be a key moderator of the effect of each individual factor. However, we recognise, too, that there are other important moderating factors. Education changes the way in which family resources impact on children, but so do ethnicity and class. Resources may be allocated in different ways for boys and girls as well as by mothers and fathers. Hence these moderating effects may apply to all of the factors that impact on attainment so that the whole model of effects may be different for children of different ethnicities, class backgrounds or gender.

Summary

As we outlined in Chapter 2, class, income and education are all strongly correlated. Education may matter because it is a proxy for those other elements and because of its own independent or supplementary effects. Probably both of these things are true. We have suggested in this chapter that there is differential allocation across families of the resources that matter for the educational achievement of children, but argued that parents' education has a particular and important role. The theoretical framework and resulting conceptual model put forward here is intended to be an aid to us and others in better understanding the mechanisms for the inter-generational effects of education. In doing so we hope to better understand some of the pathways that exacerbate social class inequalities.

The attention to proximal factors as the most central elements of the ecological framework does not relegate distal factors or indicate a lower concern for their importance. Some mechanisms for the association between social background and, for example, the attainment gap may be mediated or explained by the proximal factors and internal features of the family environment, but that does not mean that the influence of these distal factors is not real. Rather, this framework helps in understanding the elements of the background effect, the interactions between them and the role of education therein. It is also important to recognise that it is not implied here that a specific factor (distal or proximal) causes a given child outcome through a unique one-way causal pathway that would operate for all children with those specific aspects of an environment. Rather, there are complex processes of interaction between children and contexts. Bronfenbrenner (1979) argues that, in ecological research, the principal main effects are likely to be interactions between process, person, context and time. Making distinctions in this way therefore enables the detection of particular relationships and synergies among these components and allows a more complete picture of development to emerge.

This perspective also provides a framework within which to intertwine different theoretical approaches and strands of literature. The essential advantage of Becker's economic approach and its focus on the family as a little factory in producing academic attainment is its clarity and aid in the formulation of hypotheses. It does not provide alternative hypotheses about the processes by which resources impact on attainment, but assumes that attainment follows in a fairly straightforward way from the investments of parental resources. Developmental models from psychology, on the other hand, provide more insight into these processes and wider constraints on them. However, while they recognise the importance of financial and other constraints at the distal level, they have been less explicit in formulating their implications. The two approaches can thus be beneficially brought together within the ecological framework adopted here. We now turn to Part II, in which we review and evaluate the theory and evidence put forward by our model.

Part II
The influence of parents' education
A review of the evidence

4 The importance of what goes on in the family

We now turn to the centrepiece of this book and our review of the evidence on the role of education in the intergenerational transfer of success. As we described in detail in Chapter 3, our framework for conceptualising the influence of parents' education is based on Bronfenbrenner's ecological model of human development, which, at its centre, is based around the daily interactions that support, sustain or hinder development. We therefore begin our evaluation of the theory and evidence of the family-level influences on children's school achievement with these proximal family processes.

Introduction

In the field of child development, few would argue against the view that parents, families and the relationships therein are among the most important and direct influences on children and their development. In recent years, changes in the structure and dynamics of family life have fuelled the interest and debate in the topic of what constitutes responsible and effective parenting (Ramey and Ramey, 2000).

The importance of parenting and the parent–child relationship has been well documented in the literature and research here, in which answers have been sought to questions such as: What aspects of parent–child interactions affect children's development? How can these interactions differ and how do they impact on children's development? And how might parents' education influence the parent–child relationship and related child outcomes? We begin Part II with such questions in mind, looking at the daily life of the child and exploring the ways in which parent–child interactions shape developmental outcomes.

In the conceptual model put forward here, the parent–child dyad and the relations therein are defined as proximal family processes. These processes are the central element of our conceptual model of influences on children's development and refer to the daily experiences of the developing

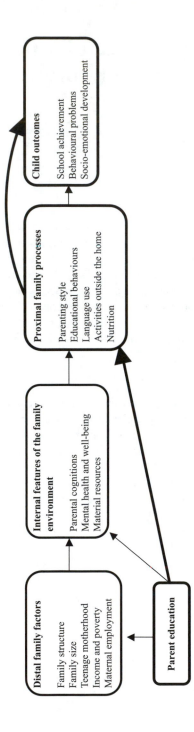

Figure 4.1 Conceptual model for the effects of proximal family processes on child development outcomes

child and the observable interactions that take place between parents and their children. Examples of family process variables include aspects of parent–child relationships such as warmth and affection, the use of discipline, control and punishment. They also concern aspects of these relationships that involve facilitating and engaging in age-appropriate developmental activities such as reading books together, teaching nursery rhymes, songs, letters, numbers and colours, or helping with homework and encouraging play and intellectual curiosity, as well as the content and style of the language used that pervades all of these interactions. Figure 4.1 shows some of these key processes and their position in our conceptual model of the influence of parents' education.

In the same way that providing books and toys can be thought of as an integral part of supporting positive parent–child interactions, nutrition can also be conceptualised as an aspect of proximal processes. However, this characteristic of family dynamics, while important for many aspects of development, takes us beyond the scope of the current book and its focus on the influence of parents' education for children's school achievement. For a thorough review on the relationship between child nutrition and school outcomes see Sorhaindo and Feinstein (2006).

As we outlined in Chapter 1, our primary focus in this book is on children's advantage and positive development with respect to school achievement. We do, however, point to relevant literature that also highlights influences of proximal processes on behavioural adjustment and socio-emotional development. We consider the theory and evidence in support of each key factor of family process and assess the strength of the link:

- from the family process factor to child outcomes; and
- from prior parental education to the family process factor.

Identifying and classifying key features of parent–child interaction

There is a large body of literature on family process factors in terms of parent–child interaction, largely from within the fields of developmental and social psychology, with many different elements of this relationship put forward as influences on child development. Based on our reading of the theory and empirical investigation here, we adopt a simple, twofold classification of types of parent–child interactions:

1   parenting style; and
2   educational behaviours.

Parenting style encompasses both positive and negative aspects of the parent–child relationship. In the literature these are typically treated separately and include features such as warmth and responsiveness (such as praising and rewarding children) and socialisation practices (such as parental use of discipline), and the strategies adopted to control, regulate and punish behaviour. In some contexts separating out these aspects of parenting is useful, as it may be, for example, that parental education impacts on discipline but not on parental warmth. However, since children and their development are affected by all of these features of parenting, it is useful to consider the evidence across them all, integrating and discussing correspondences where relevant.

Educational behaviours are clearly influenced by, and related to, parenting style but we distinguish them as separate here because they often take the form of specific behaviours rather than part of parent–child interaction more generally. Educational behaviours can include parent–child interactions such as reading to children and the provision of and engagement with a cognitively stimulating environment. These have been well documented in the child development literature and consistently associated with children's development.

This twofold classification can be related to that of others. In a fivefold classification of core processes that link family functioning and school achievement for children, Hess and Holloway (1984) identified five core family processes:

1   verbal interaction between mothers and children;
2   affective relationships between parents and children;
3   discipline and control strategies;
4   expectations of parents for achievement; and
5   parents' beliefs and attributions.

Of these five processes, the last two are considered in our model as parental cognitions and not immediate (proximal) elements of parent–child interactions. Therefore, they are considered in our later chapter on the internal features of the family environment. The second and third can be considered as elements of parenting style, our first category. Their first process cuts across both of our process categories. Hess and Holloway stress the importance of educational behaviours and the learning environment in the home, but treat them as implicitly underpinning each of these five core processes rather than as an explicit aspect of parent–child interactions.

In a later classification of family process factors essential for normal cognitive and social development, Ramey and Ramey (2000) identify seven psychosocial developmental priming mechanisms. We quote these in full because they demonstrate well how the separate categories of parent–child interaction necessarily merge in the reality of those interactions:

1   encourage exploration with all the senses, in familiar and new places, with others and alone, safely and with joy;
2   celebrate developmental advances – learning new skills, little and big and becoming a unique individual;
3   protect from inappropriate disapproval, teasing, neglect, or punishment and comfort appropriately;
4   guide and limit behaviour to keep a child safe and to teach what is acceptable and what is not, i.e. the rules of being cooperative, responsive and caring;
5   mentor in basic skills, showing the whats and whens and the ins and outs of how things and people work;
6   rehearse and extend new skills, showing the child how to practice again and again, in the same and different ways, with new people and new things;
7   communicate richly and responsively with sounds, songs, gestures and words. (p.129)

We recognise that many of these suggestions might equally well be thought of as aspects of either or both of our two categories. For example, the first of the Rameys' admonishments encompasses elements of both of our categories of interaction, namely learning ('exploration'), as well as parenting quality in terms of discipline ('safely') and warmth ('joy'). Thus, neatly classifying different elements of family process is difficult but is a necessary stage in analysis if one is to attempt measurement and evaluation.

A standard and frequently used measure of parenting quality is the Home Observation for Measurement of the Environment (HOME) scale (Caldwell and Bradley, 1984). This inventory assesses age-appropriate parental quality using both mother report and observer ratings in terms of emotional support, such as measures of warmth and discipline, as well as cognitive stimulation, including the frequency the child is read to, household resources such as the presence of toys that teach colour, size and shape in the home, and the physical environment of the home, such as ensuring that outside play areas are safe. Importantly, this broadly matches the distinction that we put forward, although it does combine elements described here as proximal process with aspects considered as characteristics of the family context. This is unfortunate for our attempt to assess the separate links in our overall model.

Language

Proximal processes are the dynamic interactions between children and parents, relationships through which resources of cultural and human capital are exchanged; they are considered as an implicit element of these processes. Language is a key element of these family relationships, a medium of communication and expression that enables transmission of these resources but also a resource itself, a key element of human and cultural capital for its value in enhancing cognitive capabilities and social relationships. Thus, language is intimately involved with intergenerational dynamics both as a mechanism of transmission and as a capability or asset to be transmitted. This chapter refers to evidence highlighting its importance where it is relevant to, or furthers our understanding of, the dynamics in parent–child interaction and the mechanisms for intergenerational transfer.

Fathers

Societal changes over recent years have forced, and continue to force, adjustments in both popular and scholarly conceptualisations of the family, especially in terms of the role of the father. According to Pleck and Pleck (1997), we have seen the evolution of father ideals from the distant breadwinner, to the more actively involved dad, to the father as modern co-parent and in some instances as primary care-giver. Changes in the paternal role and its responsibilities have led to a renewed interest in the research questions, such as how will changes in the roles and expectations of fathers affect children's development, and what type of intergenerational legacy will be left by the fathers and sons of today? However, much of the literature on parenting has tended to focus on the role of mothers, and this is reflected in the discussion below (for a review of the literature examining fathers' involvement in their children's learning and education, see Goldman, 2005).

Some issues of methodology and causality

The studies described in this section have mainly been undertaken with methodological perspectives from fields of psychology in which the focus is often on establishing that measures developed to assess a feature of parenting demonstrate sufficient validity to predict outcomes. This indicates that the instrument is a good, reliable one, not necessarily that parenting is a causal factor in policy terms. The foundation for a hypothesis of underlying causality tends to come rather from theory, qualitative or practitioner evidence. Therefore, care must be demonstrated in interpreting the results in the context of this book, namely to understand the mechanisms that might explain how and why children of parents with greater levels of education achieve better in schools than those whose parents have less education.

A related, important distinction between the studies discussed here and those reported in Chapter 6 on the influence of distal family factors is that they tend to be drawn from small samples. In the methodology commonly adopted in sociological, epidemiological or economic studies, the aim is often to build large samples with a broad range of variables so that it is possible to control for potentially confounding bias and so assess causality in a sample representative of a larger population. In the branches of the psychology literature considered here, the methods adopted tend to be based on collections of data from small but homogeneous samples. Thus, unobserved differences are conditioned out by the sampling frame rather than through the use of multivariate regression.

Each of these methodological approaches has advantages and dis-advantages depending on the objectives of the study, the assumptions made and the validity of the data and measures. For our purposes, a number of studies that have provided simple correlational evidence are reported because they demonstrate the validity of the measures and that proximal processes can be assessed reliably. Where possible we then turn to studies using longitudinal data with value-added results – that is, those that analyse changes in outcomes such as educational achievement over time – to establish causality. However, for many of the important and much-discussed links in our model there are very few or no such studies (see Collins *et al.*, 2000, for further discussion). This is a serious gap in the evidence base and one that we hope will be rectified in years to come. For a full discussion on the problem of establishing causality, see Chapter 2. However, the evidence reported does show that the instruments designed to evaluate the hypo-thesised causal processes have sufficient reliability and validity to indicate that the processes are stable and are important features of development.

Parenting style

The effects of parenting style on child development outcomes

Warmth, responsiveness and authoritative parenting

An extensive body of literature documents connections between aspects of warmth in parent–child relationships and children's development and adjustment. In particular, the importance of parental warmth and secure attachment for the development of children's cognitive and behavioural competence is widely acknowledged (see Baumrind, 1967; Bowlby, 1969, 1973; Masten and Coatsworth, 1998). Secure attachment exists within the individual and the related behaviours of a securely-attached child serve to obtain or maintain proximity to, and contact with, the person or persons referred to as the attachment figure(s), typically the mother or other primary care-giver. Attachment behaviours tend to be most noticeable when the child is scared, ill, insecure or otherwise distressed and is seeking protection, help and comfort.

Bowlby (1969, 1973) argues that the simple knowledge that an attachment figure is available and responsive provides the strong and pervading feelings of security that underlie stable and positive development. The importance of parental warmth may then be due to its effects on the child's sense of attachment and the resulting capability to develop understanding and confront uncertainty or puzzling tasks. Research has shown that children who have a sense of secure attachment, particularly as infants, subsequently approach cognitive tasks in ways that are more conducive to cognitive development. For example, their problem-solving style is characterised by more curiosity, persistence and enthusiasm and less frustration than less securely attached infants (Bretherton, 1985).

Similarly, parents who are warm but structured and use a parenting style with their children that combines clear and consistent rule-setting with high expectations for behaviour, often described as authoritative in the literature (in contrast to authoritarian or permissive parenting) (Baumrind, 1971; see also Maccoby and Martin, 1983), are more likely to promote pro-social behaviour and academic readiness and thus have children with higher academic achievement, better conduct and great social competence with teachers and peers (Masten and Coatsworth, 1998). Those children whose interactions with their mothers are warm and involved are more likely to be socially and emotionally competent and less likely to exhibit behavioural problems than children without such positive parental interactions (Maccoby and Martin, 1983). In contrast, antisocial children are more likely to have experienced harsh, punitive, rejecting and inconsistent parenting (Coie and Dodge, 1998).

A large number of studies have found correlations between the warmth of parent–child interactions and later cognitive outcomes. McGroder (2000), for example, examined different dimensions and patterns of parenting and found that children whose parents adopted styles that were defined by greater warmth in the mother–child relationship and by the mothers' tendency to explain disciplinary rules scored more highly on measures of cognitive school readiness (see also Barocas *et al.*, 1991; Diaz *et al.*, 1991). Moreover, using a person-centred analysis, McGroder shows that for particular parenting style profiles, mothers' warmth and responsiveness may actually compensate for lower levels of cognitive stimulation and so provide resilience against the otherwise negative association between low levels of cognitive stimulation and children's developmental outcomes.

It is also interesting to note that mothers who displayed both more negative patterns of parenting and whose children had poorer outcomes were also more likely to have a lower internal locus of control and higher incidence of depressive symptoms. This finding is consistent with literature suggesting that depressed mothers are less responsive with their children (Downey and Coyne, 1990; Goodman and Brumley, 1990). It also further highlights the value of using an ecological approach to understand the processes underlying children's positive development and educational success. To address this issue, one must consider the dynamics of multiple relationships within the whole family context and not just elements of discrete family functioning as they operate in isolation. The role of parental mental health and well-being is further discussed in Chapter 4.

McGroder goes on to argue that her person-centred approach offers a more fruitful approach to characterising parenting across its multiple dimensions and configurations and, as such, is better able to assess the complex non-linearities that get 'averaged out' in variable-centred approaches. Person-centred approaches examine the characteristics of similar individuals by aggregating those with similar profiles into homogeneous groups; here, for example, clusters of individuals who show comparable parenting styles or patterns of parenting behaviours. The main goal is to understand the interconnectedness among groups of individuals and to identify groups and characteristics of individuals who function in both similar and different ways to other groups. Variable-centred approaches, on the other hand, examine how variables function within a certain population of individuals. As such, they are based on the responses of the 'average' individual and so can have a tendency to ignore the heterogeneity – that is, individual differences – across populations.

However, person-centred approaches are often based only on cross-sectional data that consider the relationships across predictor and outcome variables simultaneously. These methodologies, while interesting, are therefore only able to offer correlations at a given point in time rather than look at development or changes over time, in economic language value-added analyses. That is to say, they preclude drawing any causal conclusions about the determinants of parenting or its effects on child outcomes. However, inasmuch as they attempt to deal with the heterogeneity in diverse populations by identifying associations among homogeneous groups and demonstrating validity of particular measures therein, they are useful.

One longitudinal study that estimated such value-added effects of parenting quality assessed in terms of warmth is that of Estrada *et al.* (1987).

Using longitudinal data, these authors found that the affective quality of the mother–child relationship when the child was four years old significantly predicted school readiness at ages five to six, IQ at six and school achievement at twelve. These associations remained statistically significant when the contributions of maternal IQ, socio-economic status (SES) and children's mental ability at age four were taken into account, suggesting that maternal IQ, SES and earlier ability do not themselves explain the later association between the affective relationship and children's cognitive functioning. Rather, it is the nature of the parent–child relationship itself that predicts positive development in the child outcomes considered. The authors suggest that affective parent–child interactions may have an effect on children's cognitive growth by influencing:

- children's exploratory tendencies, hence their willingness to approach and persist in tasks;
- children's social competence and consequently the flow of information between children and adults; and
- parents' tendency to engage and support children in solving problems.

Patterson *et al.* (1989) also provide evidence suggesting that maternal warmth also matters for later child behavioural adjustment and competence. Children whose interactions with their mothers were low in warmth were subsequently rated by teachers as having more behavioural problems and as being less scholastically competent in certain respects than other children. Children characterised by earlier low levels of maternal warmth also gave self-reports of their own social acceptance and cognitive competence that were discrepant from more objective information from their peers. The authors argue that these results are consistent with the idea that high maternal warmth serves as a protective factor against later adjustment difficulties.

It is also possible, however, that lower maternal warmth may be a response to a child's earlier behavioural difficulties and so reflect the reciprocal relationship between child behaviour and temperament and parenting styles. Alternatively, low levels of maternal warmth may be mediating other features of parent capability or cognition, such as poor mental health. As such, it is these other features of the family environment that drive the relationships that the Patterson study observes between low maternal warmth and poorer child outcomes, not just the lack of warmth in and of itself. This endogeneity (both factors of interest, here low maternal warmth and poor behavioural adjustment) being driven by a third factor, namely poor mental health, would be natural to psychologists interested in interactive relationships. However, it is problematic when one wishes to identify the econometric-style causality, detailed in Chapter 2, that is important for designing policy-based interventions (see also Coie and Dodge, 1998; Loeber, 1990). Nevertheless, these results indicate that warm, responsive and authoritative parenting practices are strong indicators of children's later developmental outcomes.

In adolescence, Steinberg suggests that authoritative parenting is made up of three specific components that reflect the developing maturity of the child and the parent–child relationship and contribute to continued academic achievement: parental warmth and acceptance, behavioural supervision and strictness, and autonomy granting or democracy (Steinberg, 1990; Steinberg *et al.*, 1989, 1992, 1994). These authors posit that while the definition of what constitutes authoritative parenting shifts slightly, taking on age-appropriate meanings, this parenting style nevertheless continues to make significant contributions to adolescents' school success.

Results of various investigations by Steinberg and his colleagues indicate that authoritative parenting has a significant impact on adolescent school performance and engagement during the high school years. Moreover, by using longitudinal data, their research designs allow them to examine the impact of parenting on *changes* in the outcomes assessed, enabling them to make claims about the likely direction of effects. In one investigation, for example, students whose parents were described as authoritative made more academic progress and became more engaged in school over the one-year period assessed than did students from non-authoritative homes (Steinberg *et al.*, 1992, 1994). This methodology reduces the possibility that the results follow from a causal pathway in which the child's behaviour provokes the response of the parent rather than the other way around, since with this estimation strategy the parenting style *precedes* the child's behaviour change (that is, positive development).

The authors claim that their analyses indicate that authoritative parenting leads to school success. They are, however, careful to highlight the probable reciprocal nature of this relationship: students who make good progress and are otherwise positively engaged in school may also be more likely to elicit more authoritative styles of parenting behaviour from their parents. They also note the influence that earlier authoritative parenting may play, that is, the cumulative effect of authoritative parenting over time rather than just the difference between the two points in time studied, and so remain somewhat tentative in their final conclusions. Both these issues echo the potential caveats of our conceptual model, highlighted in Chapter 3, in that its somewhat static or unidirectional approach does not lend itself to modelling the roles that children and young people play in these dynamic, cumulative parent–child relationships.

This study also notes the important mediating roles played by parental involvement in school and parental encouragement of academic success;

higher levels of authoritative parenting were associated with higher levels of school involvement and greater encouragement of academic success. Steinberg and his colleagues therefore posit that how parents convey their beliefs and valuations of academic endeavours may be as important as whether, and to what extent, they do. Parents communicate attitudes, norms and beliefs to children through both subtle and more overt ways. By involving themselves in their children's education and the school more generally, parents may send signals to their children about what they value and expect of them. The important role of parental cognitions will be further discussed in the next chapter.

The studies reviewed thus far underline many of the subtle distinctions between the different aspects of the parent–child relationship and the inevitable cross-overs between definitions or classifications that separate out, for example, warmth and responsiveness and cognitive stimulation, or authoritative parenting styles and parental cognitions. However, inasmuch as they help us to understand better the interactions that take place in the child's day-to-day life that promote cognitive development and academic success, such a distinction is helpful in 'capturing the total pattern of a child's experience' (Schaefer, 1959, p. 226). We now turn to some studies that have explored some of the associations with more negative forms of parenting and child socialisation practices.

Negative parenting and socialisation practices

Authoritative parenting is marked by warm but firm parenting behaviours coupled with high expectations and is associated with academic success from early childhood through adolescence. Negative parenting practices, on the other hand, are marked by harsh and/or inconsistent discipline, punitiveness (such as verbal punishment and physical restraint) and intrusiveness (for example, interfering behaviours such as a mother taking over a task from her child), and predict poorer cognitive outcomes (Egeland *et al.*, 1993; Fagot and Gauvain, 1997) and negative child behaviours (Bradley *et al.*, 2001; Brenner and Fox, 1998). Intrusive and overprotective parenting behaviours are hypothesised as interfering with, or otherwise preventing the acquisition of, independent and self-regulated behaviour (Levy, 1943). In clinical populations, an intrusive style of care-giving has also been suggested as an antecedent to the development of disorders such as attention deficit and attention deficit hyperactivity disorders (ADD and ADHD; see, for example, Cohn *et al.*, 1987; Jacobvitz and Sroufe, 1987).

Egeland *et al.* (1993) explored the relationship between maternal intrusiveness in infancy and children's academic and social adjustment in first and second grades. Observations of mother–child interactions were recorded during one play session and two feeding situations when children were six months old. Mothers were rated in terms of their intrusive behaviours on a scale that included Ainsworth's Scale of Cooperation and Interference (Ainsworth *et al.*, 1978) and assessed the extent to which mothers' behaviours 'break into or interrupt the baby's ongoing activities rather than being geared in both timing and quality to the baby's state, mood, interests, and activities' (Egeland *et al.*, 1993, p. 362).

Their results showed that in assessments six to eight years later, children of mothers who were judged to be intrusive at six months were doing worse in terms of academic achievement as well as in terms of their social, emotional and behavioural adjustment than children of non-intrusive mothers. The children of intrusive mothers scored lower on achievement tests in maths and reading, withdrew from new situations and were less involved with peers. These results remained significant conditional on maternal IQ and stressful life events experienced by the family, as well as mothers' own affective behaviour during feeding situations observed at six months. The authors thus argue that these results indicate a unique contribution of maternal intrusiveness, independent of mothers' affective interactions with her child, and conclude that such maternal behaviours constitute a distinct element of parenting, particularly related to negative outcomes for children.

These results also support the hypothesis that parenting styles influence children's achievement and achievement-related behaviours by encouraging exploration and active engagement in learning environments. For example, children who grow up with more intrusive parents are more likely to have problems in interacting with teachers and peers and may consequently avoid new situations and so experience less cognitive stimulation. These, in turn, may also hinder development of achievement-related skills by lowering self-concepts and reducing motivation to succeed. Again, however, these data, while longitudinal, are not value-added in the sense of establishing econometric causality and the methodology used makes it impossible to disentangle the relative importance of early, concurrent or cumulative effects of maternal intrusiveness. Nevertheless, early observations of maternal intrusive behaviour are salient in predicting later child outcomes.

Rubin *et al.* (2002) obtained value-added results, similar to those that Steinberg *et al.* reported earlier, in their study examining the role that early parenting plays in predicting socially reticent behaviour (socially wary behaviours) in pre-schoolers. Building on earlier investigations, which had only looked at these relationships contemporaneously, Rubin *et al.* explored whether maternal intrusiveness or use of derisive comments during interactions were predictive of child characteristics two years later, either directly or indirectly, via the moderation of earlier behavioural inhibition.

They found that maternal intrusiveness predicted children's internalising behavioural problems two years later, at age four, conditional on earlier levels of these problems: toddlers who had been inhibited with their peers at age two were likely to be highly reticent at age four only if their mothers had been observed to be controlling and/or derisive. The longitudinal design of this study, which allows the authors to control for earlier measures of both parenting and child behaviours, enables stronger, more confident conclusions to be drawn about the relationship between maternal intrusive behaviours and child outcomes. Thus mothers' psychologically controlling behaviours moderate the predictive association between peer inhibition when children are toddlers and their socially reticent behaviours as pre-schoolers.

Furthermore, children who were observed to be behaviourally inhibited at two years old, whose mothers did not engage in such negative parenting, displayed a more 'healthy' form of solitude – that is, solitary but not anxious – two years later. The authors therefore argue that negative parenting practices undermine the development of competence and independence in children at risk of later social or behavioural problems by not allowing them adequate opportunity to practise and improve social skills (for example, by being overprotective) and by either implicitly or explicitly signalling to them that they are simply not able to do so (derision).

Many theories regarding the causes of conduct problems and depression among children suggest that inconsistent, erratic and harsh parenting practices characterise a coercive cycle of conflict and parent–child interactions that lead to increased problem behaviour and depressive symptoms. For example, Patterson's model of the development of antisocial behaviour (1986; Patterson *et al.*, 1989) specifically implicates poor parental use of discipline as fundamental in the development of antisocial behaviour problems and conduct disorders.

Brenner and Fox (1998) found that parental discipline, such as responding to difficult behaviour with verbal and corporal punishment, was strongly related to the behavioural problems of children aged between one and five years old, including disobedience, acting aggressively and not listening. Moreover, parental discipline accounted for more of the unique variance in predicting ratings of children's problem behaviour than all demographic variables, such as education, income level and marital status, combined. The authors also found that parents who report higher rates of discipline use had children who exhibited greater problem behaviour than those who reported less frequent use of discipline (see also Bradley *et al.*, 2001). They concluded that their results demonstrate the particular importance of parental discipline. As already highlighted, however, caution is required in interpreting these results as an alternative view might simply suggest that the association operates in the other direction; children with more problematic behaviours require more discipline (Bell, 1968).

The effects of prior parental education on parenting style

Why does parents' education matter for parenting and its impact on parent–child interaction? Proponents of this view argue that education may provide parents with important skills, values and knowledge that enable them to better support and facilitate their children's learning and development (see Eccles, 2005 for a review). In turn, these cognitive strategies may influence parents' own personal resources enabling them to provide, and engage in, a family environment that presents greater opportunities and broader life chances.

Klebanov *et al.* (1994), for example, found evidence of an association between mothers' education and warm, responsive parenting styles as assessed by Caldwell and Bradley's HOME inventory (1984). While both family income level and mothers' education were related to the learning and physical environment, only mothers' education was predictive of the warmth and social climate provided by parents (see also Smith *et al.*, 1997). Moreover, of all the familial variables studied (including family income, family size, teenage birth, female headship and ethnicity), education was the most predictive of all the parenting behaviours assessed.

Similarly, van Bakel and Riksen-Walraven (2002) considered the determinants of the quality of parenting defined in terms of the quality of the support that the parent provided for their infant and the overall quality of their parental interactive behaviour. Testing a sample of 129 parents and their fifteen-month-olds, they found that parental education explained significant and unique portions of the variance in the observed quality of parental behaviour. The authors argue that parents with more education provide more supportive childcare for several reasons. In particular, they suggest that during their years of college or university education and functioning in jobs requiring higher qualifications and involving more responsibilities, these parents may have acquired other important attitudes and competencies such as tolerance or the ability to plan tasks.

Davis-Kean (2005) used data from the child supplement of the US Panel Study of Income Dynamics (PSID-CDS, Hofferth *et al.*, 1998) to examine the processes underlying the associations between key distal features of the family, such as parents' education and income and children's academic achievement. Using structural equation modelling techniques to explore some of the possible mechanisms involved in the intergenerational transmission of educational success, Davis-Kean found evidence for indirect effects of parents' education on children's achievement through measures of parents' beliefs and behaviours. Three composite measures of parenting behaviours were assessed: parental warmth (an interviewer rating scale that assessed six items of parent–child interaction, including 'parent's voice conveys positive feeling to the child' and 'how often did primary care-giver spontaneously praise child for his or her behaviour, helpfulness, looks, or other positive qualities?'), parent–child play (four items indicating parental participation with their child in activities such as board games, sports, computing and arts and crafts), and reading (how often the child reads for enjoyment and the number of books that the child has).

Her results show that education is the primary predictor of child achievement in maths and reading through the mediating mechanisms of expectations and beliefs (these results are discussed in Chapter 5), warmth and reading. Moreover, the influence of parental warmth and reading remained statistically significant even after family background and parents' educational expectations were controlled. Parent–child play-based interactions were not found to mediate the association between parents' education and child achievement. The author points out, however, that this may reflect the ages of the children in these data, who were on average 10.6 years old, arguing that by mid-childhood, parent–child play may be more closely related to sustaining the affective quality of the relationship than are achievement-related parenting activities.

These findings have recently been replicated in a large, multi-racial, longitudinal dataset. Parents' educational attainment was again found to be the most important distal factor in predicting children's achievement as well as the change in their achievement across time (Davis-Kean and Sexton, 2007). Interestingly, the mechanisms for the relationships between family SES (education and income) and child achievement differed by ethnic group (European Americans and African-Americans). The results suggest that, while the mediating mechanisms of parental beliefs and behaviours examined here explain, statistically, most of the relationship between parent education and child achievement for African-American families, the picture for European American families appears more complicated. Davis-Kean suggests that, for the European American families, home activities that encourage academic competence such as homework monitoring, assistance with school projects or going to science museums or libraries will have stronger relations with achievement.

Other evidence using the PSID-CDS data similarly reports that mothers with less than a high school education are less likely to show their child warmth than are parents with higher levels of educational attainment. For example, 75 per cent of mothers with less than a high school education hug or show physical affection to their child at least once a day, compared to 87 per cent of mothers with a high school diploma, 91 per cent of mothers with some college education and 94 per cent of mothers with college degrees. Similarly, more college-educated fathers (77 per cent) report hugging their child daily than do fathers with less than a high school education (68 per cent) or fathers with a high school diploma (70 per cent) (Child Trends, 2002). However, these results may not necessarily reflect a causal effect of education, but rather issues of endogeneity; that is, the prior emotional development of the parents may underlie both their educational success and the warmth of their parenting (see Chapter 2 for further discussion of the problems of endogeneity inherent in the estimation of causal education effects).

Developmental research has also demonstrated an association between maternal education and the mother's parenting behaviour in terms of the socialisation practices and disciplinary strategies she adopts. For example, Fox *et al.* (1995) found that scores from maternal ratings of discipline frequencies were consistently higher (that is, greater use by parents of corporal punishment, such as spanking and yelling) for women with less education. In addition, younger mothers, mothers with two or more children living at home, unmarried mothers and those from middle SES, as opposed to upper-middle SES, reported more frequent need for discipline. Studies of maternal intrusiveness have also documented statistically significant relations between higher levels of maternal intrusive behaviour and lower levels of educational and socio-economic status (Bee *et al.*, 1969; Bradley, 1993; Phinney and Feshbach, 1980).

Research from the USA also shows that, in terms of attitudes towards endorsement of physical punishment such as spanking, adults who are college graduates are less likely than adults without a high school diploma or an equivalent to say that spanking a child is sometimes necessary (Day *et al.*, 1998). In 2000, 66 per cent of men who were college graduates agreed that spanking is sometimes necessary compared to 87 per cent of men with less than a high school education. Among women, 55 per cent of college graduates agreed that it was sometimes necessary to spank a child, compared to 80 per cent of those who did not graduate from high school (Child Trends, 2002).

Educational behaviours

The effects of educational behaviours on child development outcomes

Educational behaviours in the home, while part of the parent–child relation-ships and so influenced by factors such as warmth, responsiveness and disciplinary strategies, take on more specific interactions in the parent–child dyad. These aspects of parenting often include more particular or observable forms of parent–child behaviours and include, for example, reading to children, teaching them letters, numbers, songs, poems and nursery rhymes, painting and drawing earlier in childhood and later helping with homework and being actively involved in children's schooling, as well as going on visits to places of educational value and interest such as libraries and museums. Such experiences are likely to influence both the child's skill levels and their interest in continued engagement in such activities. In turn, skill and interest level should facilitate transitions to school and motivate the pursuit of educational goals and endeavours, and so influence subsequent academic success. Authors such as Wigfield and Asher (1984) suggest that factors in the home outweigh factors in the school in predicting children's desire and ability to succeed in school.

Reading to children and exposure to print

Just as oral language development has a history that precedes the child's utterance of his or her first word, reading development also has a history that precedes the child's ability to read. Parents play an important role in fostering literacy skills in their children. Reading to children and involving them in other activities related to literacy facilitates the development of an orientation toward print, knowledge of narrative structure and function, general knowledge of the world, phonological awareness and a positive attitude towards reading (Baker *et al.*, 1994).

The Effective Provision of Pre-school Education (EPPE, for example see Sammons *et al.*, 2002) project is the first major European longitudinal study of a national sample charting the development of children between the ages of three and seven, across intellectual and affective domains. To investigate the effects of pre-school education for three and four year olds, the EPPE team have collected a wide range of information on over 3,000 children, their parents, their home environments and the pre-school settings they attended.[1] A sample of 'home' children, who had no, or minimal, pre-school experiences was recruited for the study at entry to school for comparison. Both quantitative and qualitative methods have been used to explore the effects of individual pre-school centres on children's attainment, as well as social, emotional and behavioural development at entry to school and on to outcomes at the end of Key Stage 1, the end of year 2 when pupils are six or seven years old, and most recently Key Stage 2, the end of primary school, aged ten or eleven (Sammons *et al.*, 2004b, 2007).

Among their findings, results from analysis of the EPPE study document that the frequency with which parents read to their children is associated with higher scores in language and pre-reading skills, early number concepts and non-verbal reasoning at entry to primary school. These results continue to hold when the estimation controls for distal features of the family including parents' education, SES and the number of siblings, as well as child-level characteristics such as gender and age. Rowe (1991) similarly indicates that regardless of family SES, age and gender, reading activity at home has significant and positive influences on measures of students' reading achievement and attitudes towards reading. Moreover, these results also show a strong interdependence between students' attitudes towards reading and reading activity at home, both of which had significant positive influences on reading achievement.

Other authors have found that the language used during shared book reading is richer and more varied than that used during other parent–child interactions, such as more general play sessions or mealtimes (for example, Dunn *et al.*, 1977; Hoff-Ginsberg, 1991). On the basis of such findings, many authors have concluded that 'regular, wide reading must be seen as the major avenue of large-scale, long-term vocabulary growth' (Nagy *et al.*, 1985, p. 266). However, whether parents read to their children or not is likely to depend in part on whether their children wish to be read to or not and operates as part of the dynamic and transactional processes in the parent–child relationship. As such, this measure should be interpreted as endogenous and the resulting effect sizes found may be an overestimate of the true causal effect of parent–child reading behaviours.

In their meta-analytic review on the role joint book reading plays in the intergenerational transmission of literacy, Bus *et al.* (1995) recognise the difficulty of this 'chicken and egg' relationship, but argue that it seems reasonable to assume that 'interest in reading is as much a prerequisite as a consequence of book reading' (p. 3). Looking across the results of 29 quantitative studies on the importance of parent–pre-schooler reading, Bus *et al.* conclude that joint book reading explains about 8 per cent of the variance in outcome measures such as language growth, emergent literacy and reading achievement. Furthermore, this effect is not dependent on the distal features of families but does appear to diminish as soon as children become conventional readers and cross over from learning to read, to reading to learn.

Theoretical work by Sénéchal *et al.* (1998) splits early literacy experiences with parents into informal and formal experiences. Informal literary activities are those that focus on the message contained in the print such as the story and its characters, whereas formal exposure centres more on the print itself, for example talking about letters, providing names and specific sounds. Using this distinction, Sénéchal and LeFevre (2002) assessed the relative importance of parents' storybook reading with children and parents' reports of teaching on children's oral language skills, later written language skills as well as reading acquisition in a five-year longitudinal study. Exposure to storybooks was used as the measure of informal literary activities and parental reports of how frequently they taught their child about reading and writing as the formal measure. Their findings highlight the importance of home learning, both in terms of formal and informal reading experiences, on later literacy abilities, suggesting clear links from home literary experiences from early literacy skills through to fluent reading. It is interesting and somewhat surprising, however, that parents' reports of teaching (formal) and storybook exposure (informal) were uncorrelated. This result may, in part, reflect the endogeneity issue referred to above.

Cognitive environments, teaching strategies and learning stimulation in the home

Growing up in a home rich in cognitive stimulation and educational opportunities not only influences literacy development but also has a lasting impact on a child's desire to learn (Gottfried *et al.*, 1998). EPPE research, for example, documents the importance of broad features of a young child's home learning environment (HLE). The EPPE study uses a wide-ranging index of cognitive stimulation in the HLE, which includes measures of reading to children; encouraging playing with, teaching and actively engaging children with letters and numbers; teaching songs and nursery rhymes; painting and drawing; and visits to the library. While distal factors such as mothers' educational level and family SES are highly significant, the HLE has been found to exert a significant and independent influence on attainment at three plus years of age, as well as later at entry to primary school (rising fives) and progress during this pre-school period (see also McGroder, 2000). As with their findings for the influence of parental reading with children, researchers at EPPE have found that, conditional on distal features of the family, the HLE is the strongest variable in predicting cognitive skills as well as non-verbal abilities and four measures of social/behavioural development: cooperation/conformity; peer sociability; confidence; and anti-social behaviour.

The nature of the home environment is also conceptually relevant to academic intrinsic motivation – the pleasure found in school and learning endeavours more generally. Academic intrinsic motivation can be characterised by features of the individual such as curiosity, persistence and mastery orientation, and has been shown to be consistently and positively related to pupil achievement and academic self-concept as well as negatively associated with academic anxiety (for example, Gottfried, 1990). Availability of cognitive stimulation in the home such as exposure to learning-orientated opportunities and activities would be expected to stimulate children's orientation towards enjoyment of learning through engaging in, as well as by valuing, such activities. Hence, cognitive stimulation and the provision of learning experiences in the home are likely to be positively related to children's academic intrinsic motivation. And as with the parenting practices reviewed earlier in this chapter, one might expect these behaviours and activities to have cumulative effects over time. However, these assessments of home environment are as related to the responsiveness of the child to cognitive stimulation as are the educational behaviours in relation to parent–child reading. Therefore, one must again be concerned about the potential over-estimation of pure causal effects in econometric terms. Nonetheless, these patterns of association are interesting and informative.

Gottfried *et al.* (1998) used structural equation modelling in longitudinal data to show that children whose homes were higher in cognitive stimulation (measured at age eight) had higher academic intrinsic motivation from ages nine to thirteen, conditional on parents' SES. The results of their analyses, which look at pathways for these effects over time, suggest that the effect of the home environment is continuous, as the earlier measures of the provision of cognitive stimulation positively related to subsequent motivation both directly at ages ten and thirteen, as well as indirectly though earlier measures of academic intrinsic motivation. In support of the conceptual model that we put forward in Chapter 3, the authors argue that family SES is filtered to the child through the proximal environment they experience, here the provision of a home environment rich in active academic stimulation, a social climate that supports and encourages an intellectual and cultural orientation, and a variety of learning opportunities. These proximal experiences, in turn, impact directly on the development of intrinsic motivation.

The importance of a cognitively rich home environment can also manifest itself through parents' active engagement in their children's education. Parental interest and involvement in school, for example, is considered an important component in children's educational and cognitive development and shows strong and positive links with school achievement and adjustment. Feinstein and Symons (1999) find strong associations between teachers' assessments of their pupils' parents' interest in learning and the attainment of children (see also Sacker *et al.*, 2002 and Reynolds, 1992 for comparable findings for the USA). Again, making use of the strengths of longitudinal data, these authors found that change (growth) in attainment between the ages of eleven and sixteen was related to the parents' interest in their child's education, as rated by teachers, when that child was age seven. Teachers were asked to rate their impression of the interest parents take in the progress of their child's learning and education on a scale of low, medium or high interest. Using a measure of parental interest in children's education prior to the measures of attainment (here eleven and sixteen) reduces the potentially confounding bias of teachers simply reflecting the ability of that child in their rating of parental interest. It seems likely, therefore, that this is not just a misreport by the teacher who sees a pupil doing well and infers parental interest falsely. However, this variable does not refer to parental involvement explicitly and may pick up the effect of parent cognitions, such as aspirations and expectations, rather than specific parental behaviours per se. We discuss the important role of parental cognitions in the next chapter and the relationships and interactions between families and schools in Chapter 7.

In a recent review of the literature on the impact of parental involvement, parental support and family education on pupil achievement and adjustment, Desforges and Abouchaar (2003) highlight the specific importance of 'at home' parental involvement. Noting the 'catch-all' term of 'parental involvement' and subsuming good parenting, helping with homework, talking to teachers, attending school meetings and functions, and being involved with aspects of school governance more generally, Desforges summarises a wealth of international evidence that supports the view that parent involvement has positive effects on pupil achievement and adjustment, net of parental social class and educational level. Among the key findings of this review, Desforges concludes that, during the primary school years, the HLE and the nature of parental involvement have a greater influence on child achievement outcomes than does the variation in school quality. This finding holds across all social classes and all ethnic groups. He also notes that, although the extent to which parents are involved diminishes as the child gets older, it nevertheless remains a significant factor in secondary schools where it affects pupils' educational aspirations and staying-on rates. Interestingly, parental involvement in the form of home supervision was shown to be negatively related to achievement. Desforges argues that this presumably reflects a more reactive kind of involvement, increasing in response to pupil difficulties.

Parental involvement is influenced by distal features of the family such as education, social class and single-parent status as well as characteristics of the home including maternal psycho-social health. Moreover, it is strongly influenced by the child's own level of achievement: the higher the level of achievement, the more the parent gets involved. Thus, in line with the caveats of our model outlined in Chapter 3, Desforges also notes the dynamic role that children and young people play in shaping the relations between the home and school environments.

Language pervades nearly all forms of these specific educational behaviours and many studies report an association between aspects of verbal communication in the home and subsequent school achievement. Hubbs-Tait *et al.* (2002) examined the specific influence of parental language during teaching strategies on child development, arguing that the nature of support and guidance used by parents during problem-solving tasks is also a good marker for children's cognitive performance. They state that, in general, the more parents make use of statements that challenge children to use *representational* thought, that is, to evaluate their own competence ('Are you ready for the third step?') or assess their own performance ('Well, what do you think?'), the better the child's cognitive understanding and perform-ance. In contrast, greater parental use of statements requiring only *referential* thought, that is, requiring more simple statements of labelling or observation or including no challenge for thinking, lowers the children's cognitive performance.

Arguments such as these highlight the parallels between the nurturing and responsive aspects of parenting discussed above, and the teaching strategies parents adopt during educational behaviours at home. For example, parents who communicate using praise and encouragement during parent–child interaction create a positive atmosphere in which children are more likely to take an increasing share of responsibility and, in turn, show increases in both their actual development and their sense of competence.

The effects of prior parental education on educational behaviours

In the preceding section, we argued that the influence of parents' education on measures of parenting styles may operate by providing parents with important cognitive resources that enable them to better support and facilitate their children's development. The same basic premise motivates research that explores the consistently found relationship between parental education and the provision of a cognitively stimulating environment, the teaching strategies parents use and the learning behaviours in which they engage their children. In addition, more educated parents have been shown to have greater knowledge about the environmental factors that influence children's development (Clarke-Stewart, 1973; Stevens, 1982) and are more accurate in assessing their children's developmental skills (Gottfried *et al.*, 1998). More educated mothers may also be more aware of what is necessary for intellectual development and school success and act on this knowledge to provide the experiences and the setting that facilitate such achievement.

Early work by Hess and Shipman (1965) found associations between mothers' education and the educational and teaching behaviours they used with their children. They showed that, in a group of African-American mothers, those with more formal education provided more structure, verbal guidance and elaboration when teaching their pre-school children a problem-solving task (see also Harris *et al.*, 1999). Laosa (1980) also found differences in the principal teaching strategies adopted by Anglo-American and Chicana mothers. For example, Anglo-American, more highly-educated mothers used higher levels of inquiry and praise, whereas Chicana mothers with lower levels of education relied more heavily on modelling behaviours, negative physical control and directives. The author suggests that the different approaches used may result from acculturation to the mainstream culture represented by formal schooling (see also Rogoff, 1990). Equally, however, the direction of causality may operate in reverse: mothers with less education may adjust their teaching behaviours to better fit the educational needs of their children who tend to perform more poorly on tasks of cognitive ability.

More recently, Diaz *et al.* (1991) found similar associations between maternal education and the maternal teaching strategies used with three-year-old children during tasks of selective attention and card sequencing (see also Uribe *et al.*, 1993). Differences were observed in terms of frequency of controlling directives, distancing (use of open-ended questions and adult responses designed to evoke representational and independent thinking) and maternal attributions of child competence (such as use of praise and encouragement), even when controlling for children's initial level of task performance.

Hoff-Ginsberg (1991, 1992) found differences associated with parents' level of education and mothers' conversational behaviour. Notably, mothers with only a high school education addressed less speech towards their children than college-educated mothers did. Similar to the findings for differences in teaching strategies as well as the important role of language (such as Hubbs-Tait *et al.*, 2002) reported earlier, mothers with lower levels of education also asked fewer conversation-eliciting questions, either for the purpose of initiating or sustaining conversation, engaged in fewer conversations related to topics children themselves raised and used less complex syntax and less varied vocabulary, suggesting that these children are experiencing specific differences in their language-learning environments. Moreover, research that explores the relation between SES and children's language development suggests that maternal speech is a key mediating mechanism for the relationship between SES and child vocabulary (see also Hoff, 2003a and b; Hoff-Ginsberg, 1998).

Descriptive data from the USA using the National Household Education Survey and the Federal Inter-agency on Child and Family Statistics (Child

Trends, 2002) show that mothers' education is consistently related to whether children are read to by a family member or not. Young children are more likely to be read to if their mothers have completed higher levels of education. For example, in 2001, 73 per cent of young children whose mothers had graduated from college were read to every day by a family member. In contrast, 60 per cent of children whose mothers only had some college education were read to every day, compared to 49 per cent whose mothers had only finished high school and 42 per cent whose mothers had not finished high school.

More comprehensive data and analysis from the UK's EPPE project show similar patterns in the relationship between parents' education and educational behaviours such as reading to children. Their index measure of cognitive stimulation in the home, the HLE, is significantly correlated with mother's qualifications ($r = 0.35$), more so than measures of parental socio-economic status or occupational class.

As with the conclusions of Desforges in his recent review of the impact of parental involvement, parental support and family education on achievement, the EPPE project's findings have been interpreted as suggesting that what parents do is more important than who they are. While mothers' highest educational qualification showed a strong, positive and consistent impact across all five cognitive outcomes assessed, actual parenting behaviours, such as reading to children, were better predictors of children's outcomes. As we, our model and some of the empirical studies reviewed above suggest, however, since part of the education effect is *mediated* by these behaviours – that is, since they are the channels for education effects – the fact that, in an ordinary least squares regression, the coefficient on such behaviours is greater than that on education does not necessarily mean that behaviours are more important than education. Unpacking this estimation issue requires a more sophisticated analysis. Only recently has research that systematically and simultaneously examines the multiple channels through which parent education may influence multiple features of parenting and child outcomes and give some understanding of the relative importance of different factors started to emerge.

In a recent study by Bradley and Corwyn (2003) for example, the authors examined the extent to which learning stimulation in the home mediated the relation between distal features of the family and various measures of child development, including verbal ability, achievement in reading and maths and behaviour problems. One purpose of this study was to determine whether constituent components of SES (specifically maternal education and household income) have similar influences on the mediating proximal processes of learning stimulation and maternal responsiveness and child development. In order to understand possible differences in these mediated effects, relations were examined for children from four to fourteen, split into three developmental periods (early-, middle-childhood and adolescence) and across three ethnic groups (African-Americans, European Americans and Latin Americans). Learning stimulation was defined at each developmental period by items from the HOME-SF, the short form of Caldwell and Bradley's original HOME inventory, a semi-structured interview made up from a combination of observer ratings and mothers' reports on aspects of the home environment (1984). Items include the frequency with which the child is read to, encouragement to start and keep up hobbies and visits to museums and other cultural activities.

Using data from the National Longitudinal Survey of Youth (NLSY), maternal education was shown to have stronger relations with children's scores in verbal ability and achievement in maths and reading than either family income alone or a composite measure of education and income, the Duncan Socio-Economic Index (SEI) (Duncan, 1961; see also Davis-Kean, 2005; Davis-Kean and Sexton, 2007; Smith *et al.*, 1997). In terms of developmental time periods considered, the influence of maternal education was found to be most pronounced on these outcomes during early childhood. These education effects were mediated by learning stimulation in the home: parents with higher levels of education tend to provide their children with materials and experiences that foster academic success and engage them in richer language exchanges.

While causality cannot be established using such analyses, Bradley and Corwyn's results and those from the EPPE and Davis-Kean studies do indicate that educational behaviours and particular aspects of the home environment are not just simple proxy measures for aspects of economic or cultural wealth, but real independent forces. This is an important result with implications for programmes such as Sure Start.[2] For example, if these results are accurate in a causal sense, young mothers with few qualifications, whose children typically show a higher incidence of low attainment, can improve their children's progress and give them a better start at school by engaging in those activities in the home that foster learning.

Feinstein and Duckworth (2006) have attempted to counter such estimation problems and establish whether the strong correlation between mothers' participation in education and measures of her parenting behaviours result from a primarily causal relationship or from selection effects. Using longitudinal data from the UK spanning three generations, the results suggest that, while mothers' participation in post-compulsory education has some small positive causal effects on her provision of a cognitively stimulating environment (again using the HOME inventory), much of the apparent relationship between a mother's post-16 educational participation and measures of her parenting is driven by selection bias. It is largely other factors such as her aspirations, motivation and prior achievement that determine her parenting style and affect her decision to stay on in education.

Summary

Positive parenting styles are strongly associated with positive outcomes for children. Educational behaviours in particular have real and considerable effects on children's development, particularly in the domains of cognitive ability and academic achievement. In their meta-analytic review of the similarity in parents' child rearing, Holden and Miller (1999) conclude that parenting style and parental behaviour are highly stable across time. Thus, when consistently experienced, parental influences are likely to accumulate and so produce larger, meaningful outcomes over the course of childhood and adolescence. However, much of the evidence base here comes from correlational research and so issues of causality remain. Parenting is influenced by many features of both parents, their own upbringings, their relationship together, work and social networks. In economic terminology, parenting is not exogenous, yet neither can it be allocated experimentally so as to establish causality in a true econometric way; with some exceptions, children are born into particular families and cannot be randomly assigned to different ones in order to examine the influences that different parenting experiences might produce. It may well be that often unobserved factors such as parental well-being, stress or cognitive capabilities underlie the apparent effects of parenting style on development. We discuss these influences in the next chapter.

Evaluation evidence is a useful aid here, but not conclusive as authors disagree about the extent to which parenting programmes influence children's development. Magnuson's (Magnuson and Duncan, 2004) view of the evaluation evidence is that parenting may exert a stronger influence on behaviour than on cognitive development. Webster-Stratton finds strong influences on behaviour, in line with Magnuson's reading of the evidence (Webster-Stratton, 1990b; Webster-Stratton and Hammond, 1997). The implication of the discrepancy between evaluation and survey-based evidence is that more work needs to be done on examining *changes* in parenting style over time in the large survey analyses. The evaluation evidence suggests that interventions succeed in altering children's school attainment substantially. This perhaps suggests that existing survey analysis has been wrong in assuming that the strong correlations between parental warmth and socialisation practices and cognitive development are causal.

At first glance, one may not imagine that education would impact heavily on parental warmth, which is more about affection in and enjoyment of relationships with children and parental well-being than about parental demographics. However, to the extent that education enhances efficacy and well-being, it may lead to increased parental warmth. Education does appear to enhance parents' capacity to be considerate in their use of discipline. There may therefore be an effect of education on the use of appropriate socialisation strategies; warmth with discipline provides a developmentally enhancing structure, one without the other less so. The evidence supports this theoretical conjecture but, again, there have not yet been sufficient large sample longitudinal studies to test causality as robustly as available techniques would allow.

There is substantial theory and evidence to support the view that parents' education influences educational behaviours in the home. The magnitude of this effect, however, has not been fully identified as the evidence for the causal role is not robust to reverse causality problems. And as Desforges highlights in his literature review, while it is easy to describe what parents do and how they are involved in their children's education, it is difficult to establish in quantifiable terms whether that particular behaviour or interaction makes a difference to school outcomes. Feinstein and Duckworth (2006) suggest that assumptions regarding the causal interpretation of the relationship between parents' education and the educational behaviours that they adopt should be drawn with caution. They argue that simply extending the length of time that women spend in education may do little to directly affect the educational attainment of their children. Rather, it is more likely to be the ability and aspirations of women that motivate their partici-pation in post-16 education, their subsequent parenting style and the attainment of their children. It may be through intergenerational contin-uities in factors such as these that inequalities in educational success are transmitted through the generations. This suggests that supporting children in learning through early and continued investment in good quality education and developmental opportunities is more important in addressing social immobility than simply extending the average length of participation, important though that may be.

5 Internal features of the family environment

Introduction

The previous chapter examined the associations between prior parental education, family proximal processes and children's developmental outcomes. While much early development is viewed primarily as a function of the quality of parenting and the child's own characteristics, the quality and nature of parenting itself is shaped by broader factors. This chapter takes a step back from the immediate parent–child relationship and turns to the internal features and characteristics of the family environment as factors influencing the context within which these relationships occur. We continue our focus on the context of family and on the relative importance of its key characteristics as mechanisms for passing down educational success and advantage to children. Key internal features of the family context identified here are:

- parental cognitions;
- mental health and well-being; and
- material resources.

Put broadly, parental cognitions refer to the ways in which parents think about parenting, the dynamics of the parent–child relationships and the family management practices. Cognitions may include values, attitudes, knowledge and beliefs, as well as expectations, aspirations and lifestyle philosophies, and are crucial in shaping the family environment. Mental health and well-being are also fundamental in influencing children's developmental context.

As in the previous chapter, for each key characteristic, we consider the theory and evidence for:

- its importance as an influence on children's development; and
- an influence of parental education on the characteristic.

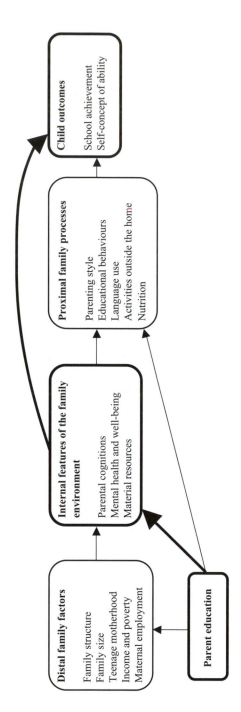

Figure 5.1 Conceptual model for the influence of the key internal features of the family environment

Much of the literature exploring the nature of the family environment and its importance for child outcomes views these characteristics as part of the complex relationship between distal and proximal factors rather than as separate mechanisms important in their own right. As such, there is less evidence on the specific importance of the individual characteristics of the family contexts for children's development per se. This chapter is therefore largely grounded in theory, drawing on evidence where it is available. Evidence based on more complex modelling of distal factors operating through these family-level characteristics on proximal processes and, in turn, on children's developmental outcomes will be discussed in our conclusions in Chapter 9.

We also note the importance of interactions between the characteristics of families; each of the key features identified here is likely to moderate the effects of others. Thus, parents' beliefs are likely to be moderated by poor parental well-being and/or high levels of stress. For example, parents who are depressed may also feel less able to implement their parenting beliefs and goals (Elder and Ardelt, 1992). Some interesting interactions between characteristics of context will be noted.

A note on resources

The expenditure of resources on material goods, from housing to food, is the primary mechanism by which distal factors such as income, family structure and maternal employment achieve real impact on children's lives in the economic model. Economic models of child development (for example Becker, 1973, 1981) view the family as a little factory in which child achievement is produced and suggest that families with higher economic resources are better able to purchase or produce important goods or inputs for their children's development. A family's resources can also be conceptualised in terms of time. Becker highlights, for example, the import-ance of time resources in terms of substitution effects: time spent on one activity cannot then be spent on another (see Chapter 3 for a full discussion of the application of economic models to children's attainment).

According to our model for the influence of parents' education, because resources mediate the effects of distal factors on children's lives, evidence on their importance belongs in this chapter. However, there are many more studies on the effect of resources in terms of family income or family structure than there are on breaking down the effects of expenditure on specific resources into component channels, for example the differential effects of spending money on toys, books and computer games versus extra-curricular activities or different types of childcare. As such, the influ-ences of resources and their importance within the context of the family on children's developmental outcomes are discussed in detail in Chapter 6, and we do not provide specific evidence on them here.

Parental cognitions

The previous chapter explored the parent–child relationship in the context of the day-to-day experience of the developing child, highlighting specific aspects of familial interactions such as warmth, discipline and socialisation practices and educational behaviours in the home as important channels for the intergenerational transmission of educational success. However, understanding the relationships between what parents do with their children and children's achievement is only part of the picture, and even with good measures of parenting behaviours and parent–child interaction there are many reasons why we should also be interested in the relation between parental beliefs and child development. Why do parents parent in the ways that they do? What do parents think about children's development and abilities and how do these differ? Do differences in the ways parents think about their children matter for their children's development?

Research in the field of parental cognitions is based on the premise that the aspects of parenting discussed in the previous chapter are largely influenced by parental beliefs (Goodnow and Collins, 1990; Murphey, 1992). Direct observation of parent–child interactions is, however, unlikely to encapsulate all the important and dynamic elements of parenting and the parent–child relationship. Miller (1988) asserts that attitudes towards, and expectations of, parental and household responsibilities, as well as the ways in which parents structure and resource their home environments, are examples of potentially important decisions that are difficult to capture in observable behaviours or discrete measures.

Moreover, parents learn to parent by parenting and, as we suggested in the previous chapter, some beliefs may only be conveyed over time in a cumulative way. For example, a child may have understood (and so internalised) from an early age that their parent values intellectual curiosity and exploration, yet there is no single measure that can sufficiently account for or convey such a construct. Measuring parental cognitions such as beliefs, aspirations, expectations and values may therefore provide a more fruitful insight into the dynamics and processes underpinning the parent–child relationship and so offer a more complete understanding of the intergenerational pathways for educational success and the role that parents' education plays.

Theoretical perspectives on why parental cognitions matter

Current work on the influence of parental cognitions on children's development is grounded in theoretical perspectives of motivation and the social and psychological features of individuals that influence choice and persistence. These theories help to explain how and why the different cognitions parents hold impact upon children's achievement outcomes. For example, *attribution theory* (Graham, 1991; Heider, 1958; Weiner, 1985) emphasises how interpretations of achievement, rather than motivational dispositions or actual outcomes, determine subsequent achievement in both positive and negative ways. Bandura's (1994) social-cognitive model, *self-efficacy theory*, emphasises human agency and perceptions of efficacy in determining achievement. Bandura proposes that individuals' efficacy expectations are the major determinant of goal-setting, activity choice, willingness to expend effort and persistence. Perceived self-efficacy is determined by previous performance, vicarious learning, verbal encouragement by others and one's own psychological reactions.

Self-worth theory of achievement motivation (Covington, 1992) defines the motive for achievement as the desire to establish and maintain a positive self-image. Thus, achievement-related behaviours and activities reflect students' attempts to maintain their self-esteem by constructing an image of themselves as academically competent. Accordingly, approaches to learning, engagement in class, school and educational endeavours more generally, academic goals and so on are set, raised and lowered in order to preserve this self-image.

Modern expectancy-value theory (Eccles (Parsons) *et al.*, 1983; Eccles, 1993; Wigfield, 1994; Wigfield and Eccles, 1992) assumes that expectations for success and its value directly influence motivation, performance, persistence and activity choice. These expectancies and values are also influenced by beliefs such as perceptions of competence, perceptions of the difficulty of different tasks and individual goals. These are, in turn, influenced by individuals' perceptions of other people's attitudes and expectations for them and by their own interpretations of previous success or failure. Much of the following review of literature is couched within this expectancy-value framework.

Defining parental cognitions and their possible influences

The term 'parental cognitions' used here is meant in a broad sense and encompasses any sort of cognition that parents might have or form concerning children's cognitive development and abilities. These cognitions can take the form of beliefs (both general and more specific to individual children), attitudes (including stereotypes of gender, culture and activity), aspirations and expectations, interest, values and knowledge. This umbrella term also subsumes other possible terms and classifications put forward in the literature, such as schemas, attributions, judgements and ideas.

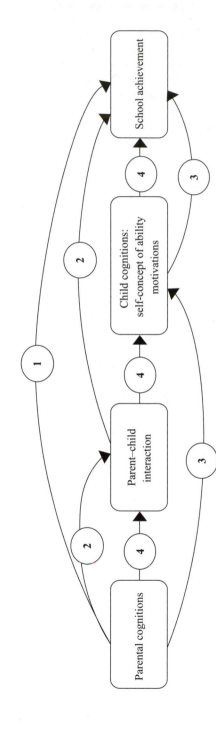

Figure 5.2 Some hypothesised direct and indirect influences of parental cognitions

These parental cognitions do not stay fixed, nor do they exist in isolation. Rather they change in dynamic ways, interacting with each other and with children's own cognitions, as well as with both distal factors and proximal family processes to influence child development in a number of ways and for a number of different outcomes. Figure 5.2 attempts to show graphically some of the possible pathways of influence. Again, it is important to note that the pathways depicted here are not mutually exclusive and that their influence is embedded within wider family and social contexts.

Parental cognitions can have a direct effect on children's achievement (arrow '1' in Figure 5.2). Parents communicate their perceptions of the child's abilities and their expectations for performance and these can directly impact upon children's success and achievement outcomes.

As noted above, parental beliefs and attitudes about childrearing may also be important determinants of parental behaviour more generally and so influence the environment through parent–child interaction and, in turn, the subsequent development of the child (arrows marked '2'). This association builds on the key elements of the parent–child relationship and its effects on children's outcomes discussed in the previous chapter. Higher levels of maternal knowledge regarding the developmental abilities of infants, for example, are associated with greater structuring of activities in the early years and with providing a more stimulating physical and learning environment (Luster and Dubow, 1990; Stevens, 1984). Moreover, parents who are more knowledgeable of children's development generally and in terms of their own child's ability show more sensitive teaching behaviours (Miller, 1988). By providing specific toys, home environment, cultural and recreational activities for children, parents structure their children's experiences and model what children see and are involved in outside the home (D'Amico *et al.*, 1983).

The effect of parental cognitions on achievement may also operate through children's own cognitions, as parents' cognitions also matter in that they shape and influence children's own beliefs and self-concepts of ability, interest, motivation and aspirations (arrows marked '3'). Children's cognitions may thus mediate the relationship between parental cognitions and achievement outcomes. Young children in particular are not very good at assessing their own level of competence (for example, see Harter, 1982; Nicholls, 1978) and so rely heavily on their parents' interpretations of their own performance when interpreting their own ability. This parental valuation and interpretation of reality may be communicated in both subtle and more overt ways.

Parents may equally influence their children's development by modelling involvement in valued activities during parent–child interaction, and again may affect children's outcomes by influencing children's own cognitions.

For example, parents who place great value on education may expose their children to lots of educational opportunities in their communities (Furstenburg *et al.*, 1999). Children may then internalise the importance of these activities and so integrate them into their self-concepts and value systems, in turn working harder and being more involved in school life and, accordingly, showing greater gains in their own educational achievement. Parents' cognitions may similarly manifest themselves by way of the experiences they provide, such as enrolment in extra-curricular activities and/or the behaviours they display at home; for example, the nature-loving parent who regularly takes their child to parks, forests and zoos and watches specialist nature programmes on television.

Figure 5.2 also shows that all these channels for the influence of parental cognitions may operate together (arrows marked '4') and highlights the complexity in understanding not only their effects but also the mechanisms involved. For simplicity, and because we are interested in the intergenerational transmission of educational success from parents to children, the graphical representation in Figure 5.2 and the subsequent review of parental influence holds constant the dynamic and reciprocal influences between children's achievement, their cognitions and parent–child interaction. We also do not consider here the likely transactional relationship between parent and child cognitions. While we recognise the importance of such feedback loops, these specific relationships are not central to our current focus on the role of parents' cognitions in influencing child outcomes.

As with other chapters of this book, our interest is on children's development primarily in terms of school attainment and achievement outcomes. Our evaluation of the theory and evidence therefore focuses on the associations between parents' cognitions and child achievement, discussing the mediating role of children's own cognitions where relevant. Since the importance of parenting and parent–child interaction has been discussed in the preceding chapter, we do not repeat this review here.

The effects of parental cognitions on child development outcomes

As we have attempted to demonstrate in Figure 5.2, parental and familial beliefs and expectations are conveyed to children in many subtle and more overt ways: encouraging particular activities and discouraging others, telling children what they are good at and making comments about the value of talent versus ability. The following section describes some of evidence that tries to explain these relationships and their effects on children's achievement in more detail.

Parent involvement in their children's education has been consistently related to school achievement (Eccles and Harold, 1996; Epstein and

Sanders, 2002; Hill, 2001; Kohl *et al.*, 2000). Through direct involvement in their children's education, parents establish relationships with teachers and other members of staff and parents and learn important information about the school, its policies, structures and its own expectations (Epstein and Sanders, 2002). These, in turn, may increase parents' ability to shape their child's interactions with school as well as enhance their own confidence in engaging with, and responding to, educational institutions. Parental involvement may also have positive effects on children's achievement by conveying messages about the importance of education and participation. In this way, parents act as role models and socialisers of valued behaviours, the importance of which has been well documented in the developmental literature (Bandura and Walters, 1963). Moreover, parents' academic involvement may serve to ensure that children and adolescents obtain academic skills and knowledge that prepare them for adult life and the educational and occupational choices available to them (Young and Friesen, 1992; see also Hill *et al.*, 2004).

Support for such propositions comes from both UK and US evidence. In the UK, for example, Desforges and Abouchaar's (2003) recent review of the impact of parental involvement and support on children's achievement and adjustment argues that parents' educational attitudes, aspirations and values are the most significant elements of parenting, controlling for social class and educational level (see Chapter 4 for further discussion). In Feinstein and Symons's investigation of parental interest in their children's education (1999), also reviewed in Chapter 4, the authors found that both mothers' and fathers' interest had large effects on progress in secondary school, conditional on individual, family, neighbourhood and school factors. The methodology used provides a robust, unbiased estimate that puts forward parental interest in children's education as the most powerful parental inputs. Given the limitations of the parental interest variable considered, the authors are unable to say conclusively what features of the parent, family and the relationships therein are being assessed. However, the authors maintain that it is likely to reflect parental cognitions such as motivation as well as related features of family-management practices such as discipline and parents' selection of children's peer group through school and neighbourhood choices. This paper also reaffirms seminal work by Douglas (1964) and Plowden (1967), who found that parental interest dominates other social class factors.

There is a well-established association between parents' expectations for their children's educational attainment (such as whether or not their child will attend college) and the child's current and later achievement (Alexander and Entwisle, 1988; Marjoribanks, 1988; Schneider and Coleman, 1993; Seginer, 1983). Halle *et al.* (1997) investigated the influence of parents' expectations for their children's level of future educational attainment and found that higher expectations were related to higher levels of achievement in both maths and reading. However, as has been highlighted in previous research (for example, Entwisle and Hayduk, 1978; Murphey, 1992) and throughout this book, problems of causality are inherent here. The reciprocal relations and feedback loops between child outcomes and parents' beliefs, valuations and expectations are highly complicated and constantly shifting, so to say that one definitively causes the other is often beyond the scope of most research designs.

In the Halle *et al.* study, however, the relationship between parents' expectations and children's later achievement remained significant even when children's prior achievement in the same subject was controlled for. Continuity in cognitive ability is well established; children who are already doing well in school should continue to do so. Therefore, expectations for their future attainment are also likely to be higher. By controlling for children's earlier levels of achievement, the effect of parents' expectations for future attainment is not biased by their knowledge of how well their children have already been doing at school. As such, we can be more confident that these results reflect the actual effects of parents' expectations and not the combination of expectations and achievement together.

In a large, diverse sample drawn at random from twenty schools in the Baltimore city system, Alexander *et al.* (1994) examined the effectiveness of expectations on future school performance. Children and their parents were interviewed regarding expected marks for the following year and asked to recall the previous years' marks. Consistent with other literature, their results showed that parents' higher expectations for their children's education resulted in children's greater educational attainment. Moreover, these higher expectations exerted a significant independent influence on performance levels, conditional on other factors such as social background (including parents' education, income level and ethnicity), as well as children's scores in standardised tests in the same domain. These results also hold for children's own expectations. Furthermore, the effects of parents' (and children's) expectations on children's performance are greater when recall of marks is accurate than when it is inaccurate. The authors posit that the abilities to form accurate beliefs and expectations are essential in structuring and scaffolding children's learning environments. They go on to argue that parents are 'agents of positive socialisation' and failure to attend to the feedback provided by schools on their child's performance will result in parents being less able to frame appropriate expectations for future performance.

Other research on the influence of parents' achievement-related beliefs has also highlighted the positive association of accurate perceptions of ability with higher attainment in children. Miller *et al.* (1991) for example, examined the accuracy of parents' judgements of their children's cognitive abilities across five different tasks, as well as the relation between parental accuracy and child's actual performance. The authors used a small sample of parents and children drawn from three elementary schools in Florida. They were split equally across second grade (mean age = 8 years, 2 months) and fifth grade (mean age = 11 years, 3 months) in order to investigate possible age moderation effects.

Their results show that accuracy was positively related to child performance: more accurate parents tended to have higher-performing children. Results also demonstrate that parents were typically 'above chance' in assessments of their child's ability, but nevertheless far from perfect. Parents' most common error of judgement was of overestimation, both with respect to absolute performance and with respect to relative standing; that is, parents showed a marked tendency to be more accurate in their judgements of the abilities of children in general than their own children's cognitive skills (see also Hunt and Paraskevopoulos, 1980; Miller, 1988).

This is a consistent finding in this literature; parents are more likely to both overestimate their own child's abilities and at the same time show accelerated normative expectations in comparison to other children of the same age. In the study outlined above, Halle *et al.* (1997) also found that the predominant error by parents in comparative assessments of children's performance was of overestimation of achievement (see also Hiebert and Adams, 1987; Miller and Davis, 1992). For Miller *et al.*, although parental accuracy in predicting their child's ability did not vary by age or gender, there was some variation across the different tasks assessed. Most notably, parents were least accurate in judging their child's memory and far more accurate in judging maths ability. The authors posit that this in part reflects parents' greater awareness of how their child is doing in maths relative to their memory as a result of the feedback received from school.

Ma (2001) extended the typical scope of influence here and investigated the effects of expectation and influence of peers and teachers as well as of students and their parents on participation in advanced maths classes and expectations for future attainment. The effect of parents' expectations and plans for college were strong in predicting participation and, when controlled for, the effect of students' own future expectations declined. Interestingly, peer influence and teacher expectations did not have strong effects participation and the effects of student future expectation were independent of peer and teacher effects. Moreover, when controlling for students' prior maths achievement and attitudes toward maths, the effects of parents' expectations and plans for the future still held (see also Fan, 2001; Singh *et al.*, 1995).

The mediating effects of children's cognitions

As discussed, one of the ways in which parental cognitions impact upon children's achievement is through their influence on children's own cognitions. While children's self-concepts of ability can be considered as outcomes in their own right, it is interesting here to see how children's cognitions mediate the effects of parental cognitions on achievement. Advocates of this perspective argue that parents influence children's belief systems by, for example, acting as 'interpreters of reality' through the messages they provide regarding their perceptions of the child's world and experiences (Eccles *et al.*, 1997; Goodnow and Collins, 1990). Young children in particular are not very good at assessing their own competence and so rely on parents to do so. Over time, the interest and value that become incorporated into the child's self-concepts are likely to affect future task choice as well as performance and, later, educational choice. Children's own cognitions and achievement motivations influence what they do, how they choose to approach a given task and its resulting outcomes.

Extensive work by Jacquelynne Eccles, her colleagues and others consistently finds that parents' perceptions and estimates of their children's academic abilities are significant predictors of children's own ability and interest in maths, English and sports (for examples, see Alexander and Entwisle, 1988; Eccles *et al.*, 1989a, 1993a and b; Jacobs and Eccles, 1992; Miller *et al.*, 1991; Pallas *et al.*, 1994). Eccles (Eccles *et al.*, 1993b) finds that, over time, parents' ratings of their child's ability in maths and English predicted changes in children's own ratings of their ability in maths, controlling for their actual mathematical ability. Moreover, the rate of decline found in pupils' confidence in their own ability over the course of secondary school is influenced by their parents' initial confidence in their children's ability as assessed in primary school (Fredricks and Eccles, 2002). This relationship remains even when teachers' ratings and children's own standardised test measures in maths assessed in primary school are controlled for.

Evidence here also suggests that parents' ratings of, and the related attributions that parents make about, children's ability are influenced by child gender. For example, despite contradictory evidence from both teacher ratings and assessment of time diaries, girls and girls' parents think they work harder in maths than in English, as well as harder than boys in maths (Eccles *et al.*, 1993a). Furthermore, when girls do well in maths, their parents are more likely to attribute this success to hard work rather than natural ability, whereas parents of boys attribute success in maths to both hard work and natural talent. What is particularly interesting here is that parents' rating of their daughters' abilities in English appeared to undermine girls' interest in maths. Thus, independent of actual ability in maths, if parents think their children are better in English than maths, then their children come to believe that too.

It is noteworthy that the relationship between parents' perceptions of children's ability and children's own self-ratings holds even when taking actual ability is taken into account. However, the role of causality in this association is still unclear. Clearly, parent and child perceptions are reciprocally related. Nevertheless, research suggests that mothers' perceptions of their children's ability appear to influence the change over time in the children's own self-perceptions of ability more strongly than vice versa (Eccles *et al.*, 1991).

Halle *et al.*'s (1997) study of parents' expectations and the influence on children's level of future educational attainment in a sample of disadvantaged African-American families also finds that the relationship between parents' expectations and children's later achievement remained significant even when children's beliefs were controlled for. It may be that such findings reflect greater accuracy in mothers' perceptions than in children's perceptions. It may also be the case that as children learn and become better at evaluating their own performance, so the perceptions of mothers and children converge. The causal direction aside, these results draw attention to the fact that parents' expectations are particularly important determinants of attainment.

These authors go on to suggest that optimistic self- and parent-appraisals of achievement may serve as a protective factor for children at risk of poor academic achievement or developmental problems such as emotional or behavioural adjustment difficulties (see also Garmezy, 1991). Wagner and Phillips (1992) argue that children who underestimate their academic abilities may be at risk of underachievement and low motivation. Alexander *et al.* (1994), however, note that holding 'too high expectations' does not necessarily serve the interests of minority ethnic and low socio-economic status parents and their children in terms of achievement, though it may help to maintain positive self-esteem. As a result of their findings, however, Halle *et al.* (1997) suggest that children from disadvantaged backgrounds may be more likely to show higher motivation and greater persistence towards academic achievement if they are able to see themselves as capable and successful in school, regardless of the accuracy of their assessments. Thus, the positive attitudes of these students and their parents may aid, rather than hinder, their achievement. There is therefore a need to understand the relevant contexts surrounding expectations and how these either impede or facilitate successful follow-through. Such results highlight the importance of studying 'person-in-context' interactions, as what applies to one group might not necessarily fit the dynamics of another (see also Entwisle and Hayduk, 1978; Ogbu, 1988).

Other research suggests that parental beliefs influence not only academic outcomes but also those in other areas of children's development. Jodl *et al.* (2001) investigate the pathways linking parental values, beliefs and behaviours to young people's occupational aspirations. These authors, like Alexander *et al.* (1994), highlight the role of parents as socialisers of values related to achievement and young people's occupational visions of themselves in the future. Using an ethnically diverse sample of early adolescents growing up in non-divorced families, they demonstrate that parents' valuation of the importance of success in academic subjects predicted youths' valuations directly rather than indirectly through parenting behaviours. In turn, these valuations predict occupational aspirations. In these processes, parents' views impact on children not just because they lead parents to behave differently but because parents' views matter in and of themselves to children.

The effects of prior parental education on parental cognitions

The central aim of this book is to better understand the mechanisms that might explain how and why children of parents with longer participation in education do better in standard tests of school attainment than those whose parents have had less education. As was detailed in the last chapter, one of the most direct explanations for this well-established association is based on the assumption that parents learn something during schooling that influences the ways in which they parent and interact with their children, particularly around teaching behaviours and learning-related activities in the home.

Proponents in this field argue that education provides parents with important cognitive resources that enable them to better support and facilitate their children's learning and development. In terms of general maternal knowledge for example, Brooks-Gunn *et al.* (1995) showed a positive association between higher maternal education (that is, having more than a high school education) and mothers' greater knowledge of child rearing and general child development theory. This relationship held, even when controlling for poverty. As noted above, maternal knowledge may impact on parental cognitions but can also be considered as one aspect of proximal family processes.

Those with higher levels of education are more knowledgeable of and familiar with the education system and what criteria typically define and determine success at school. Parental education may facilitate parents' ability and willingness to seek out expert advice about rearing their children and can increase parents' ability to synthesise information, leading to better decision-making and greater efficiency in meeting goals. More educated parents may therefore be better able to support and reinforce traditional academic goals (Hess and Holloway, 1984; Slaughter and Epps, 1987) and act as more sophisticated advocates of their children's schooling. For example, parents' education is associated with the accuracy of parents in rating their children's school performance and in forming expectations that are more related to actual performance. In their sample of low-income African-American families, Halle *et al.* (1997; see also p. 85 above) also found that mothers with more education had higher expectations for their children's academic achievement. As noted above, the authors argue that, in these data, optimistic self- and parent-appraisals of achievement may serve as a protective factor for children otherwise at risk of academic under-achievement (see also Garmezy, 1991).

Alexander *et al.* (1994) found considerable social stratification differences in the efficacy of parents' expectations for their children's school success. Parents with moderate to high education and income showed greater accuracy in predicting both their children's expected marks as well as in recalling previous grades. Parallel findings were found for the children of parents with more and less education: children of parents with less education were far less accurate in both recall and in predicting future success than those children whose parents had more education. These findings are particularly striking when social advantage is combined with correct recall: children of parents with moderate levels of education and income who correctly report their previous marks gain more advantage from their high expectations than do their counterparts from similar SES levels whose recall of prior marks is mistaken. Furthermore, children from less educationally advantaged backgrounds appear especially ineffective in capitalising on their performance expectations and are far less likely to benefit from parents' high expectations, irrespective of whether or not they reflect ability.

Alexander *et al.* (1994) argue that the social patterning found here results from differences in the human and social capital of parents and their families that originate in differences in class background and life experience reflecting social marginality (see Coleman, 1988). They suggest that the skills of dealing with the institution of school, understanding the flow of information from school to home and relating such understanding to their own lives are relatively lacking in lower SES and minority ethnic households. Kohn (1977) argues that such results reflect the socially stratified differences in the aspects of education that are rewarded. He claims that more educated and higher-SES parents place greater value on academic skills and 'doing well' in school. By contrast, less educated and lower SES families place greater emphasis on conduct and behaviour-related skills such as 'being good'. See Chapter 7 for further discussion of the relationships between parents, families and schools.

Davis-Kean (2005) used longitudinal data from the US Child Development Supplement of the Panel Study of Income Dynamics (PSID-CDS) to examine the link between parental education and measures of parental expectations for children's achievement. Parents' education was measured in terms of number of years of education of both mother and father. Here data were available for both parents; the highest education in the household was used as the indicator of family education. The mean number of years of completed education for this sample was just over thirteen, slightly more than a high school education. Parents' expectation was measured with an ordinal variable that asked the parent: 'how much schooling do you expect that your child will complete?' Choices ranged from eleventh grade or less; that is, less than high school (education = 1) to M.D., Ph.D. or other doctoral degree (education = 8). The mean for the sample was 5.0 indicating that, on average, the parents in this sample expected their children to graduate from a four-year college course.

Correlational analyses of these results showed that having a higher parental education was significantly related to parents having higher expectations of child achievement ($r = 0.42$). Subsequent structural equation analyses also showed parent education level as having the strongest impact on parental expectations of the family demographic variables assessed (income, employment status and ethnicity). Davis-Kean claims that parental education impacts directly on parental expectations of their children's achievement, but also notes the mediating effect of parental beliefs on parenting behaviours as explanations for children's increased achievement (see review in Chapter 4 for further detail). However, while an effect of parental education on parental expectations is one explanation for the correlation, it is also likely that parents with higher education have higher-attaining children for whom they therefore have higher expectations. In other words, expectations may be driven primarily by parents' observations of the apparent ability of their children. More recently, therefore, these results have been replicated in longitudinal data to control for the earlier attainment of the child and the pattern of results implicating both direct and indirect channels for education effects remain (Davis-Kean and Sexton, 2007).

Other analyses of the US PSID-CDS data show an association between the types of values that parents seek to instil in their children and parents' own level of education (Child Trends, 2002). For example, 74 per cent of mothers educated to college degree level ranked thinking for oneself as the most important quality children can learn compared to just 35 per cent of those with less than a high school education.[1] Conversely, 34 per cent of mothers with lower educational achievement report obedience as the most important quality for their children to learn compared with only 8 per cent of mothers with a college degree.

Ganzach (2000) argues that the enhanced skills and knowledge of more educated parents enable them to create and provide an environment that facilitates learning, present greater opportunities and so make way for broader life chances. He examines the interactive effects of children's cognitive ability and parents' education in an estimation model that attempts to understand the role of educational expectations and finds that parents' education accounts for significantly more of the explained variance in children's cognitive ability than other possible factors, including self-esteem, ethnic background, family composition and income. Furthermore, his findings (from NLSY data) are consistent with an offsetting relationship between mother's and father's education: the more educated of the two parents exerts more influence on the formation of educational expectations than the less educated parent. These results also suggest interaction effects between mothers' (but not fathers') education, the formation of educational expectations and the child's own cognitive ability. These findings are consistent with others that highlight the protective features of high maternal education, particularly for at-risk groups, here those children with low ability.

Ganzach finds evidence of a curvilinear relationship between parents' level of education and their children's own educational expectations. This relationship suggests that for parents with fewer than twelve years of education (less than a high school graduate), the relationship between parents' education and their children's educational expectations is only slightly positive, while for more than twelve years of education this relationship is much more positive. Ganzach suggests that this result reflects differences between 'normative' levels of education, twelve years in the USA, and the choices of those who invest in greater amounts of education. He argues that parents whose belief in, and valuation of, education was high when they were young are likely to both choose more education for themselves and have higher valuations of education for their children. Simple correlation of educational valuation and parental education is not therefore proof of an effect of education, although the theoretical grounds for such a link are strong.

Issues of causality

Many of the points about causality made in Chapter 4 in relation to the evidence for the effects of proximal process apply equally to the evidence about parents' beliefs and aspirations. It is difficult to disentangle pure causal elements in the complex interactions between attainment and the beliefs and aspirations of parents and children. It requires a methodological focus that differs somewhat from that of the dominant authors in the field. Clearly, aspirations are likely to rise in response to success but, equally, positive aspirations may drive success.

Parental mental health and well-being

The effects of parental well-being and mental health on child development outcomes

Parental mental health has important influences on parents' interaction with infants. Both the inability to control the source of stress and the inability to cope or handle the stress itself contribute to the deleterious effect on psychological functioning (Makosky, 1982). Psychological distress, depressive symptoms and parent irritability, in turn, may lead to less responsive parent–child interactions and other forms of poor or impaired parenting behaviour (McLoyd, 1990; McLoyd and Wilson, 1991). Parents' ability to cope with emotional stress, financial and economic pressures and additional social stressors are known to influence the performance and attainments of children, both directly through living in a more stressful environment and indirectly through negative impacts on parenting and diminished parent–child relations. For example, proximal family processes such as rewarding, explaining, consulting and negotiating with children require patience and concentration, qualities typically in short supply when parents feel harassed and overburdened.

Even when stressful life events occur in the context of otherwise low-risk families they can have a deleterious effect on parent–child interaction. Elder (Elder and Ardelt, 1992; Elder *et al.*, 1995) suggests that increased numbers of social and environmental risks force parents to adopt less effective parenting styles. High stress levels may prevent parents from efficiently adapting their parenting strategies to the developmental changes in their children's needs. For example, parents may be over-controlling or, at the other end of the scale, too detached and/or permissive (see also Lempers *et al.*, 1989).

A number of recent studies have also identified specific implications of maternal depression for longer-term difficulties in infant development. Infants between twelve and twenty-one months have shown a range of adverse outcomes including behaviour problems (Murray, 1992), cognitive impairments (Lyons-Ruth *et al.*, 1986; Murray, 1992), particularly in boys (Murray *et al.*, 1996), interaction difficulties (Stein *et al.*, 1991) and insecurity of attachment (Hipwell *et al.*, 2000; Lyons-Ruth *et al.*, 1986;

Murray, 1992; Teti *et al.*, 1995). These adverse developmental outcomes have been observed in infants even in cases where mothers' depressive symptoms have remitted (for example, Murray, 1992; Murray *et al.*, 1996; Stein *et al.*, 1991). This suggests that poor outcomes can have origins in mother–child interactions from as early as two months after birth. These authors suggest that it is possible that, despite the mother's recovery from depression, early negative attitudes to the infant may set up a cycle of particularly marked difficulties that influence later child behaviours. This view is consistent with other research (for example, Bendell *et al.*, 1994; Field *et al.*, 1993), which reports that depressed mothers' early perceptions of their infants tend to be more negative than those of independent observers and show considerable continuity throughout the pre-school years. This re-emphasises the fact that characteristics interact with each other. Here postnatal depression interacts with maternal attitudes, both of which affect child outcomes, mediated by mother–child interactions.

It is also interesting to note that fathers may buffer the negative effects of maternal depression on their children. Hossain *et al.* (1995) found that infants' interactions with their non-depressed fathers were more positive than they were with their depressed mothers. The authors suggest the negative association between maternal depression and infants' own depressed mood style is therefore specific to the mother–child interaction and not generalised to, or associated with, interactions across care-givers.

Evidence on the importance of psychological well-being and stress also emerges from studies that consider *how* stress is the mediator for the effect of poverty on children's outcomes. The adverse consequences of poverty affect family well-being generally but also affect children's emotional and social well-being indirectly through the negative impacts on parents' well-being and their parenting style and practices (Conger *et al.*, 1997; Evans and English, 2002; Jackson *et al.*, 2000; McLoyd, 1990; McLoyd *et al.*, 1994; Mistry *et al.*, 2002).

Cummings and Davies (1994) review the research on the association between parents' mental health and children's development. While they acknowledge the influence of genetics and hereditary factors, they emphasise the need to study the contextual and environmental risk factors associated with depression in families (Downey and Coyne, 1990; Reiss *et al.*, 1991; Rutter, 1990). Their framework for examining the relationships between parental, particularly maternal, depression and children's development mediated by parent–child interaction is a good example of the application of the developmental model. However, their main concern is to show that proximal family processes mediate the effect of family characteristics on outcomes. This evidence has already been considered in Chapter 4.

The effects of prior parental education on parental mental health and well-being

There are a number of reasons why education may have an effect on adult mental health and well-being (Feinstein, 2002; Hammond, 2002, 2003). Hammond puts forward four possible pathways through which education positively enhances mental health and well-being: economic benefits; access to health services; adoption of health-related practices; and coping with stress. These benefits result from the positive effects that education has on self-efficacy, cognitive skills and communication.

It is well established that at all levels of education, depression rates among women are higher than those of men. Using data from individuals born in one week in 1958 and followed up through their life (the National Child Development Study, NCDS), Parsons and Bynner (1998) found that, for individuals aged 37 in 1995, 36 per cent of women and 18 per cent of men who had very low literacy skills suffered from depression, compared to 7 per cent of women and 6 per cent of men with good literacy skills. The relationships were smaller but nevertheless substantial in relation to numeracy skills: 18 per cent of women and 11 per cent of men with very poor numeracy skills suffered from depression, compared to just 5 per cent of men and women with good numeracy skills.

This association, however, may result from a spurious relationship reflecting the consequences of upbringing, individual attributes and attitudes, and socio-economic background. To guard against such arguments, researchers frequently adopt research designs that employ longitudinal data. Mirowsky and Ross (2002) investigate the role of education as a protective factor against depression in the context of entry age of parenthood, controlling for a large set of earlier background characteristics. Using the US 1995 Survey of Ageing, Status and the Sense of Control, results show years of schooling to be associated with a decrease of 6 per cent in the likelihood of depression. When other socio-economic variables and physical health are introduced as controls in the analysis, the estimated coefficient is reduced to 2.3 per cent. Feinstein (2002), using data from the UK 1958 and 1970 birth cohorts, shows that controlling for childhood abilities, health and family background factors, women from the 1958 cohort with qualifications at UK National Vocational Qualification (NVQ) Level 1 – roughly equivalent to lower secondary education – have six percentage points lower likelihood of depression than women with no qualifications. For women born later, in the 1970 cohort, the estimated effect is ten percentage points. For men these effects are weaker.

Chevalier and Feinstein (2006) again rely on a rich longitudinal dataset to control for childhood determinants and measures of mental health over an individual's life span. They use matching methods to account for selectivity and instrumental variables to estimate the causal effect of education. Their instruments include teachers' expectations concerning the schooling of the person when she was a child and the number of cigarettes smoked per day at age sixteen (as a proxy for time-use preference). In their estimations, the impact of the highest qualification is strengthened and independent of work- or family-related controls. They consistently find that achieving qualifications significantly reduces the risks of adult depression. The effect is non-linear and is larger at low- to mid-levels of educational qualifications. Their most reliable estimate suggests that individuals with at least O-levels reduce their risk of adult depression by 6 percentage points. This effect is similar for men and women.

The effect of education on depression may, however, be ambiguous since there may be contrasting mechanisms for its influence. For example, a higher occupational grade is associated with greater control over working lives, more varied and challenging work and thus has a positive effect on mental health and reduces rates of morbidity (Kubzansky *et al.*, 1999; Marmot *et al.*, 1991). However, higher occupational attainment also leads to higher levels of stress (Rose, 2001). There may be important trade-offs between stress and satisfaction that may lead to a complex and non-linear relationship between educational success and mental health (see, for example, Hartog and Oosterbeek, 1998). Miech and Shanahan (2000) look at the relationship between education and depression over the lifecourse. Using data from the 1990 Work, Family and Well-Being Study in the USA, they find that the association between education and depression strengthens with age, and that individuals with higher education are more successful at lowering the likelihood of depression because they have better physical health.

Empirical studies using cross-country data have shown that wealthier countries have a low positive correlation between education and happiness and life satisfaction. Helliwell (2002) estimates a multivariate regression using individual level data from the World Values Survey for forty-six countries. Results show that the association between well-being, defined as overall life satisfaction, and education is strong and positive. However, when other individual and national variables were included in the regression model, this statistically significant association disappears. This suggests that educational effects may be mediated by other factors. Ross and van Willigen (1997) and Dench and Regan (1999) obtain similar results for the USA. They find that the relationship between education and well-being is mediated by psycho-social resources. In contrast, using data from Switzerland in 1992–4, Frey and Stutzer (2002) estimate that achieving middle and high levels of formal education increases life satisfaction by 2.19 and 2.09 percentage points.

Issues of causality

The pattern of causality in the association between parents' education and their mental health and well-being is somewhat complicated. First, although no single gene or set of genetic characteristics is responsible for, or conclusively identified in, the inheritance of depression and mental health problems (see Cummings and Davies, 1994), we cannot ignore the substantial evidence implicating the importance of hereditary factors here. Second, the role of reverse causality cannot be ruled out. For example, parents of children with developmental disorders are, understandably, under increased pressures. Stress and depression may then result not from the parent, but rather as a consequence of the increased demands they face (McLoyd and Wilson, 1991).

Finally, an inherent methodological problem here is that self-reported information may itself be influenced by the mental health and well-being of parents, resulting in complex bias in the estimation of results. Some caution in interpreting the empirical studies reviewed here is therefore required. Moreover, mothers depressed by their strained financial situations may be more likely to perceive their children as being distressed as well. Duncan *et al.* (1994) found that mothers' accounts of their child's behaviour correlate only modestly with other sources of information, such as teachers' reports, and are confounded with mothers' own mental health. Thus, correlations between family economic status and maternal reports of children's problems may be a spurious reflection of the association between financial difficulties and mother's psychological distress.

Summary

This chapter focuses on features of the family context that shape the proximal environment in which parent–child interactions take place. In particular, we emphasise two broad areas that influence the family context, parental cognitions and mental health and well-being. Parental cognitions is a catch-all term used to refer to the way parents think about parenting and family dynamics. Cognitions may include values, attitudes, knowledge and beliefs, as well as expectations, aspirations, hopes and desires.

Parents learn to parent by parenting and measuring parental cognitions offers a useful insight into the dynamics and processes underpinning the parent–child relationship. However, although the overall correlational evidence for the effects of education on parents' cognitions on children's development is strong, there is not yet enough evidence to suggest that the relationship is causal. From a theoretical standpoint, cognitions are a key mediator of education effects. They are important both in themselves and as a channel for intergenerational transmission of learning and achievement, and studying them is likely to afford a more complete understanding the mechanisms that promote educational success.

Parental mental health and well-being also have important influences on children's outcomes. Mental health and well-being affect proximal processes in the home and can interact with other characteristics of the family such as parental cognitions. The evidence supports the view that such mediating relationships exist even if the precise causal role is unproven.

There may be some important benefits of education in lowering the risk of depression, although there are many potential mechanisms such as work satisfaction, income and/or resilience. Research has shown that substantial bias can be introduced into statistical analysis if earlier life circumstances and other health factors are not taken into account when estimating the effects of education on depression. An important finding of these studies is that the relationship between qualification level and depression changes depending on the level of qualifications. In the UK, for example, results suggest that the main effects of education on the reduction of the risk of depression occur at the level of completed compulsory secondary education and the attainment of Level 2 qualifications – that is, five A*–C passes at GCSE (or equivalent). Recent research has gone some way to testing the causal effect of education using econometric approaches such as IV and matching methods. Again, results for the UK show that attainment of at least Level 2 qualifications reduces the risk of adult depression by around six percentage points. This effect is similar for men and women. More work is needed to replicate the methodological approach in other contexts and cohorts. Overall, evidence in this area suggests that education may affect life satisfaction through both psycho-social and economic mechanisms. The observed association between education and well-being is significantly reduced when variables are introduced to account for confounding bias. Educational effects on life satisfaction seem to be non-linear, reaching a maximum at intermediate levels of education. However, this conclusion is drawn from analyses that do not deal with the endogeneity of education and further research on the relationship between education and life satisfaction is therefore required.

6 Distal family factors

Introduction

Parental education is not the only variable that affects intergenerational relations. Other distal factors can also affect child development through proximal processes and features of the family environment. Children's educational attainments can be affected by the number of siblings, the structure of the family, or the age of parents at first birth. These factors are distal in that, while they shape the experiences of children's lives and so their educational outcomes, their influence is not immediate in an ecological sense. Rather, the impact of distal features on children's development is mediated by the features and nature of the contexts experienced by the child already reviewed in Chapters 4 and 5.

In this chapter, we will describe the most salient distal factors of the family commonly found to, or thought to, have important effects on children's outcomes:

- family structure;
- family size;
- teenage motherhood;
- income and poverty; and
- maternal employment.

Evaluating the separate effects of specific distal factors is not an easy task. Distal factors may impact on certain developmental outcomes but their effect may well depend on children's characteristics, such as age and gender, and other family distal factors, such as birth order and number of children. Therefore, interactions between distal factors themselves may be very important. While we try to separate the effect of distal factors on developmental outcomes, it is important to remember that it is often cumulative disadvantage and compounding risk that matters more than any one risk

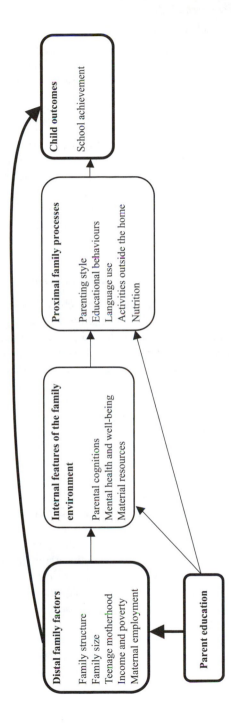

Figure 6.1 Conceptual model for the influence of distal family factors

associated with a single distal factor. Children raised in poverty, whose parents lack qualifications, and who live in a large family headed by a single parent are likely to experience a higher risk of low or under-achievement at school than children raised in a one-parent household out of poverty.

Family structure

Family structure can be defined according to the number of parents, either biological or non-biological, living in a household, but in the literature it is typically categorised into one- or two-parent families. Each of these groups contains sub-categories differentiated by marital status and the nature of the relation between parents and children. In this sense, cohabitation differs from marriage and living with both biological parents differs from living with step-, foster- or adoptive parents.

The effects of family structure on child development outcomes

The social science literature has analysed how child development may be affected by the structure of the family in these terms. One of the main concerns is with developmental effects due to changes in family structure. For instance, the break-up of a family, regardless of the causes, brings new interactions between parents and children as well as new parental roles within the household. Resources at home, such as time and income, as well as the mental health and well-being of parents may be affected and, in turn, influence child development. However, the majority of studies point out that what matters for child development, more than the presence of parents in the household as providers of care and resources, is the stability of the family and the strength of the relations between household members. These factors affect both the internal features of the family context and the proximal family processes described in our model.

One important theoretical basis for the role of family structure as a distal factor comes from economic models of household production. According to these models, the presence of two parents in the household increases the quantity of parental investment in children's development (Haveman and Wolfe, 1995). A single parent is likely to be both the main earner of the household and the main carer for the children. The resulting trade-off between income and care in single-parent households may also increase stress and so further decrease the quality of parental resources.

Psychologists, on the other hand, focus more on the nature of parental relations in the family (McLanahan and Bumpass, 1988). In these models, family structure itself is seen as having a direct influence on the parental well-being and proximal processes. In particular, the frequency and length of fathers' or mothers' absence from the child's home may affect children's sense of security as well as disrupt day-to-day life and general family management practices. These theories emphasise that unstable relations, perhaps characterised by intra-household violence, conflict or periods of parental absence, can impact on children's behaviour as well as their achievement and likelihood of gaining school qualifications. The complementarities between economic and psychological approaches and advantages of considering them alongside one another were discussed in Chapter 3.

Empirical evidence has shown that children who experience the breakdown of their parents' relationship, involving a move to a one-parent household due to divorce or separation, differ from those who do not in terms of their behaviour at school and completed years of schooling (Brooks-Gunn *et al.*, 1997; Ermisch and Francesconi, 2001; Hill *et al.*, 2001). Other studies point to the importance of parental stability, measured by the presence of both biological parents living in the house, for a broad set of child development outcomes that include cognitive achievements and behavioural indicators (McLanahan, 1997). In addition, some studies suggest that the arrival of a step-parent can have both positive and negative consequences for child development (Cooksey, 1997). Among the negative effects we find low educational qualifications (Boggess, 1998; West *et al.*, 1995).

Recent work, however, suggests that the experience of a parental separation in and of itself may not have a causal impact on children's educational outcomes. Aughinbaugh *et al.* (2005) and Ginther and Pollak (2004) investigate how the apparent relationship between parental separation and children's educational outcomes is significantly reduced, or even disappears, when controls for income, education and other socio-economic variables are included in the analysis. This is because, in the simple correlation, parental separation may be capturing the effect of other variables that impact upon children's outcomes; for instance, education may be a strong mediator of intra-household conflict in the case of parental separation. Hence the inclusion of this variable can significantly reduce the impact of parental separation. Another study by Björklund and Sundström (2002) uses data on Swedish siblings to estimate the effect of parental separation on children's educational attainment. The authors measure differences in educational attainments between siblings who experienced parental separation and those who did not and found no statistically significant differences between the two groups.

Other studies have focused on family structures beyond one- and two-parent families and have found mixed results. DeLeire and Kalil (2002) found that young people who lived with a mother who had never married in a multi-generational household had better educational outcomes, were less likely to smoke and less likely to have engaged in sexual activity before leaving high school than children who lived with a single mother alone. In contrast, Sigle-Rushton and McLanahan (2002) found that children from multi-generational households were in fact at higher risk from certain negative outcomes. Loury (2006) finds differences by gender and reports that sons' educational attainment and college attendance are affected by uncles' and grandfathers' levels of education, whereas daughters' schooling outcomes are affected by aunts' and grandmothers' educational background. Loury's findings are robust to factors observed in the data that may impact upon family structure as well as children's educational attainments.

Several important issues have emerged from this evidence. Conflict and instability in the relationship between parents have negative consequences for child development regardless of the structure of the family (Joshi *et al.*, 1999). Using a longitudinal sample of Norwegian students, Mastekaasa (2006) finds that changes from married or cohabiting to single increases the levels of psychological distress in individuals, regardless of whether children are present in the household. Family structure does not influence children's cognitive ability when income is included in the model (Joshi *et al.*, 1999; Peters and Mullis, 1997; Smith *et al.*, 1997). The impact of parental separation on children's educational achievement seems to be, if any, very small (Haveman *et al.*, 1997; Manski *et al.*, 1992). This suggests that the main underlying cause of the effect of family structure is the conflict associated with broken or unstable relationships. The effect of conflict can occur in both one- and two-parent family structures and the causal pathway is not necessarily from structure to conflict, but may equally operate the other way around.

The effects of prior parental education on family structure

Of all the distal factors, family structure has the weakest or most unclear relation to parental education. In economics, theoretical models developed by Becker (1973, 1981) suggest that unmarried men and women enter into partnership because they have more, comparatively, to gain by marrying than by remaining single. Traditionally, women had greater advantage (or higher productivity) at home, whereas men had the comparative advantage in the labour market. On this basis, Becker predicts that increasing education is likely to delay marriage.

Trends in partnership formation show that individuals with similar levels of education tend to marry each other. This is known as 'educational assortative marriage' (Schwartz and Mare, 2005). But is this because of the level of education itself? In Germany, Blossfeld and Huinink (1991) find that engagement in education rather than the level of education is significantly associated with the timing of marriage. Results for the USA (Michael *et al.*, 2006) and Japan (Raymo, 2003) are similar. Michael *et al.* (2006) find that being enrolled in school reduces the likelihood of entering into marriage, but that the number of years of education also matters. It is important to note, however, that they estimate the impact of school enrolment to be more than ten times greater than the impact of educational attainment. Similarly, Raymo finds that delayed marriage is associated primarily with longer school enrolment. These findings suggest that it may be participation in education that delays marriage and relationship formation. It may then be the circumstances surrounding education and the constraints it places on individual choices that lead to assortative mating as opposed to education itself driving who marries who.

Other theories have focused on the role of education in predicting partnership dissolution. Economic and psychosocial theories propose that a husband's lack of resources and a wife's economic success tend to destabilize a marriage (Choo and Siow, 2006; Jalovaara, 2003). Hoem (1997) suggests that education would decrease the risk of partnership breakdown if people with high levels of education are better at selecting their partners or spouses and making their relationship work. In contrast, individuals with more education stand to gain more than their counterparts with less education in ending a relationship that turned out to be unsatisfactory. The total effect of educational attainments on partnership dissolution depends on which effect dominates.

It is unclear, however, whether the critical factor that affects partnership dissolution is the absolute level of education in the household or the relative level of education between partners. The relative education hypothesis suggests that as women's position relative to men increases, the marriage is more susceptible to disruption because of lower gains from specialisation. In Becker's theory this means that the gains from marriage as compared to remaining single are reduced as both partners have now comparative advantages in the labour market. Therefore, husbands and wives have less to lose by separating from each other. The absolute level of education is also important in partnership dissolution as it provides independence for women.

Studies from the USA (Martin and Parashar, 2006; Tzeng, 1992) and from Finland (Finnas, 1996; Jalovaara, 2003) have reported an inverse relationship between spouses' levels of education and partnership dissolution. This means that couples with low levels of education are at greater risk of partnership dissolution than couples with high levels of education. Kiernan and Mueller (1998) suggest that the observed increase in risk of partnership dissolution among those with less education in the UK may be in large measure due to the formation of early partnerships and poverty (see also Berthold, 2000; Hobcraft, 2000). Kiernan (1997) and Hoem (1997) have estimated effects of education on the formation and dissolution of partnerships but have found that family structure appears to be fairly independent of parental education.

We conclude, therefore, that education can have both positive and negative effects on the probability of parental separation, but that these positive and negative effects more or less cancel each other out. Consequently, we do not see family structure as a key mediator of education effects.

Family size

Two main dimensions of the role of family size as a distal factor have been analysed in the literature: number of children and birth order. As a quantity or total number of individuals in the household, family size affects the amount of resources available per child. The resources available per child also depend on the relative birth position, as well as the ages between children.

The effects of family size on child development outcomes

Because of resource constraints at the household level, some economic models predict that the greater the size of the family the lower the future educational attainments and earnings for children, since every additional child receives relatively fewer parental resources (Becker and Tomes, 1976). This, however, may be offset somewhat by the positive influence that older children can have on their younger siblings (Blake, 1981), as well as by resources or activities that parents can share with one or many children; for example a visit to the zoo, referred to as 'public' time in Hanushek (1992).

Empirical evidence from the USA and the UK suggests that children from small families tend to achieve higher educational qualifications than children raised in large families (Baydar *et al.*, 1997; Hauser and Sewell, 1983; Iacovou, 2001). These effects are significant and fairly stable. However, the effect of family size on educational attainment depends on birth order (Behrman and Taubman, 1986; Dearden, 1999). In Norway, Black *et al.* (2004) show that the effect of family size on children's attainment becomes negligible once controls for birth order are introduced. It is possible, then, that first-born children achieve higher educational qualifications not because of parental favouritism, but by having a higher probability of belonging to a small family (Hanushek, 1992). But at the same time, younger children tend to benefit from their older siblings and from interactions with other children (Iacovou, 2001).

Overall, based on replication and good longitudinal evidence there is a relatively strong effect of family size on children's school achievement. Although family size and birth order matter for child development, a number of interactions remain empirically unexplained. Parental experience gained from raising the first-born child may be important. This may have positive as well as negative effects for second and subsequent children. Similarly, how much young children benefit from their older siblings is relatively unresearched. It may be the case that young children are negatively influenced by their older siblings, particularly with respect to social and behavioural development.

The effects of prior parental education on family size

Evidence on the raw negative relationship between parental education and family size is robust: a simple correlation analysis shows that parents with more education have, on average, fewer children (Ferri and Smith, 2003). However, the interpretation of the causality of this association is difficult.

In economic theory, there are four general pathways by which education can be thought to affect family size, mainly via effects on parents' choices regarding the number of children. First, parents with higher levels of education may have fewer children in order to maximise each one's individual attainment (Becker, 1991; Joshi, 2000). Second, education may increase the opportunity cost of employment; that is, income forgone due to participation in education. This may induce a substitution away from fertility and into employment (De Tray, 1973; Hobcraft and Kiernan, 1999; Mooney, 1984; Schultz, 1981). Third, education may reduce childbearing time (Dale and Egerton, 1997) and, fourth, may lead to better understanding of contraception and so enable the achievement of desired family size (Blackwell and Bynner, 2002; Rosenzweig and Schultz, 1989). It is extremely difficult to test for these mechanisms and consequently evidence here is rather limited.

One of the few studies to examine the effect of education on family size was carried out by Wolfe (1980). She examined the effect of more education for women on their fertility behaviour using data from the US National Bureau of Economic Research – Thorndike-Hagen sample (NBER-TH). The effect of education on family size is analysed through several distinct factors: contraceptive efficiency; age at marriage; preferences towards children; desired standard of living; wage lost due to full-time parenthood, and efficiency in raising children. Perhaps unsurprisingly, the results show that individuals who have strong preferences towards having children and who enjoy raising their children and spending time with them are likely to have large families. The factor that has the greatest impact on family size is the wage lost due to engagement in full-time parenthood: the higher the wage lost, the smaller the size of the family.

A number of factors, which unfortunately are not measured in surveys, may affect these relationships and cause confounding bias, such that what appears to be the effect of education on family size is caused by other individual characteristics that affect both education and family size decisions, for example ambition. Also important is the reverse causality of family size on education, as having a child may also affect the choice to continue in schooling. As a result, low education is in part attributable to early entry into parenthood. In general, weak evidence exists on the causal effects of parental education on family size. However, overall there is a clear inverse correlation between family size and parents' education and theory to support the view that an element of this is a causal effect of education.

Teenage motherhood

Closely related to the topics of family structure and size is mothers' age and, in particular, teenage motherhood. Mothers' learning experiences may be associated either directly or indirectly with mother–child interactions and may improve parenting skills and thus positively influence children's outcomes (Conger *et al.*, 1984). Therefore, the age at which a woman has children may have a positive impact on children's outcomes and education may play an important role in this relationship.

The effects of teenage motherhood on child development outcomes

On average, children of young mothers score more poorly on cognitive measures and are at higher risk of poor school attainments than children of older mothers (Feinstein *et al.*, 1999; Furstenburg *et al.*, 1987). Other studies also suggest behavioural differences between children of teenage parents and other children (Pagani *et al.*, 1997). Moreover, studies of intergenerational effects show that children of teenage parents are more likely to become teenage parents themselves (Kiernan, 1997; Manlove, 1997).

One possible explanation is that young mothers may be unprepared for motherhood and so have less adequate parenting skills (Furstenberg *et al.*, 1989). Other theories suggest that the differences in children's achievements may not be the consequence of young maternal age per se, but that teenage motherhood emerges as a consequence of prior socio-economic disadvantages, which are transmitted across generations and are responsible for jeopardizing the future of the child (Geronimus *et al.*, 1994). In general, empirical studies find that the effect of age of the mother, if any, is small relative to other risk factors. Once income, parental education and SES are controlled in the model, the effects of age of the mother tend to disappear – or become statistically insignificant. Hence, age of the mother is not a significant distal factor that affects child development on its own. The fact that children of teenage mothers tend to have poorer developmental outcomes is mainly due to the multiple adverse factors that tend to co-occur with teenage parenthood.

The effects of prior parental education on teenage motherhood

Education affects the age at which women become mothers through three main channels, which are similar to those for the effect on family size. First, education increases the opportunity cost of having children. High educational attainment is likely to both increase future earnings and subsequently increase the income lost due to full-time or part-time parenthood. Second, women with higher levels of education spend longer in schooling and so delay marriage and childbearing. Third, education increases women's agency, that is women's ability or sense of power to take control of their lives, empowering them in making choices concerning fertility, partly through effects on self-esteem and aspirations (Hammond, 2002), but also through changes in life possibilities. This may lead many women to delay child-rearing into later adulthood.

Empirical studies show that women with lower levels of educational qualifications tend to have children younger than their better-educated counterparts (Rowlingson and McKay, 1998). Statistics from the UK Labour Force Survey show that less than a third of women with degrees had children by the age of thirty, compared to 80 per cent of women with no qualifications. As in the case of family size, the correlation is clear but may be driven by a number of underlying mechanisms, which make it problematic for empirical analysis to unpack the causal relationship between education and fertility.

The main difficulty in estimating the causal effect of education is the reverse causality of fertility on education (Hobcraft, 1998). The presence of a child could prevent young mothers attending school and, consequently, decrease the likelihood of gaining qualifications or high school completion. Thus it may be that fertility causes low educational attainment. In order to deal with the problem of reverse causality, Hobcraft estimates the effect of early educational test scores on the likelihood of becoming a teenage parent, using test scores during childhood as a measurement of likely educational attainment. For both males and females, the probability of becoming a young parent – either a father before the age of twenty-two or a teenage mother – are more than three times higher for children attaining the lowest reading and maths test scores than for children with the highest test scores. Note, however, that this is an effect of low cognitive attainment, not of educational participation.

Ermisch and Pevalin (2003) investigate the family background and childhood factors that are associated with teenage pregnancy using two longitudinal datasets: the NCDS and the British Household Panel Survey (BHPS). Two factors are found to be important determinants of teenage motherhood. First, daughters of teenage mothers are more likely to become themselves teenage mothers. Second, mothers' education has a significant impact in reducing the likelihood that their daughters will become teenage mothers themselves. This effect remains after the inclusion of earlier variables that may impact upon their probability of becoming a teenage mother, for example cognitive attainment, as well as measures for behavioural and emotional development.

School experience more generally, both positive or negative, can also affect sexual behaviour and teenage pregnancy. Bonell *et al.* (2005) consider the relationship between dislike of school and sexual risk-taking and pregnancy using longitudinal data on girls between the ages of thirteen and sixteen in schools in central and southern England. The authors used data from twenty-seven mixed comprehensive schools randomly selected to either receive a sex education intervention or to serve as a control. Even after adjusting for measures of SES, expectation of parenting, lack of education or training expectations and lack of knowledge or confidence about sexual health information, girls who disliked school were twice as likely to become pregnant in their teenage years. This research does not demonstrate a causal relationship, but rather highlights the strong relationship between attitude to school and risk of teenage pregnancy.

Another problem in estimating the causal relationship of education on teenage parenthood is the role of unobservable factors that affect both education and mother's age, for example labour market ambition. Women with high levels of ambition tend both to choose higher schooling and delay childbearing, leading to an association of education and age of mother that is in fact due to labour market ambition. In order to deal with this issue, Black *et al.* (2004) use the variation provided by the compulsory schooling legislation in the USA and in Norway to estimate the impact of schooling on teenage pregnancy. They find that increased compulsory schooling does reduce the incidence of teenage childbearing in the USA and in Norway and that the estimated effect in both countries is very similar.

We conclude that, because of the stage of the lifecourse at which teenage parenthood necessarily occurs, there is not a clear causal pathway for an effect of parents' education on child development. School failure or low school engagement may be an important cause of teenage parenthood in some circumstances. However, this is more a matter of relations with the school and academic success in childhood and early adolescence than of qualifications themselves. If education is defined in terms of cognitive attainment or participation in schooling rather than qualifications, then teenage parenthood is an important mediator of intergenerational effects of education on children's development.

Income and poverty

Studies have shown that children living in low-income families have a higher probability of dropping out of school, being convicted of committing a crime, misbehaving at school and attaining lower educational qualifications (Hobcraft and Kiernan, 1999). Children from low-income families also score lower than children from richer families on health assessments, cognitive development, school achievement and emotional well-being (Brooks-Gunn *et al.*, 1997). In this section we consider why this may be so and how income and education interact. We restrict the concept of 'poverty' to income and other material assets, such as housing, car ownership and durable goods. We acknowledge, however, that poverty is multi-dimensional and that the effects of wider material deprivation, including lack of access to institutions, may not be completely captured by income poverty (McCulloch and Joshi, 1999).

The effects of income and poverty on child development outcomes

Family income is a very important determinant of child development and provides families with the means to offer their children nutrition, health and care, which are essential features of the home environment. It affects outcomes through deprivation of material needs that aid educational success – for example, a learning environment with adequate housing, books, clothing and educational games – and through the lack of provision for children's physical needs. Research has consistently found that experience of income poverty during childhood has long-term detrimental effects on educational attainments (Duncan and Brooks-Gunn, 1997; Gregg and Machin, 2000). In addition to estimating the extent of income and poverty effects, researchers have sought to establish whether the duration and timing of poverty affect children's educational attainments. Are children who always lived in poverty more likely to underachieve in school than children who lived in and out of poverty? Does poverty have worse effects on educational attainment if it occurs during childhood than during adolescence?

Carneiro and Heckman (2003) suggest that transitory parental income, measured as annual net take-home income, does not explain children's educational attainment but permanent income, measured as average income over the lifecourse, has a positive role. Evidence from the USA has supported this argument (see Acemoglu and Pischke, 2001; Plug and Vijverberg, 2005; Shea, 2000). Using a sample of adopted children from the Wisconsin Longitudinal Study, Plug and Vijverberg (2005) estimate a positive and significant impact of parental income, measured before children started school and again once schooling had been completed, on the educational attainment of adopted children. Their estimates are genetically unbiased and so do not reflect hereditary factors. They also condition out the possible impact of parental ability, which means that this is not because parents with high ability may be more able to assist their children on educational matters, and the potential effect that the non-random allocation of adopted children may have on their educational attainment; that is, the result is not because white children tend to be allocated to white families and black children to black families. The authors conclude that family income, permanent rather than transitory, has a causal impact on children's educational attainment.

In the UK, Blanden and Gregg (2004) estimate a causal effect of family income on the probability of achieving qualifications using the differences in educational achievement of siblings. Chevalier *et al.* (2005) investigate the impact of permanent and transitory parental income on the likelihood of children staying on in post-compulsory education in the UK. Their results suggest that parental permanent income has a causal impact on children's decisions to stay on in schooling, even when controlling for education and for transitory income. Other empirical studies have found the effects of income on children's attainment to be substantial but non-linear (Gregg and Machin, 2000; Hobcraft, 1998). That is, below a certain level of income, the effects of poverty on children's attainments and behaviour are large and have long-term impacts. Above this level, additional increments to income have less substantial effects, although where resources are spent on educational provision these continue to have wide-ranging benefits.

The duration of poverty is also important for children's developmental outcomes. The longer children live in poverty, the lower their educational attainment and the worse their social and emotional functioning (Duncan *et al.*, 1994). In the USA, studies have shown that children who always live in poverty have the highest probability of dropping out of school (Haveman *et al.*, 1997). In both the UK and the USA children living in and out of poverty are also at risk of underachievement compared to children who have never lived in poverty (Haveman *et al.*, 1997; Hobcraft, 1998).

The effects of prior parental education on income and poverty

A large body of literature links educational attainment to income. Blundell *et al.* (1999, 2005) and Card (1999) investigate the causal effect of education on income and the rate of return to education.[1] Blundell *et al.* (2000) investigate the impact that education has on changes in income over time and Heckman and Vytlacil (2001) provide evidence for the role of ability in explaining changes in returns to education. Research in this area has been carefully designed to control for confounding factors, for example ability, which can affect both educational attainments and future labour income. Longitudinal datasets and large-scale surveys such as the Labour Force Survey have been used to condition out the impact of factors that occurred prior to, or at the time of, achievement of educational qualifications, which may also impact upon later economic outcomes. These would include parental expectations and aspirations, as well as cognitive, emotional and behavioural development during childhood. In addition, twin studies have been used to investigate the relative importance of genetic factors versus family background characteristics in predicting income differentials among identical twins.

Returns to education have been calculated for vocational and academic qualifications, as well as for individual qualifications for men and women, and for different sectors of the economy (Dearden *et al.* 2002). The rate of return for obtaining a university level degree from an upper secondary level of education is 4.8 and 3.4 per cent in Denmark, 8.6 and 7.2 per cent in Sweden, and 15.8 and 15.4 per cent in Finland for men and women, respectively (Organisation for Economic Cooperation and Development (OECD), 2005). The economic benefits of education differ considerably across OECD countries and the gender gap remains high for some countries. Finland and Portugal show some of the highest returns to schooling and Norway the lowest. Ireland has the largest gender gap and Finland has an insignificant gender gap.

Estimates based on identical twins samples show that returns to schooling are of considerable magnitude. Arias *et al.* (2003) estimate that the impact of education on income in the USA is never lower than 9 per cent and can be as high as 13 per cent for individuals at the top of the wage distribution. Ashenfelter and Krueger (1994) estimate that education increases earnings by 13 per cent per year of schooling. In Australia, the impact of education on income in 1985 was estimated to be 3.3 per cent for a sample of male twins and 5.8 per cent for a sample of female twins (Miller *et al.*, 1997). In Sweden, the estimated impact of education in 1990 for the pooled sample of twins was 5.2 per cent (Isacsson, 2004) and, in the UK, 7.7 per cent in 1999 (Bonjour *et al.*, 2003). In Denmark, education was estimated to increase income by 9.4 per cent for male twins and by 5.3 per cent for female twins in 2002 (Bingley *et al.*, 2005).

Low educational test scores are powerful predictors of low earnings (Hobcraft, 1998, 2000). Even after controlling for educational success and family background, individuals with the lowest test scores are more likely to have low income (Hobcraft, 2003). Average levels of education are associated with countries' aggregate productivity. Sianesi and Van Reenen (2003) estimate that a one-year increase in average education raises the level of GDP per capita by between 3 per cent and 6 per cent. However, the impact of increases at different levels of education seems to depend on the countries' level of development, with tertiary education being the most important for growth in OECD countries.

Maternal employment

Maternal education and employment are strongly linked. In recent decades, women's educational attainments have improved together with opportunities in the labour market. At the same time, mothers' participation in the labour force has been hypothesised to influence children's developmental outcomes, in particular cognitive ability and educational attainments. We review the evidence on the role of maternal employment as a distal factor.

The effects of maternal employment and type of employment on child development outcomes

Parental employment increases household income and hence the availability of monetary resources to invest in developmental activities for children. In the economic model, this is known as the 'income effect'. At the same time, parental employment implies time away from children and the activities that promote their development, which reduces future attainment. This is known as the 'substitution effect'. Other models have included factors that affect both the income and substitution effects, such as availability of formal and informal pre-school mechanisms, number of hours worked, flexibility of the labour market, age of the child and part-time employment. The strength and nature of income and substitution effects have been subject to considerable debates.

There are valid theoretical grounds for some potential negative effects of maternal employment on child development, the basis of which arise mainly from the time that mothers spend away from the child because of work-related activities. It has also been argued that work may increase levels of stress and tiredness, which may, in turn, affect mother–child relations.

Berger *et al.* (2005) find that children whose mothers return to work early are less likely to receive regular medical check-ups, be breastfed in the first year of life and have all their immunisations. Similarly, Anderson *et al.* (1999) find that working mothers breastfeed for shorter periods than full-time mothers and highlight that early switching to formula feeding may have detrimental effects on children's developmental outcomes. Han *et al.* (2001) also argue that combining employment with the use of pre-school education may lead to greater tiredness and more stress, which could negatively impact on the child.

However, other factors such as pre-school education and quality of parenting could offset these negative effects. Bianchi (2000) presents evidence from American mothers' time diaries to indicate that the actual reduction in time devoted to children from working mothers is small compared to non-working mothers. In the UK, Gregg and Washbrook (2003) find that, while employed mothers report significantly higher levels of stress and of tiredness, this stress does not appear to have any significant impact on children's developmental outcomes. Joshi (2000) maintains that as long as employed women purchase 'quality' pre-school education and goods and services to improve children's cognitive and educational skills, the future of their children should not be jeopardized.

Although many interesting empirical studies have tried to quantify the magnitude of the effects of maternal employment on child development, the estimation has been complicated for several reasons. First, unobservable characteristics can induce a spurious relationship between employment and outcomes, rather than reflect a causal one. For example, highly-motivated parents may be more focused on their careers as well as more involved in their children's education. Hence, the positive relation between employment and educational attainment may be the result of motivation. Second, a full structural model should allow for the fact that the decision to participate in the labour market and the choice to have children are not made in isolation. Finally, it is important to realise that the average effect of maternal employment may not be a true representation of the population, as there are many types of employment arrangements and opportunities both between and within industries, which may have differential effects on child development.

Contrary to the theoretical predictions mooted above, empirical evidence has shown that there is little effect of maternal employment on child development. Most of the recent evidence finds that the role of the mother as care provider has been supported, complemented and in some cases substituted for by the availability of pre-schools, a more active role of fathers as carers and assistance from grandparents. Gregg *et al.* (2005), however, find that it is the use of paid childcare, as opposed to friends or relatives, which protects children from any adverse effects of early maternal return to employment in the UK. Their result highlights the interdependence between quality of parental care and non-parental care in determining the effects of maternal employment on child development.

Furthermore, most evidence from the UK and the USA suggests that the timing of mothers' return to work decisions is what matters for child development. Maternal employment, particularly full-time working, in the first year after birth has a small negative effect on children's early cognitive outcomes, measured by reading and literacy test scores (Berger *et al.*, 2005; Gregg and Washbrook, 2003; Hill *et al.*, 2001; Joshi and Verropoulou, 2000), although this result is by no means universal (Ermisch and Francesconi, 2000). This effect may be more than offset by positive effects of working in the second and third years of the child's life. In any case, the key moderator of any effects is the availability of pre-schools or adequate child-care facilities. Very few studies have looked at whether maternal employment has lasting effects on children's educational attainments and later adult outcomes. Ermisch and Francesconi (2000) find a small negative effect of maternal employment on A-level results in the UK, but no effect on unemployment or teenage pregnancy.

Recent empirical evidence from the UK highlights the moderating effect of education on the relationship between maternal employment and children's educational attainment. Gregg *et al.* (2005) show that children of mothers with low levels of education are not disadvantaged when their mothers work. The small negative effects of maternal employment on child development described above are concentrated among women with high levels of education, both in the UK and the USA (Berger *et al.*, 2005; Gregg *et al.*, 2005; Han *et al.*, 2001). These results are consistent with the possibility that alternative childcare provision may be beneficial for mothers with low levels of schooling, as the quality of the alternative care may be higher than the quality of care provided by these mothers. Again, this indicates the importance of the availability of childcare as a moderator of these relationships. In general, we conclude that employment effects are limited on the whole, if any exist at all.

The effects of prior parental education on maternal employment

Greater educational participation for women has been matched by the attainment of better-paid jobs, flexible working hours and better working conditions. In Britain the increase in female education has been accompanied by higher wages, which has driven further participation in education (Davis *et al.*, 1996). In the USA, women's participation in the labour market has slowed down since 1990. For example, labour force participation only rose from 57.5 per cent to 60 per cent between 1990 and 1999. Blau and Kahn (2006) explain that this is the result of how the female labour supply has responded to increasing male and female wages. In Canada, Oreopoulos (2006) uses compulsory schooling and child labour laws to estimate schooling effects on employment. His results show that compulsory schooling reduces the likelihood that affected individuals later report not working or looking for a job. The probability of being unemployed is reduced from an average of 4.4 per cent to 4.1 per cent: a small, but statistically significant, reduction.

However, education does not have a straightforward relationship to maternal employment, particularly in terms of the elements that may impact on child development. With a more educated female workforce, the composition of the labour force has changed. There is, for example, a higher proportion of women in skilled jobs, and their unemployment rate is lower (Saint-Paul, 1996). This introduces job security during economic downturns, reduces stress from losing a job and allows long-term planning for childcare. It is also possible that the increase in female labour force participation may lead to replacement of male labour (Sternberg and Wikstrom, 2004). In this case, some households may benefit from the increase in female labour force participation whereas others may face redundancies, which will increase family stress.

Education is also positively related to mothers' employment opportunities, and this leads to two further countervailing effects. On the one hand, the market power of educated mothers increases their earning, making it more difficult for them to opt out of the labour market into full-time caring for children. On the other, educated women in the labour market tend to have generous maternity rights and the ability to space work more comfortably around maternity needs. In this sense, education has both protective elements and elements of risk, which tend to cancel each other out.

Summary

Of all the distal factors analysed, family size and household income have the strongest effect on child development. These two factors are also the most important mediators, or channels, for educational effects from parents to children, though the causal effect of parental education on family size remains relatively unexplored.

Teenage parenthood is a potentially important risk factor for child development. Whether teenage parenthood is an important mediator of educational effects depends on what we mean by education. If education is defined in terms of school attainment during childhood or by increased participation in post-compulsory schooling, then teenage parenthood is an important mediator of educational effects. This is not the case, however, if education is defined as achievement of qualifications. Family structure in itself is not important for child development; what matters is the degree of conflict and instability in parental relationships. Educational effects on family structure are complex and produce both positive and negative outcomes, which more or less cancel one another out. Hence we do not see family structure as an important mechanism for educational effects. Finally, we do not find evidence to support the role of maternal employment as a key distal factor for child development. Nor do we find evidence that maternal employment is one of the main mechanisms for the transmission of educational effects across generations.

7 The importance of other developmental contexts

Introduction

The preceding three chapters have put forward theory and evidence to understand the family-level mechanisms that explain why parents' education matters for the educational success of their children. This focus on intergenerational transfer necessarily places the family as the central focus of interest. However, as has been highlighted throughout these discussions, the family is not the only context within which individuals develop and it is not independent of many other important social environments. The strength of the ecological framework that motivates our own conceptual model for describing the pathways through which education has its effects lies in its emphasis on understanding the individual and his or her development within multiple, interrelated contexts.

During childhood, early contexts such as pre-school and childcare settings, later schools and peer groups, as well as neighbourhoods and wider communities, are vital for shaping individuals, and the interactions between these environments are fundamental to our model. While the development that occurs within these other settings is important in its own right, it is beyond the scope of the current book. Our interest in this chapter is in understanding the channels through which parents' education may influence children's achievement beyond the immediate context of the family, through interconnections with other developmental contexts. Therefore the evidence presented here is not intended to be a comprehensive review of the influence of these other settings, but attempts to highlight their role in understanding the influence of education in the intergenerational transfer of advantage.

We include in this chapter evidence on the importance of three particularly important contexts for development, namely pre-schools, schools and neighbourhoods. We also recognise the importance of other children as an integral part of these contexts and that the peer group can be seen as a developmental context in and of itself. However, for simplicity we present information on the importance of peers within the two topics of schools and neighbourhoods rather than as a separate context. As with the preceding chapters, in order to better understand the mechanisms that explain why parents' education matters for their children's success, we first consider the theory and evidence demonstrating the importance of a given context for children's development and then consider the potential influence of parents' education on that context.

It is important to note that the specific influence of parents' education as a key driver in inequalities has rarely been the focus of investigation. Associations here have more commonly been made with related distal features, such as family income or social class. However, there are good theoretical grounds to believe that education itself has a real and important part to play in these relationships. These theoretical connections are made for each of the three developmental contexts examined here, and empirical evidence is evaluated where it exists. Where it does not, we make hypotheses about the likely mechanisms for education effects based on the evidence of associations found with other features of the family background.

Conceptualising the importance of other contexts and their relationship to the family

In Bronfenbrenner's (1979) ecological model, context is defined as the location and/or institutional locale within which particular sets of processes occur. These contexts are conceptualised as being developmentally appropriate (constructive) or inappropriate (destructive) depending on whether they are positively or negatively associated with patterns of achievement, behaviour, motivation and mental health. In infancy, key contexts typically include the family and pre-school or other childcare settings. As children get older, they enter more formal education institutions and so schools, after-school settings, extra-curricular activities and the peer group become important places of influence on the developing individual. The effects of different social contexts vary with the particular characteristics of the child. The peer group, for example, becomes increasingly influential during adolescence and into young adulthood. Accordingly, relations within a neighbourhood change considerably and so influences on a young child are very different than for an adolescent. Handler *et al.* (1995) suggest that, as children age, community-based organisations seem increasingly less relevant, making it ever more difficult to keep them attached to the groups wanting to serve them, while concurrently some activities and areas seem both more dangerous and exciting than earlier (see also Cook and Murphy, 1999). Thus, the relative importance of these settings necessarily changes as children get older. Regardless, these wider environments continually interact with the family context and so shape the phenomenological world of the child, as well as directly influencing the experiences of the child. Thus at any one time the connections, or disconnections, between these contexts are significant in conceptualising questions of development and social mobility.

Cook *et al.* (2002) investigated the interconnectivity between social contexts and the ways in which they jointly contribute to positive change during early adolescence. The authors considered the influence of four developmental contexts – the family, neighbourhood, school and peer group – taking into account the interactions between these contexts. Effects were generally cumulative across the nine outcomes studied so that each 'good' context promoted healthier development and thus may have provided some buffering effects against 'bad' ones, but no combination of contexts implied a special degree of protection. Rather, each context produced particular effects, some having stronger or unique links to some outcomes. Families tended to show greatest influence on changes in participation in conventional out-of-school activities, lack of misbehaviour and positive self-image; neighbourhoods were most often associated with school attendance and participation in social activities; peers were more potent in influencing negative social behaviour, such as more 'acting up' and drug use; schools led to positive changes in attendance, academic performance and participation in conventional out-of-school activities. No single, individual context was dominant on all outcomes. These results thus further stress that individual development takes place in many complicated, overlapping contexts and that a given context can operate as either a risk factor or a protective factor depending on its characteristics, those of the child and the relations between them.

Modelling the importance of other contexts

The influences of other important contexts can be similarly modelled within the distal/proximal conceptual structure used throughout our analysis. For example, as shown in Figure 7.1, the quality or characteristics of neighbourhoods are influenced by neighbourhood-level distal factors such as the educational level, affluence and social class of the residents.

Cook *et al.* (2002) note the distinctions between a context's structural features (distal factors) and its more micro-level processes (proximal processes). Structural features of the neighbourhood include neighbourhood socio-economic status and ethnic composition, while process encompasses neighbourhood social cohesion, social control and aspects of the interactions between community members (see also Sampson *et al.*, 1997). The key

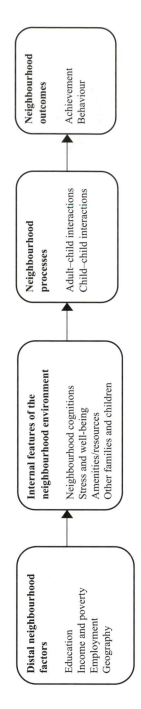

Figure 7.1 Conceptual model for the influences of neighbourhood

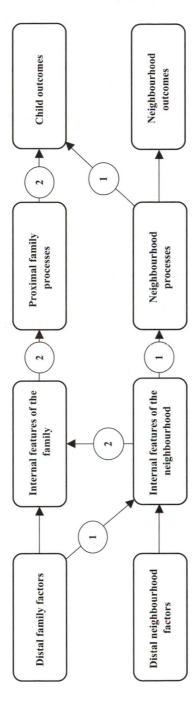

Figure 7.2 Conceptual model for multi-level interactions between family and neighbourhood contexts

characteristics of neighbourhoods are in many cases the same ones that matter in the home, but assessed at the neighbourhood level – that is, factors such as neighbourhood beliefs and attitudes and local resources. The difference in conceptual level here makes the nature of the links different, but many, if not all, key characteristics are the same. Similarly, the proximal processes include the same issues of responsiveness, discipline and cognitive stimulation as at the family level, but instead operate at a local level in terms of multi-faceted relations between individuals in complex communities.

Moreover, the interactions between different contexts can also be modelled in this framework. Figures 7.2 and 7.3 consider some of the possible connections and reciprocal influences between the family and other contexts, taking the examples of neighbourhood (Figure 7.2) and schools (Figure 7.3). Many other interrelationships might also be described but we focus on two.

First, neighbourhood is a pathway for the effect of family-level distal factors such as income (arrows marked '1'). Family-level distal factors influence neighbourhood-level (or other level) characteristics in the sense that richer families choose leafier suburbs or more educated families choose neighbourhoods with more successful schools. These neighbourhood characteristics in turn influence outcomes. Second, neighbourhood characteristics influence family characteristics (arrows marked '2'). The values and well-being of families are not immune to their wider context. Thus, neighbourhood characteristics impact on family process, and so on child development through the family as well as through the extra-familial relationships of children.[1]

To take another example, consider the interactions between family and school contexts (Figure 7.3). Distal family factors influence the characteristics of a given school in a similar way as they do for neighbourhoods. More affluent families are able to choose better-resourced and more desirable schools. Similarly, more educated parents may be better equipped to assess quality and so choose the more successful, higher-achieving schools. In turn, characteristics of the school, such as material resources and ethos, in terms of the attitudes and beliefs of the teaching staff, influence outcomes through the mediating channel of school and teacher processes (arrows marked '1').

A second channel for the effect of family distal factors is through an impact on the relationships with teachers and the school (arrows marked '2'). For example, teachers may have higher expectations for middle-class children and so treat them preferentially, leading to a relationship between family background and pupil–teacher interactions. Similarly, the cognitions and values of parents are important characteristics of the family context. Parents bring these characteristics to the interactions they have with their children's school. They may, for example, be more proficient in interacting

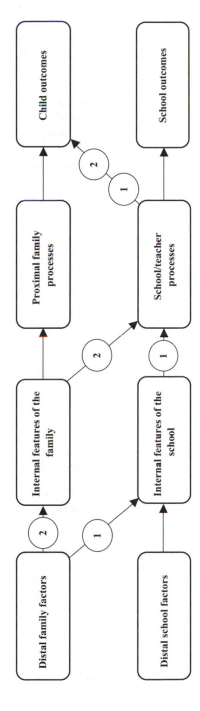

Figure 7.3 Conceptual model for multi-level interactions between family and schools

with teachers as well as better able to support and reinforce traditional academic goals (Hess and Holloway, 1984; Slaughter and Epps, 1987). Similarly, teachers are likely to recognise these characteristics of children and their parents and may respond more positively to them. There may also be a channel for effects here, based on differences in the language used by middle- and working-class families; teachers may favour middle-class children by using language that assumes certain background knowledge and shared understanding of meaning (Bernstein, 1990, 1996; see also Burns, 2001).

Teachers may come to make assumptions about parents, their cognitions and values from signals provided by the distal features of the family discussed in Chapter 6, such as parental education, income and occupational status, or by perceived features of family structure, without these necessarily being mediated by actual family characteristics. These, in turn, can impact on teachers' views of pupils at both general and specific, individual levels and so influence the resulting interactions one-on-one in the classroom as well as more widely in the school (Mortimore and Blackstone, 1982; Mortimore *et al.*, 1988).

Pre-schools

Next to the family, pre-schools and childcare settings are among the most salient social contexts for infants and young children. There are many different types of pre-school settings and the nature of those effects may depend, in part, on family income and parental employment decisions and patterns (see, for example, Gregg and Washbrook, 2003). Furthermore, the availability, accessibility, affordability and quality of pre-schools are also influenced by neighbourhood characteristics; indeed, the quality of local pre-schools may equally be thought of as a neighbourhood characteristic.

The effects of pre-schools on child development outcomes

As with educational behaviours in the home such as reading to children and exposure to print (Chapter 4), participation in an early childhood education programme can provide pre-school children with skills and enrichment that facilitate transitions into primary school and increase their chances of educational success. Many studies report a positive association between pre-school attendance and a variety of later outcomes for young children. More specifically, they note that high-quality, developmentally appropriate childcare in the pre-school years is associated with enhanced social, emotional and, in some cases, linguistic competence for low- and middle-income children alike. Early research by Osborn and Milbank (1987), for example, used the 1970 British Cohort Study (BCS 70), a longitudinal survey tracking all those born in the UK in a particular week in 1970, and found large and significant benefits of pre-school experience on most of their attainment measures at ages five and ten.

The EPPE project has also highlighted the impact that attending pre-school centres can have. It has underlined the importance of the quality and practices of pre-schools, as well as differences between pre-school settings and the influence of home learning (see Melhuish *et al.*, 1999; Sylva *et al.*, 1999). This research documents the positive effects of high-quality pre-school provision on children's intellectual, social and behavioural development. The quality of pre-school centres is directly related to measures of better cognitive development and social behaviour such as independence, concentration, cooperation, conformity and relationships with other children at entry to primary school. Children with no (or limited) pre-school experience have been found to have poorer cognitive attainment, sociability and concentration when starting school. These findings hold when observed differences between the pre-school and home groups in child, family and home environment characteristics are taken into account.[2] This research has also highlighted the positive influence of more qualified staff and pedagogies that position educational and social development in parallel.

In addition, EPPE research indicates that pre-schools can play an important part in combating social exclusion and promoting inclusion by offering disadvantaged children a better start to primary school. As they benefit particularly from good-quality pre-school centres this helps to reduce the risk of underachievement. Thus, while not eliminating disadvantage, pre-school experiences can help to lessen its effects and can provide children with a better start to formal education.

The EPPE researchers' most recent evidence demonstrates the continuing positive effects of attending higher-quality or more effective pre-school settings on children's educational outcomes in maths and reading at the end of Year 5 (age ten), controlling for the possibly confounding influences of family background (Sammons *et al.*, 2007). Children who attended low-quality pre-school settings did not show the same continued gains and, in contrast to earlier research suggesting benefits of all pre-school experience, their results did not differ from those who did not attend pre-school. The EPPE results indicate that attending a better pre-school and a more academically effective primary school, as rated by independent national assessments, improves cognitive outcomes substantially. The effect is similar in size to the impact of having a high rather than a low HLE or a mother with the highest level of educational qualifications (a degree or above). These findings are therefore particularly significant in that they highlight the combined effects of pre-school and primary school in shaping children's educational outcomes.

The positive association between good pre-schools and later outcomes is consistent with other large-scale longitudinal research, including data from the National Institute of Child Health and Development (NICHD) and Childcare Quality and Outcomes (CQO), which similarly report positive relations between good-quality pre-school experiences and later attainment (Howes, 1990; NICHD, 1997, 1998; Ramey and Ramey, 1998). Another influential study from the USA by Schweinhart *et al.* (1986) investigated pre-school systems for children in Ypsilanti, Michigan, considered to be at risk of failing at school. They randomly selected a group of children to receive pre-school education and found that the average Stanford-Binet IQ of the treatment sample rose by 27 points during the first year. The control group's average IQ rose by only four points. By age seven, the average IQ of the treatment group had stabilised at between 90 and 100, compared to between 85 and 90 for the control sample. One of the most important findings of this study was that different curricula in pre-school seem to have different effects. It is important to emphasise here, however, that the benefits of pre-school participation for disadvantaged children are likely to be eroded if the intervention or programme does not extend beyond the early years (Ramey *et al.*, 2000; Ramey and Ramey, 1992). Thus, pre-school programmes are very important but are not a panacea for all social ills.

The effects of prior parental education on pre-schools

As has been noted for the contexts above, the direct influence of parents' own education on their choice of pre-school arrangements and settings has rarely been the primary focus of research. However, there are grounds for thinking that pre-school contexts may mediate the relationship between parents' own education and their children's positive development. For example, more educated parents are likely to be better able to assess the quality of pre-schools as well as have greater access to them.

Research by EPPE (for example, Melhuish *et al.*, 1999) examines the characteristics of families using different types of pre-school by parents' qualification levels. Those mothers using private day nurseries had higher levels of educational qualifications than other mothers. In contrast, the majority of mothers using local authority centre pre-schools had no qualifications. The qualification levels are similar for mothers using nursery classes and playgroups. It is important to note, however, that in terms of the quality of these types of provider, EPPE found that local education authority (LEA) centres (nursery schools, nursery classes and nursery schools combined with care) generally had scores in the 'good' to 'excellent' range. Playgroups and private day nurseries were consistently found to have 'minimal' to 'adequate' scores (Sylva *et al.*, 1999). These findings reflect similar results from Ofsted inspection reports. Therefore the expected relationship of parental education and pre-school quality may not hold in practice. However, this conclusion needs to be tested in multivariate analysis that considers not simply the correlation between parental education and pre-school type, but rather the relationship between parental education and the quality of the pre-school, controlling for the particular type of pre-school setting.

Schools

The literature on the role of schools and schooling for children's achievement and attainment is voluminous and covers influences such as pedagogy; curriculum and assessment; size of school; teacher effects; teacher expectations; pupil–teacher interactions, and the impact and consequences of school choice and diversity. However, as noted earlier, the focus of this chapter is not to describe in detail the determinants or outcomes of effective schools but to situate, within the framework of this book, the school as an important developmental context and a possible channel for the effects of parents' education.

The effects of schools on child development outcomes

School effects

The Coleman report, *Equality of Educational Opportunity* (Coleman *et al.*, 1966), was one of the first attempts to provide a comprehensive insight into the critical factors relating to the education of minority ethnic children. It found variations between US schools in terms of achievement and went on to explore the question: what accounts for this difference? The report concluded that schools had a remarkably similar effect on pupil achievement, once the socio-economic background of the student was taken into account. Thus, when controlling for these characteristics, the differences between schools accounted for only a small fraction of differences in pupil achievement. The report noted, however, that schools did have differing impacts on different minority ethnic groups, with white pupils' achievement being less affected by the school's facilities, curricula and teachers than that of the average minority ethnic pupils. The report also stated that the variability between individual pupils within the same school was approximately four times as large as the variability between schools.

More recently, however, Mortimore *et al.* (1988) examined the progress of 2,000 pupils in fifty London primary schools and found that the school effects on progress were much larger than the effects of pupil background characteristics. For example, school membership accounted for 24 per cent of the variation in reading progress during the primary years, compared to only 6 per cent due to background factors.

The wealth of evidence that exists in this area, however, suggests that schools are differentially effective. For example, pupils make greater progress in schools with more socially advantaged intakes. Similarly, children from lower socio-economic backgrounds are more likely to attend socially deprived schools and, in turn, make comparatively less progress than their socially advantaged counterparts. Value-added analysis of pupil progress during Key Stage 1, the period from when children enter reception year at primary school (age five) to the end of Year 2 (age seven) in Wandsworth LEA showed that the composition of a school's intake can have a substantial effect on child outcomes over and above effects associated with individual prior attainment or family background (Strand, 1997; see also Feinstein and Symons, 1999; Mortimore *et al.*, 1994; Robertson and Symons, 2003). Moreover, league tables may give schools an incentive to select children in order to maximise their results. Other findings highlight the cumulative effects of educational experiences, indicating that attending a better-quality or more effective pre-school can protect against the limitations of a less academically effective primary school (Sammons *et al.*, 2007).

Ability-grouping

Ability-grouping practices are often justified by a person–environment fit perspective. This is the match between an individual and their environment, based on the assumption that individuals are likely to learn more effectively and be more motivated to do so if the material can be adapted to capture their own level of competence. However, much of the available evidence suggests that ability-grouping practices only serve to widen the attainment gap; students assigned to high-ability streams do better than those in mixed-ability groups, while placement within low-ability groups has a negative impact on pupil attitudes to school and motivation. Evidence suggests that pupils in lower-ability groups are, however, disadvantaged, primarily because they are often provided with an inferior education experience and diminished support (see Ireson and Hallam, 2001).

Peer group influences

Peers are an important context in and of themselves but are a particularly salient part of children's experiences at school. Much of the classic work on peer group influences has focused on the negative effects of the peer context. More recently, however, investigators have given greater credence to the positive influences that peers can have. The evidence suggests that children cluster in peer groups sharing similar motivational orientations and preferences and in doing so further strengthen in-group identification (Ball, 1981; Berndt *et al.*, 1990). Positive and negative influences thus depend on these group characteristics. High-achieving children who seek out other high achievers develop even greater positive academic motivation over time. Conversely, children with lower motivational achievement are at increased risk of becoming even less motivated (see Brown, 1990; Kinderman, 1993).

Both theory and evidence suggest that children should be able to focus attention and therefore be better learners when they feel socially supported and well liked by both peers and adults in their learning context (see Goodenow, 1993; Ladd, 1990). Studies focusing on social competence and motivation at school have shown that children who are accepted by their peers and who have good social skills do better in school, have more positive academic achievement motivation and place greater value on learning generally. In contrast, socially rejected children are at increased risk of negative outcomes (Asher and Coie, 1990; Hinshaw, 1992; Wentzel, 1993).

Peers also act as co-learners and aid understanding and learning through group discussion, sharing of resources and modelling of academic skills (Slavin, 1990; Stevens and Slavin, 1995). These aspects of pupil–pupil interaction may influence achievement and related behaviours through their impact on children's expectations for success, self-evaluation and self-efficacy. Furthermore, peer group effects are likely to vary across age. As children get older and become adolescents the role of the peer group becomes more salient. Group acceptance is more important and the time spent with peers is increasingly unsupervised. Consequently, adolescents are likely to be especially susceptible to peer group influences, both positively and negatively, on their interests, goals and values (see Eccles *et al.*, 1989b; Wigfield *et al.*, 1991).

Separating out the unique contribution of peer group effects is empirically very complicated and therefore it is difficult to be sure that peer group influences do not also include aspects from other processes, such as pupil–teacher interactions and ability grouping. Econometric analysis has attempted to overcome this issue and parse out the specific effects of peer group effects on achievement and school attainment. Results here, however, are also mixed and range from almost no effect (Angrist and Lang, 2004) to substantial ones (Ammermueller and Pischke, 2006).

Ammermueller and Pischke (2006) estimate peer effects for fourth-graders in six European countries – Germany, France, Iceland, the Netherlands,

Norway and Sweden – using data from the Progress in International Reading Literacy Study (PIRLS). Their identification for peer group effects is based on the assumption that, within the primary schools in these countries, classrooms are formed randomly with respect to family characteristics. Their results suggest that being in a class with children from more socially advantaged backgrounds leads to gains in reading test scores, assessed in fourth grade, across each of these six countries. The estimated effect within each country was greatest in France and lowest in Norway. The average effect for these countries is relatively large compared to other studies. Sacerdote (2000) uses the random assignment of room-mates and dorm-mates at Dartmouth College in the USA to identify peer group effects and also finds a positive relationship between the achievement of peers. That is to say, on average, the better the room-mate's achievement, the better the individual's own performance. Sacerdote also finds evidence that peer background has an effect on individuals' grade-point average. The strongest result is found for peer effects on the decision to join social groups, such as fraternities.

In contrast, Gibbons and Telhaj (2006) find that, for the population of state secondary schools in England, the influence of the ability of schoolmates can only explain 0.6 per cent of the variance in progress between the ages of eleven and fourteen. In Norway, Sandgren and Strom (2006) find that male students who are in classrooms with relatively older peers do better in maths than other male students. This result, however, does not hold for reading scores or for female students.

Pupil–teacher interactions and teacher expectations

Researchers studying pupil–teacher interaction and the classroom climate have separated factors such as teacher personality and warmth from teacher instruction and managerial style. As within the context of the family, these proximal class–school processes are influenced by other aspects of a teacher's cognitions and related practices. For example, student achievement and attitudes are maximised when teacher warmth and supportiveness occur alongside clear and efficient structured and focused teaching (Fraser and Fisher, 1982; Moos, 1979).

A common claim in the literature is that working-class pupils receive less teacher time and attention than their middle-class peers (see Foster *et al.*, 1996, for a review). These classroom inequalities are often explained as the product of differential teacher attitudes towards or expectations of pupils from lower socio-economic backgrounds. For example, Mortimore *et al.* (1988) found that, even when controlling for reading, writing and maths attainment, social class background was still related to teachers' ratings of pupils' abilities. Though a small effect, teachers nevertheless tended to have a more favourable view of those from non-manual backgrounds; that is, they would underrate the ability of working-class children and overestimate that of middle-class children. The findings from school effectiveness literature compound such classroom inequalities by highlighting high teacher expectations as a key determinant of effectiveness and pupil progress (Sammons, 1999).

The effects of prior parental education on schools

Parental education is implicated in the context of the school, primarily through the channels of cultural and social capital as well as income. The introduction of open enrolment in England and Wales in 1988, for example, allowed parents to choose which secondary school to send their children to, rather than being limited to the nearest. Consequently, many popular schools have become oversubscribed and are therefore able to select pupils. An increasing body of qualitative evidence highlights the importance of this 'quasi-market' in terms of its impact and consequences on school choice and diversity. Middle-class parents, for example, are more inclined and have greater capacity to engage with the education system (Gewirtz *et al.*, 1995). Middle-class parents and their children might also be better equipped with the cultural capital needed to 'succeed' within the school context. Furthermore, several authors argue that both curriculum and pedagogy favour those with more education in terms of their language codes and the discourse used as well as the age-appropriateness of educational behaviours in the home for classroom practices (Bernstein, 1977; Bourdieu, 1973).

In addition, the feedback loop from prior attainment in relation to aptitude selection and ability grouping is also likely to be influenced by parental education. Children from more highly educated families are more likely to do better in their early years. Schools that select on attainment may, in turn, benefit those from better-educated backgrounds. There are also important interactions between neighbourhood and school contexts here: better-educated, higher-income parents are better able to buy houses in the catchment areas of 'better' schools.

Neighbourhoods

The effects of neighbourhoods on child development outcomes

Much of the large-sample, quantitative research looking at the impact of neighbourhoods on children's development comes from the USA. Direct applicability to the UK is therefore limited, among other factors, by differences in terms of the funding of institutional resources and the different composition of communities. However, as there is little UK research looking specifically at the relationship between neighbourhood characteristics and children's and adolescents' development, we use this US evidence as a basis. One exception is Gibbons (2002), who finds, in the 1958 UK cohort, that neighbourhoods explain a small proportion of the variation in school performance once family background effects are controlled for.

In general, studies on child development outcomes find that neighbourhood conditions, particularly measures of neighbourhood SES, are accounted for, in part, by family SES. However, living in an economically deprived neighbourhood may have a negative effect on children's achievement independent of family and school characteristics (Garner and Raudenbush, 1991; Leventhal and Brooks-Gunn, 2000). The theoretical models and evidence put forward for understanding the ways in which neighbourhoods exert their influence on children and adolescents focus on two central mechanisms: local infrastructure (including physical infrastructure, institutional resources and networks) and collective socialisation.

Local infrastructure

The institutional model suggests that neighbourhood effects operate through the quality of resources in the local area. Libraries, family resource centres, literacy programmes and museums in the community are likely to foster children's school readiness and subsequent achievement. The availability of social and recreational activities, including the presence of parks, sports, art and theatre programmes, is likely to promote their physical and social development. Brooks-Gunn *et al.* (1993, 1996; see also Crane, 1991) report that low-SES neighbourhoods generally provide fewer and lower-quality resources than more affluent ones. Thus poorer children may fare badly in part because of their communities, not simply because of their family's economic situations. Similarly, Neuman and Celano (2001) found that low-income communities provide children with fewer literacy resources, such as books, libraries and printed material, than middle-income communities in a large industrial city. Such differences in access to print resources may have important implications for children's early literacy development.

Neighbourhood also influences the availability of social supports. Several studies have indicated that support systems may serve as protective moderators of negative life stressors, enhancing adults' psychological well-being and consequently impacting upon parenting efficacy and behaviours (Campbell and Lee, 1992; Taylor *et al.*, 1993).

Collective socialisation

Collective socialisation (Jencks and Mayer, 1990) posits that adults pass on their behaviours to young people in the same neighbourhood. Neighbourhood role models and monitoring provided by more successful adults are thus considered important ingredients in children's socialisation.

Brooks-Gunn *et al.* (1993) examined the impact of neighbourhoods singly and in concert with family-level variables, on school leaving and out-of-wedlock childbearing among teenagers. They found that, to the extent that economic characteristics of neighbourhoods affect child development, it appears that the absence of affluent neighbours is much more important than the presence of low-income neighbours (see also Duncan, 1994). These authors suggest that neighbourhoods with dense concentrations of white-collar workers provide children and young people with models of more conventional behaviour, which serve to reproduce the same or similar behaviours in the next generation of residents. The presence of negative peer groups may similarly serve as environments for the development of negative attitudes and behaviours. Effects here have been linked to school drop-out rates, teenage pregnancy and labour-market participation (Case and Katz, 1991; Evans *et al.*, 1993)

Multiple risks

Taken together, these neighbourhood influences demonstrate the kinds of strains and stresses that can accumulate for some parents and their families. The presence of multiple risks, in turn, makes the tasks of day-to-day family management that much more complex. Eccles *et al.* (1992) and Furstenberg (1992) show that families living in high-risk, low-resource neighbourhoods have to rely more on in-home strategies to help their children develop and to protect them from the dangers of the neighbourhood. Conversely, families from low-risk neighbourhoods are better able to use resources from their community, such as organised youth programmes, to help their children develop the same talents and skills. Fewer risks also mean that neighbourhoods are comparably safer and thus the need to protect children from the potential hazards of their environment is less pressing.

The effects of prior parental education on neighbourhoods

Distal factors, such as familial income and social class, constrain where families live through combinations of their preferences (where they would like to live) and their constraints (where they can afford and/or need to live) (Massey and Denton, 1993; Wilson, 1997). Thus, although there is little evidence looking specifically at the effect of prior parental education on location, there are strong theoretical grounds to expect a relationship between parental educational level and location. More educated families may choose to (or be able to choose to) live in neighbourhoods with better amenities such as high-quality pre-schools, successful schools, low crime and open areas.

Gibbons (2002) looked at the relationship between the educational strength of an area and house prices. Controlling for other factors, neighbourhood house prices increased with the presence of better-educated neighbours. Gibbons argues that the education levels of a neighbourhood and its community matter because of spillovers in the production of human capital in children. He concludes that house purchasers are prepared to pay to live in neighbourhoods with greater potential for human capital formation. Similarly, Gibbons and Machin (2003) show a positive effect of school quality, measured by national league tables and property prices. These findings suggest that parents value characteristics of a good neighbourhood, such as its educational richness and the quality of its schools. If parents' own education influences the development of their children's educational opportunities and their aspirations for them, then the implication is that there is a strong relationship between parents' education and their choice of neighbourhood.

Summary

The family is not the only context within which children develop and is not independent of important social environments. During childhood, pre-schools and childcare settings, later schools and neighbourhoods and wider communities also play key roles in children's developmental outcomes. This chapter has outlined some of the theory and evidence describing how these other developmental contexts operate and interact with each other to shape the lives of individuals.

Pre-school settings are important for children's early development, but their effects may depend importantly on distal features of the family context such as income, family structure, size, maternal employment flexibility and opportunity. It is government policy that pre-schools should become universally available. To the extent that the policy is rolled out nationally and across the other UK nations, the effect of these distal family characteristics on provision is therefore likely to be reduced. An effect of parental education on pre-school quality may remain, but there is no strong evidence to support that conjecture. Nonetheless, we conclude that until, high-quality pre-schools are universally available and accessible, pre-school experience will be strongly implicated as one of the mechanisms for the intergenerational transmission of education.

Similarly, there is strong evidence that schools are important for child outcomes, although since Coleman *et al.* (1966) schools have been seen as less important, relative to families, than influences on children's attainments. Parental education has important benefits for parents in terms of their capacity and desire to manage the system. In a similar way as for the contexts of neighbourhood and pre-schools, this specific role of parental education operates largely through income, aspirations and cultural capital. Therefore schools mediate the effects of education in an important way, being part of the explanation for the intergenerational transmission of education.

Substantive and relatively robust evidence also exists to support the view that neighbourhoods matter for children as a developmental context, although the effect is not a major one. Parental education impacts on neighbourhood choice through income, aspirations and lifestyle. The stratification of neighbourhoods is not manifested entirely through social class or education, but is strongly apparent in most urban environments. Evidence strongly supports this association. However, although the theoretical grounds for an effect of parents' education on neighbourhood choice are strong, there is no evidence of which we are aware that identifies and establishes empirically a causal role for parents' education here. We conclude therefore that neighbourhoods are a mediator of education effects, but only moderately so.

Part III

Policy and the wider responsibilities of education

Early preventive action

8 A framework for supporting resilience in childhood

As we have discussed throughout this book, the contexts in which the intergenerational transmission of education takes place do not exist in isolation and the model described in this book portrays some of the main interactions between them. Families, pre-school and school environments, as well as neighbourhoods and peer groups, all influence the lives of individuals and the interactions between these developmental settings are vital in determining children's educational success.

Policy interventions are also likely to cross the boundaries between these contexts, giving rise to important unintended consequences. For example, Sabates and Feinstein (forthcoming) show that the introduction of an educational policy to increase participation among young people has had an impact on crime reduction. These interactions can constrain policy success or enhance it but it is important that policy be developed on the basis of holistic thinking that recognises the likely interactions between interventions and other system-wide elements of policy. The ecological model presented here provides an example of the kind of holistic perspective that may help in these policy formulations, as it sets out how individuals exist in multiple, multi-layered contexts with complex interactions between them.

Preventive action to enhance equality of opportunity and of outcomes

The education system is a good example of a context for the support of children in need or at risk of negative and harmful outcomes in adulthood. In this chapter, we present analyses from the UK birth cohort data that describe the extent to which it is feasible to target support to those most in need and to do it in such a way as to address the compounding risk factors set out in earlier chapters and so enhance resilience and capability. We also explain how the education system may be a vital element in the development of such a system of social policy.

The statistical analyses presented were undertaken in the summer of 2006 to inform the development of the British government's Social Exclusion Action Plan and the 2006/7 Comprehensive Spending Review. The first of these documents (HM Government, 2006) sets out the actions that the UK government planned to take in 2006 to 'improve the life chances of those who suffer, or may suffer in the future, from disadvantage'. The second is the review by HM Treasury of expenditure across all UK government departments within its jurisdiction in order to determine the allocation of funds over the medium term and to set objectives for spending departments in the form of Public Service Agreements.

The objective of these dual pieces of research was to provide an assessment of the extent of persistence and change in childhood risk of adult outcomes as children pass through childhood and adolescence. We assessed the levels of change in risk status and modelled the implications of this for the value and cost of different types of policy intervention.

Our starting point was assessing the practicality of early preventive intervention to reduce the risk of adult deprivation and with this the intergenerational persistence of inequality and disadvantage. Readers seeking to avoid statistical material may wish to move to Chapter 9, in which we summarise the key findings.

Methods and research resources

Data

We draw on two datasets, the 1958 NCDS and 1970 BCS 70. The sampling frame for the NCDS was the population of all children born in Great Britain in the first week of March 1958. Data was collected at birth and then again at ages 7, 11, 16, 23, 33, 42 and 46. During childhood, interviews were conducted with parents, teachers and medical officers. Since age sixteen the sample members themselves have responded to extensive interviews and questionnaires. The BCS 70 has a similar structure to that of the NCDS with sampling in the first week of April 1970 and data collected at ages 0, 5, 10, 16, 26, 30 and 34. Again, there has been extensive data collection by interview and questionnaire with the sample members, parents, teachers, health visitors and medical officers. Testing of cognitive development has also been undertaken.

Together, these two cohorts have strength in that they include information on individuals' social and economic circumstances and family lives during adulthood. This information is useful as it enables us to construct indicators or outcomes of adult deprivation such as depression, unemployment, income poverty, residence in social housing, overcrowding at home and the lack of formal educational qualifications. The datasets also contain multiple measures collected throughout childhood; for instance, school attainment, behavioural and emotional development, characteristics of the context in which the child grew up, parental engagement and parental educational behaviours. These measures had been reported by the sample member, the parents or main carers, the teachers and health professionals such as health visitors.

Signalling of risk is not causality

Under a model of progressive universalism in policy delivery – that is, the objective of providing support and intervention on the basis of need within a system recognising the entitlement of all to such support – an important objective may be to identify those with greatest need at the earliest possible opportunity and to provide appropriate support. If one recognises the objective of minimising the social costs that result from social exclusion and related outcomes of low productivity, social division and intergenerational inequity, then identification of the relative risk of these outcomes for different individuals, households and communities is required. A great deal of intervention has been targeted at the community level but, because of important within-community differences in need and access to resources, the individuals and families most in need are often missed by such intervention. An ideal approach to policy intervention would be one that recognises each of these different units of analysis and uses all of them in the identification of individuals most 'at risk'. This is the contribution of the analysis presented in this chapter.

It is important to emphasise that the use of individual-level longitudinal information is not by itself sufficient for an accurate assessment of the value of intervention or of the relative effects of interventions at different ages. That assessment would require knowledge in relation to three types of question:

1   What are the factors that indicate risk? (signalling question)
2   What are the related causal mechanisms? (causal question) and
3   To what extent is each mechanism amenable to policy intervention? (policy effectiveness question)

The signalling question

The analysis in this chapter focuses on the first of these questions. Our key research objective was to describe the extent to which accurate predictions can be made during childhood about who will experience various forms of deprivation later in adulthood.

The precise level of accurate identification required to make intervention cost-effective depends on three factors: the cost of the intervention, the likely success of the intervention and the cost associated with the failure to intervene. Unfortunately, there is no a priori information about the minimum proportion that is required to be identified to make an intervention cost-effective. For example, we might need to identify at least 70 per cent of children living in poverty to make a programme such as Sure Start cost-effective. Other interventions such as the Educational Maintenance Allowance may have lower or higher rates of accurate identification. In fact, one might assess the rate of accurate identification of children at risk ('hit rate' or 'sensitivity') for a particular adult outcome to be as low as, say, 30 per cent, but if the cost of failure to intervene is high and the intervention is highly successful, then the intervention may nonetheless be cost-effective. The required minimum level of identification depends on the trade-off between costs and benefits of policy intervention and can only meaningfully be identified on the basis of an assessment of this trade-off (Feinstein and Sabates, 2006).

The causality question

We undertook our work within a coherent theoretical framework that clarifies the relationship of the measures used to the outcomes described. In other words, if the outcome of interest is unemployment during adulthood and we have information about the experience of poverty during childhood, it is important to know the reasons why child poverty may have long-lasting effects and also the processes by which child poverty may impact upon the likelihood of future unemployment. Therefore, our analysis was not a simple data-mining exercise as we considered issues of causality and process. However, we stress that our analysis should not in any way be equated with statements about causal mechanisms.

The policy question

Our goal was not to assess the feasibility and effectiveness of specific interventions, but to provide information that could be used to ascertain the cost-effectiveness of intervention under a range of assumptions about intervention effectiveness.

Nonetheless, the identification of individuals at risk raises issues for intervention design, or, put in other words, what the Government can do to assist these individuals effectively. It is important that the policy response fits with, and is responsive to, the identification of these individuals. This means that the identification of individuals at risk should not necessarily trigger an instant, costly intervention. A well-designed and intelligent system of risk management would recognise the need to monitor levels of risk over time and aim to intervene at the time of greatest effectiveness. The identification of this time and of the appropriate intervention may be best judged not only with the use of administrative or quantitative information, but also drawing on the skill, judgement and experience of lead professionals who know the child and child's contexts. This extra layer between identification of risk and subsequent action is vital if stigmatising effects and badly targeted interventions are to be minimised.

Risks of identification

There are costs associated with excessively rigid targeting schemes. For example, targeting children according to special education needs may trigger stigmatisation of these children which can damage their self-concepts, thus adding to their level of risk. It is also important to recognise that the identification of who is at risk will change over childhood, as children's balance of risk and protection interacts with their own development to change the nature of the identification for them. Thus, a five year old identified as high risk for developing mental health problems in adulthood will not necessarily be high risk for this same problem at another age.

Defining 'at-risk' groups

At each age at which information is collected in the British cohort studies, we can ascertain the likelihood that each individual will experience an outcome of deprivation during adulthood. We can do this because the cohort studies contain self-reported information on whether or not individuals did in fact experience an outcome of deprivation, and information about childhood and adolescence. Therefore, we can use statistical analysis to test the extent to which each observed feature of development from childhood into adolescence is, on average, associated with the adult outcome. Once these features are identified, we can make predictions about the probability that the adult outcome will occur. Children with the highest level of likelihood of experiencing the adult outcome can in these terms be defined as 'at risk'.

For clarity of exposition we use an example from the NCDS. The NCDS contains information on maths and reading attainments for sample members at the age of seven. This information was collected in 1965. It also contains information on sample members' employment status at the age of forty-two. This information was collected in 2000. We can use maths and reading test scores as measurements of school attainment during childhood to predict, using this information, the probability of being unemployed at the age of forty-two. Therefore, we use school attainment at age seven to identify those individuals most at risk of future unemployment.

The next step is to compare the actual adult outcomes to those forecast by the statistical analysis. As one would expect, there will be cases where the prediction is correct, which are called 'true positives' in the statistical literature, and others where it is incorrect, called 'false positives'. We make an assessment of how precisely the statistical model identifies those with poor outcomes. The assessment is developed using information from individuals at particular ages (for example childhood and adolescence), from particular sources (for example self-reported, reported by the mother, the teacher, the health visitor) and in terms of particular domains of measurement (for example distal, proximal or internal features of the family context). In other words, we investigate changes in how precisely our statistical analysis predicts true and false positives. In this way, the implications for the prediction of adult outcomes of information from these different ages, sources and domains can be tested and compared.

In this chapter, for simplicity of presentation, we work with a single arbitrary cut-off to define being at risk. If an adult outcome has a prevalence of 20 per cent, we identify a risk group that has the same rate of prevalence. To use our previous example from the NCDS, if the proportion of sample members unemployed at age forty-two is 5 per cent, then we identify using maths and reading test scores at age seven the 5 per cent most at risk of unemployment at age forty-two. We acknowledge that this cut-off point is arbitrary and, if such arbitrary risk groups were used as the sole method of policy targeting, it would probably lead to inefficient and ineffective allocation of interventions. This is because it is very unlikely that an effective intervention would be of benefit only to those with the highest risk (the 5 per cent identified in our previous example) and not to those with only marginally lower risk (individuals identified just above the 5 per cent cut-off point). So, it may be appropriate to target interventions at a higher or lower proportion than the prevalence of the outcome that is observed or experienced by the sample of the population in the data.

The risk groups identified here are not constructed in order to target policy intervention but to assess the relationships between being at risk at one age and at risk at another. The method has the virtue of relative simplicity and easy presentation. The fact that the statistical analysis relies on strong linearity assumptions does not interfere with the decision to use a single arbitrary cut-off point. However, we should remember that this is a caveat that impacts upon the interpretation and understanding of the findings.

True and false positives

The simplest statistical model takes the form of a linear prediction equation, where each relevant adult outcome, or measure of deprivation, is treated as a separate dependent variable. Explanatory variables are entered on the right-hand side of the equation. Some of these variables may indicate risk whereas others may be protective factors. The findings from the linear predictions indicate the extent to which risk and protective factors at different ages enhance the predictive capability of the model.

There are a number of ways of assessing the predictive power of measures of risk and protection. It is common in statistical analysis to assess the quality of the prediction in terms of the proportion of variance in an outcome explained by the predicting measures, or in terms of the statistical significance of predictor variables. These conventional approaches focus on the quality of the factor for the prediction of the outcome rather than on the quality of the factor for identifying a group that is at risk of the outcome. In other words, the conventional approaches indicate whether a measure of child development is associated with an adult outcome, whereas our approach requires the identification of those at risk of the adult outcome using information from the measure of child development.

To focus on the issue of the identification of individuals at risk, we use an alternative approach. For each explanatory variable, either risk or protective, the statistical model effectively generates weights that reflect the importance of the measure for the risk that the adult outcome will occur. These weights are then linked to the observed childhood information to generate predictions of the probability that the individual will experience the adult outcome. Much of the analysis then focuses on this probability, which can also be termed a risk propensity score.

For each individual, the data provide an observation of whether or not they actually experienced the outcome of adult deprivation (truth). The statistical analysis provides a prediction of the likelihood of experiencing the outcome in adulthood based on information from childhood (prediction). This approach creates a two-way table of probabilities, as shown in Table 8.1.

Two proportions provide a very good indication of the predictive capability of the measures that were used to generate the predicted outcome, namely:

1 The true positive proportion $P(TP)$: the proportion of those who actually experienced the outcome who are accurately predicted to do so by the statistical model;[1] and

2 The false positive proportion $P(FP)$: the proportion of those who did not experience the outcome who are erroneously predicted to do so by the statistical model.

Table 8.1 A tabular description of forecast accuracy for binary outcomes

		Truth		
		Positive (T⁺)	*Negative (T⁻)*	
Decision (predicted outcome)	Positive	True positive	False positive	
	(D⁺)	A	C	P(D⁺) = A+C
	Negative	False negative	True negative	
	(D⁻)	B	D	P(D⁻) = B+D

Note: $A+B+C+D = 1$ $\qquad$ $P(T^+) = A+B$ $\qquad$ $P(T^-) = C+D$

Note that as defined here:

$$P(TP) = \frac{A}{A+B} = \frac{P(D^+,T^+)}{P(T^+)} = P(D^+ \mid T^+)$$

$$P(FP) = \frac{C}{C+D} = \frac{P(D^+,T^-)}{P(T^-)} = P(D^+ \mid T^-)$$

These two proportions provide an indication of the accuracy of the identification of those at risk of adult deprivation.

As Table 8.1 highlights, the usefulness of the prediction can be in assessing the relative likelihood of first accurately identifying those individuals not requiring extra support (true negatives); second, wrongly identifying individuals not requiring extra support (false positives); third, not identifying individuals who require extra support, which leads to failure to intervene (false negatives), and, fourth, identifying individuals requiring extra support, which leads to an accurately targeted intervention (true positives).

It is important to note that, as the threshold determining the prediction changes, there will be important implications for the proportions of true and false positives. A low threshold, which creates a prediction that most individuals will experience the outcome, is likely to identify accurately a large proportion of those who eventually do have the outcome (a high true positive proportion) but also to suggest falsely that the outcome will be experienced by a lot of those who did not in reality experience the outcome (a high false positive proportion). Thus, the impact of the threshold on the proportions of those who are to be classified as at risk is a crucial factor in the model.

The prediction data and outcomes

There are a great many features of the background and development of children that may provide signals about likely future adult outcomes. Among these features we find parental income; socio-economic status and education; health behaviours of mothers when pregnant; child birth weight; cognitive emotional and behavioural development during childhood; parental beliefs, values and aspirations; and the characteristics of the home environment in which the child grew up, among others. Therefore, it is important to structure the analysis and to provide a foundation for interpreting the results from the statistical analysis.

Theoretical framework

The general theoretical framework for considering the relationships between background, child development and future adult outcomes is derived from the ecological model of Bronfenbrenner (1979), which we set out in previous chapters, together with more recent developing science in bio-medical and psychological social science fields. From these theoretical perspectives, we summarise the following key principles of human development, which are particularly important during the period of childhood and adolescence:

- There are features of biology and temperament that are determined by inherited, genotypic characteristics and that have important implications for subsequent development and outcomes.
- These genetic features interact with features of the environment, which therefore also have important implications for development and outcomes.
- There are many features of the environment that may impact on human development to influence the relative likelihood of adult outcomes for different children. But key amongst these influences, particularly but not exclusively in the early years, are those experienced in the family context.
- Other contexts also matter, increasingly through childhood. Particularly important other contexts are peer groups, schools, neighbourhood factors and wider social and community networks. As children move through childhood into adulthood, a wider array of contexts start to play an increasingly important role, particularly factors such as labour markets, work and college environments, close personal relationships and other interactions with adults in positions of authority and influence.

- These contexts interact in their influence in the development of children and young people.
- The personal skills, attributes, characteristics, temperaments and self-concepts of children and young people also contribute to their success in negotiating the pathway through childhood into adulthood. Children have some degree of agency in their own development but many of the underlying attributes that support agency will also be strongly influenced by background and contextual features.
- Thus development occurs through a multi-faceted and complex series of interactions between the developing child and the other agents and agencies with which the child forms relationships.
- Pathways are not set in stone as a result of early development or contexts and there is always the possibility of discontinuity or plasticity, which can change likely outcomes. However, disadvantage and background stress exert continuous and compounding pressures on young people such that the discontinuities in development tend to privilege those from more advantaged backgrounds – that is, with more supportive, nurturing and well-resourced environments.

It should be emphasised that not all of the factors that influence development can be measured in standard data collection exercises. Many important causal mechanisms are the result of very rapid intrapersonal neurological and biological processes that cannot easily be observed and that interact with features of the developing child and of social and family contexts in dynamic transactions that are not yet well understood. Therefore, it would be wrong to expect that causal processes can be easily manipulated in a theoretically grounded science of policy delivery. However, as a result of these causal processes there are relatively stable features of personal development and of social and family context, which indicate the general trends in development and carry strong signals about likely outcomes during adult life.

Domains of measurement

Using the above framework it is possible to identify seven domains of measurement, namely:

Family context

- Distal family factors, which (as discussed in Chapter 6) include family structure, family size, income and poverty, teenage parenthood and maternal employment.

- Proximal family processes, which (as discussed in Chapter 4) include measures of parenting style and educational behaviours of parents.

Other contexts

- Neighbourhood characteristics such as recreational and educational facilities.
- School characteristics, for example type of school attended; whether the child attended pre-school education; whether the child settled easily at school; and school resources.

Child factors

- Features of the cognitive development of the child as measured by school achievement in maths, reading and English.
- Features of the affective and behavioural development of the child, as measured by externalising and internalising behaviours: having soiling problems still at the age of five; bullying; being bullied; often feeling miserable; often being disobedient; and regularly fighting with other children, among others.
- Child health factors such as weight, height and having any medical condition.

Most of the measures used to predict outcomes in adulthood and adolescence can be classified into one of these seven domains. There are, however, some complex issues in the classification of constructs that are not always straightforward to resolve. For example, if a child attends an independent school, does this provide a feature of the school context or is it more indicative of family characteristics such as wealth and aspiration? Similarly, if a young person spends a lot of time in the company of peers engaged in activities that might be classified as antisocial, does this provide a signal about the peer group, properly categorised as part of the peer context, a separate domain of measurement, or is this involvement more indicative of the affective and behavioural development of the young person?

These issues cannot be easily resolved and result from the complexity of the underlying causal mechanisms. Our strategy here is to be transparent about the ways in which measures are classified so that inferences can be appropriately discussed as required.

Commensurability of measurement

The longitudinal datasets used for this study are of a high quality and internationally renowned as being a major scientific resource of a kind not

Table 8.2 Sources and ages of data collection in the NCDS and BCS 70

									Age (years)								
Source	0	1	2	3	4	5	6	7	8	9	10	11	12	13	14	15	16
1958 cohort	Teacher								✓				✓					✓
	Parent	✓							✓				✓					✓
	Medical												✓					✓
	Child												✓					✓
1970 cohort	Teacher											✓						✓
	Parent	✓				✓						✓						
	Medical											✓						
	Child																	✓

available in such depth and breadth anywhere else in the world. They are the result of long-term investments by scientific research councils, academics and sponsoring government departments and make possible an in-depth and detailed analysis of the research questions of concern in this book. However, it is important to recognise the limitations of these sources of information and the implications for our analysis.

One particularly important issue is that, for a number of reasons, comparability across ages within and between studies must be undertaken with considerable care. The measures were collected as part of separate studies that were in differing ways and at different times intended to meet the changing research objectives of bio-medical science, social science and policy. The NCDS, for example, was originally intended to support analysis of perinatal mortality and was developed on the basis of a research design appropriate for that study. The BCS 70 suffered because a teachers' strike disrupted the age sixteen data collection and led to big problems of missing information. Furthermore, the datasets use different forms of data collection at different ages of the study children. The sources of data collection in each study by age are set out in Table 8.2.

Because of differences in focus of the study at different ages, the quality of measurement across domains and ages varies quite considerably, such that there are not an equal number of measurements across the seven domains. Measurement of the neighbourhood context is particularly weak, there being few easily available measures in the data and the relevant constructs being less well understood and possibly harder to measure in individual-level data than those for the family context. Thus, scientific comparison of the relative importance of these different constructs as indicators of development must be undertaken with caution.

The purpose of the analysis presented here is to assess the differences in relative predictive power of the measures at different ages rather than across domains. Therefore, the identification of individuals at risk at each age depends on the measures available at each age. The fact that one child is identified as at risk at one age but not another may result from the differences in measurements used to assess the risk and not from the level of risk changing from one age to another for this child. This should be borne in mind.

In order to clarify the issue of the commensurability of measurement across domains and ages in the different datasets, Table 8.3 reports the number of constructs assessed at each age in each domain. It can be seen, for example, that although the 1970 cohort had assessments of twelve different distal factors at age five, only one was assessed at age sixteen. Partly this is a restriction of the data collection process itself, partly of what has been coded to date, but it should be considered when comparing the

Table 8.3 Number of constructs in each dataset, by age and domain

	NCDS (1958 cohort)				BCS 70 (1970 cohort)			
	0	7	11	16	0	5	10	16
Distal family factors	12	14	8	9	10	12	12	1
Proximal family processes	2	11	6	6	0	6	7	0
Neighbourhood context	0	0	1	0	0	2	0	0
School context	0	10	2	15	0	0	5	0
Cognitive development	0	9	10	10	0	7	4	0
Affective and behavioural development	0	15	19	16	0	3	14	12
Health	1	8	8	6	1	1	1	0

predictive power of distal factors at the two ages in this dataset. Other important points to note are:

- the 1970 cohort at age sixteen only includes measures in the domains of affective and behavioural development, with the exception of one distal factor;
- few measures of the neighbourhood context are assessed;
- few health measures are included, particularly for the 1970 cohort;
- few school context measures are included for the 1970 cohort; and
- in both cohorts there are more measures of distal factors than of proximal processes.

Outcomes

In order to maximise the level of generality of the findings, analysis has been undertaken across the two datasets of a very wide range of outcomes. There are many important features of adult deprivation. Since particular measures of child development may have differential predictive power for different outcomes of adult deprivation, we have tested across a wide range of outcomes so as to provide as detailed an investigation of these relationships as possible and to limit the likelihood that results are only relevant to very specific single outcomes.

Of key interest here are the results for multiple outcomes, or what may be described as indices of multiple deprivation. For the 1970 cohort we constructed an index of five important outcomes, assessed at age thirty, namely referral to mental health services; residence in social housing; high levels of not in employment, education or training (NEET) before age thirty; overcrowding at home; and financial problems. Approximately 15 per cent of the sample had two or more of these five outcomes at age thirty. We take this as a first indicator of multiple deprivation.

We also constructed a measure indicating how many of the broader outcomes each individual had experienced at age thirty. Among these factors we have smoking; obesity; depression; psychiatric disturbance; being single, separated or divorced; teenage parenthood; single parenthood; residing in social housing; homelessness; being a victim of crime; dissatisfaction with life; not having formal qualifications; criminality; racial intolerance; not voting; low self-efficacy; low income; receipt of social benefits from the Government; unemployment; overcrowding at home; long periods of time not in employment, education or training; financial problems; and addiction to drugs or alcohol. We found that roughly 11 per cent of the sample had experienced nine or more of these outcomes and we take this as a second high-risk group. The correlation between these two indicators is fairly high at 0.61.

For the NCDS, we constructed an index of multiple deprivation outcomes based on use of six of the measures assessed at age twenty-three. These six measures are being in an unskilled or semi-skilled occupation; having problems with literacy or numeracy; the number of children before the age of twenty-three; teenage parenthood; depression; and low income. We used a cut-off of three of the six outcome measures, with 8.7 per cent of the sample experiencing three or more of these six outcomes. We also constructed a second measurement of multiple deprivation based on the broader outcomes utilised for the 1970 cohort but measured at the age of forty-two for the 1958 cohort. We found that 12 per cent of the sample had experienced seven or more these outcomes.

Results

The relationship between childhood factors and deprivation in adulthood

In terms of raw statistical associations across time, the extent of association between family background at birth and adult deprivation for the 1970 cohort is shown in Figure 8.1.

Nearly 30 per cent of individuals aged thirty born to parents with fathers in SES V (unskilled, manual occupations) reported multiple deprivation at age thirty, compared to 5 per cent of those born into families with fathers in SES I ('professional' occupations). The gradient is fairly striking, although it is also notable that 5 per cent of those from the most advantaged homes also experience multiple deprivation in this cohort.

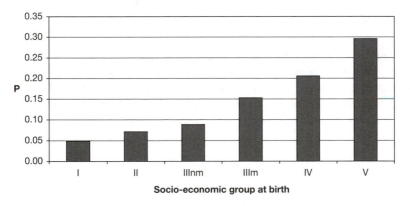

Figure 8.1 Probability of multiple deprivation at age 30, by birth SES (BCS 70)

Table 8.4 Predicting outcomes at age 30 from age 10 measures (BCS 70)

	P(TP)	P(FP)
Workless household with children	50.0	1.3
Mental health problem	45.3	16.3
Serious addiction to drugs or alcohol	52.2	1.1
Long periods not in education, employment or training (16–30)	51.6	2.5
On benefits at age 30	41.6	3.6
Multiple offending	51.6	1.3

However, this result is only drawing on one measure of family context, obtained at birth. Table 8.4 shows the extent to which childhood data can be used to predict a range of different aspects of adult deprivation. Here we are drawing only on measures available in the age ten data collection, that is to say, information collected at one point in time and used to predict outcomes twenty years later.

In Table 8.4, *P(TP)* is the probability of a true positive prediction, and indicates the proportion of those who actually experience the outcome who would have been predicted to do so from the age ten data. For most of these outcomes, half of those experiencing eventual deprivation could have been identified as having been at risk at age ten. On the other hand, *P(FP)* is the proportion of false positives, the proportion of those who did not experience the outcome who were considered to be at risk from the age ten data. For mental health problems at age thirty the model falsely identifies a relatively large proportion of children at risk from age ten information who did not experience this outcome (16.3 per cent). For the other outcomes, the proportion of false positives identified is relatively low, for example only 1.1 per cent of those not suffering serious addiction to drugs or alcohol were falsely identified by the model as at risk. Another way of showing this level of forecast accuracy is shown in Figure 8.2.

In Figure 8.2, we have grouped children according to their level of risk at age ten and report the probability of experiencing multiple deprivation for each of three groups represented. Along the horizontal axis is an increasing measure of deprivation. The point at one, for example, indicates the experience of one or more of the thirty-two outcomes of adult deprivation; the point at two indicates the experience of two or more outcomes, and so on. The vertical axis represents the probability of experiencing this number of outcomes. Thus, the lines in the graph all decline from one at

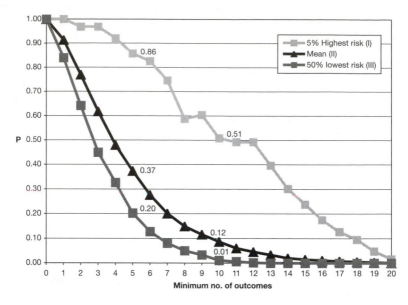

Figure 8.2 Probability of multiple deprivation at age 30, by level of risk (BCS 70)

the origin (since it captures the fact that all children experience either none of these outcomes or at least one of them), to zero at the farthest extent of the horizontal axis (no one experiencing twenty or more of the outcomes).

The highest line reports the multiple deprivation probabilities for the 5 per cent with the highest level of risk based on the age ten data. The middle line reports the probabilities for the average child. The lowest line represents the 50 per cent with the lowest level of age ten risk. The difference between the risk line for the 5 per cent most at risk and the 50 per cent with lowest risk or the average child is striking. To take the risk lines at the point of ten or more of the outcomes of multiple deprivation, this is experienced by 12 per cent of the cohort as a whole but, whereas only 1 per cent of the large low-risk group experience this level of adult deprivation, this rises to 51 per cent for the 5 per cent with the highest level of risk.

This figure indicates the extent, depth and persistence of childhood deprivation in the 1970 cohort. Using information about context and development available at age ten, it is possible to identify a group of the most at-risk children of whom 51 per cent will experience very severe disadvantage in adulthood. We can distinguish this group from the majority of the population, whose risk is substantially lower.

Movements into and out of risk throughout childhood

We also explored in more detail childhood pathways of movement into and out of risk. We are concerned with the implications of continuities and discontinuities in risk for the process of identification and intervention for those at risk. There will be some children who are at risk at one period and stay at risk in subsequent periods, but also many others who move in and out of risk. This creates important challenges for attempts at targeted support.

Our starting point is a consideration of the static relationship between the level of risk at each age at which data are collected in childhood and the actual experience of adult deprivation. A summary is shown in Table 8.5 for the multiple deprivation outcomes. Note that prediction is based on information at the indicated age only, not also accounting for information from prior ages.

It can be seen that the odds of experiencing the adult outcomes are very high for those who are defined as at risk at each age. For example, for children identified as at risk from information available at birth in 1958, the odds for outcomes of multiple deprivation at age twenty-three in 1981 are 4.2 times higher than for children identified as not at risk. Therefore, being at risk in childhood is very strongly associated with the likelihood of experiencing the indicated outcome. There is, however, a substantial difference between the two cohort studies. For the 1958 cohort, the odds for outcomes of multiple deprivation increase with the age at which risk is defined (from 4.2 at birth to 9.5 at age seven, 11.1 at age eleven, and 11.7 at age sixteen). For the 1970 cohort this effect is less marked, as the odds only increase from 3.9 at birth to 4.4 at age five, 4.9 at age ten and 4.4 at age sixteen. To some extent this may be due to the weakness of the age sixteen data collection in the 1986 survey of the 1970 cohort, which coincided with a teachers' strike and also suffered other unusually great problems of attrition and missing data.

Another interesting finding for the 1958 cohort is that the odds for the outcome of multiple deprivation obtained for children at risk at age seven are substantially larger than the odds for children identified as at risk from birth. Age five risk in the 1970 cohort, however, is closer to birth risk than to age ten risk in the strength of its negative implications for adult outcomes. There are several plausible inferences from this result. What we infer is that predictions made at age seven are stronger than those at age five because children have spent longer in school, which leads to more useful teacher information in the formation of predictions.

The persistence of risk

Before considering in detail the dynamic movements into and out of risk status, we first consider the number of periods at which individuals are so

Table 8.5 Odds of multiple adult deprivation given childhood risk categorisation

Outcome	No. of observations	Age	Odds	t-statistic
1958 cohort				
Probability of multiple	10,123	Birth	4.22	16.32
deprivation (three or	8,423	7	9.5	24.33
more of the six	7,647	11	11.07	24.76
outcomes at age 23)	7,424	16	11.75	25.3
1970 cohort				
Probability of multiple	10,148	Birth	3.86	21.08
deprivation (two or	11,112	5	4.36	24.42
more of the five	11,038	10	4.95	26.51
outcomes at age 30)	11,112	16	4.43	24.67

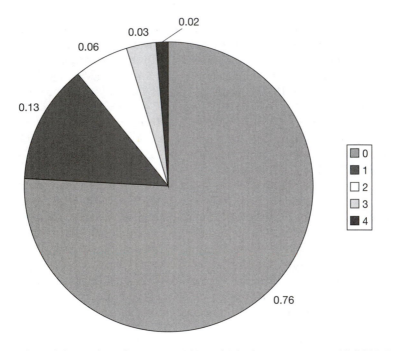

Figure 8.3 Number of sweeps 'at risk', multiple deprivation at age 42 (NCDS)

classified. Results are shown graphically in Figure 8.1 for age forty-two deprivation in the 1970 cohort, and in Figure 8.2 for the age thirty deprivation in the 1958 cohort. As well as showing the number of times children are classified as at risk, we also show in Figure 8.3 and Figure 8.4 how the likelihood of each adult outcome increases with the number of times at which individuals are said to be at risk during childhood.

Figure 8.3 shows that 13 per cent of individuals are classified as at risk from information at birth and again at ages seven, eleven and sixteen. An additional 6 per cent are classified as at risk in three of the four periods in which we have information, 3.2 per cent are identified as at risk in two of the four periods, and only 1.5 per cent are identified in only one of the four periods.

Similarly for the 1970 cohort, which is shown in Figure 8.4, we find that 14.4 per cent of individuals are identified as at risk in all four periods (at birth and at ages five, ten and sixteen). An additional 7.6 per cent are identified as at risk in three of the four periods and 2.9 per cent are identified

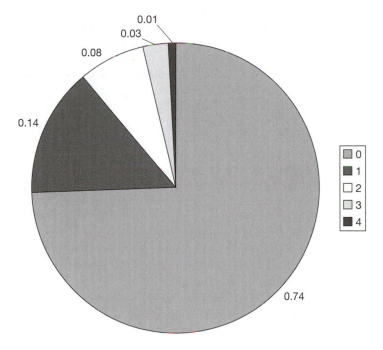

Figure 8.4 Number of sweeps 'at risk', multiple deprivation at age 30 (BCS 70)

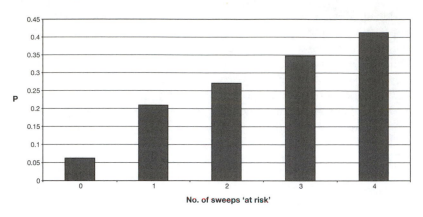

Figure 8.5 Probability of multiple deprivation at age 42 by number of sweeps 'at risk' (NCDS)

as at risk in two of the four periods. Finally, we only identify 0.7 per cent of individuals as at risk in one of the four periods.

In summary, across both sources of information we find that once an individual is identified as at risk at one age it is very likely that he/she will be identified as at risk at a later period.

Figure 8.5 shows the probability of multiple deprivation at age forty-two according to the number of periods at which individuals in the 1958 cohort are identified as at risk. The greatest likelihood of multiple deprivation is shown for individuals identified as at risk in each period of information, from birth to age sixteen. These individuals show a probability of multiple deprivation at age forty-two of 42 per cent. For individuals identified as at risk in three of the four periods, the probability of multiple deprivation at age forty-two is nearly 35 per cent, which is six percentage points lower than for individuals who were identified as at risk in all periods. The probability of multiple deprivation at age forty-two is reduced to 26 per cent and 21 per cent for individuals identified as at risk in two and one of the four periods, respectively. Finally, the lowest probability of multiple deprivation is for individuals identified as not at risk at any of the four sweeps of data collection (only 6 per cent).

The analysis for the 1970 cohort is shown in Figure 8.6. With this cohort, individuals who are identified as at risk in all periods of information have 70 per cent probability of multiple deprivation at age thirty. The probability of multiple deprivation for individuals who are identified as at risk in three periods is nearly 60 per cent and for individuals identified in two periods is just below 40 per cent. The probability of multiple deprivation at age thirty

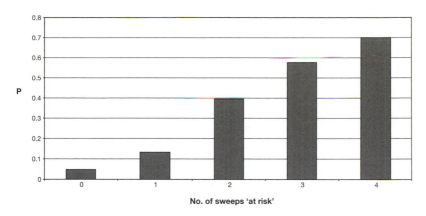

Figure 8.6 Probability of multiple deprivation at age 30 by number of sweeps 'at risk' (BCS 70)

is much lower for individuals identified as at risk once (12 per cent) or not at risk (less than 5 per cent).

Overall, the risk gradient is steep and fairly linear with respect to the number of episodes of risk. The lowest likelihood of multiple deprivation is shown for individuals not at risk and increases according to the number of periods at which individuals are identified at risk.

Dynamic risk movements

We also use information from the cohort studies to investigate continuity and discontinuity in risk from birth to adolescence. In order to do this, we treat risk status at each age in childhood as an outcome to be predicted by information from previous ages and then consider the proportions of true and false positives in this prediction. We use all information from all constructs at the previous age to predict risk status at the later age. This also leads to greater accuracy in prediction. Results using this method are presented graphically in Figure 8.7 for the 1958 cohort and in Figure 8.8 for the 1970 cohort.

Figure 8.7 shows the proportions of true and false positives (above and below the arrows, respectively) for transition from the situation of risk at one age to risk status at a later age. Of those classified as at risk at age seven, for the age twenty-three outcome of multiple deprivation in the 1958 cohort, 37 per cent would have been predicted to be so classified on the basis of their birth data (the true positive rate). Thus, 63 per cent of those at risk at age seven would not have been identified as at risk from the birth

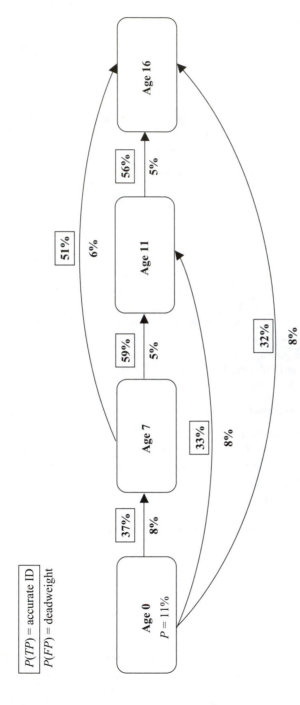

P(TP) = accurate ID
P(FP) = deadweight

Figure 8.7 Risk continuity: true positives and false positives for multiple adult deprivation at age 23 (NCDS)
Note: 100 − P(TP) = P(FN) = missed cases

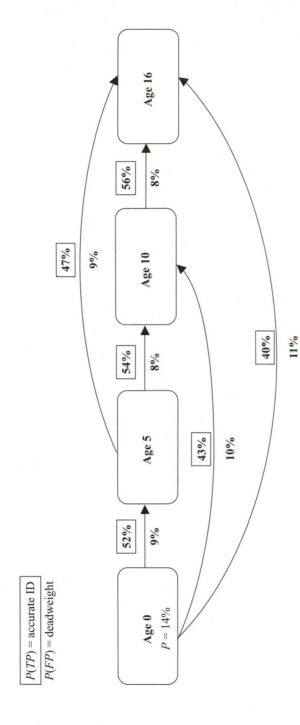

Figure 8.8 Risk continuity: true positives and false positives for multiple adult deprivation at age 30 (BCS 70)

Note: 100 – *P*(*TP*) = *P*(*FN*) = missed cases

data, if an arbitrary cut-off was used to classify all cases at birth as either at risk or not at risk. Note, too that the false positive proportion from birth to age seven for this outcome is 8 per cent, which is to say that 8 per cent of those who were not at risk at age seven would have been falsely predicted to be at risk from their birth data.

Overall, this figure demonstrates quite a high degree of discontinuity in risk between birth and age seven and therefore inaccuracy in risk predictions made from birth.

Another important finding for the 1958 cohort is that there is much greater accuracy in risk forecasting from age seven onwards than from birth onwards. This reflects the fact that the age seven data include wide-ranging assessments of the development of the sample member whereas the birth data only include assessments of the context of the child. By age seven, many of the impacts of family risk are apparent (though not immutably) in the school attainments and behaviours of children and it becomes possible to better discern those children who are resilient to family risk or under-achieving despite risky circumstances. These factors improve predictions considerably for the 1958 cohort.

Additionally, there is much higher continuity of risk from birth and so accuracy of forecast in the 1970 cohort than in the 1958 cohort. For example, for the multiple deprivation outcome, the true and false positive proportions for the 1958 cohort predictions, based on information from birth, are 37 per cent and 8 per cent respectively. For the 1970 cohort, the equivalent statistics are 52 per cent and 9 per cent. This is a big rise in the true positive proportion without an equivalent rise in the false positive proportion. These findings are mirrored across all outcomes.

Finally, for the 1970 cohort risk continuity from birth to age sixteen is not much lower than that from birth to age five or from birth to age ten. In some cases it is even higher. This reflects the impact of compounding risk. A fairly high proportion of those who exited risk status between birth and later ages re-enter it subsequently.

A context for policy responses

In our view it would be irresponsible and socially and economically inefficient to ignore this very high level of capacity to identify early on those at risk of multiple deprivation in adulthood. An intelligent system of policy implementation would both respond to these signals of risk and learn from the resulting evidence on implementation to improve its own identification capacity and policy responses.

However, it is also vital to remember that the issue of identification is distinct from that of causation. The fact that we can identify those at risk of high cost and high harm outcomes using a small number of key measures does not at all mean that these measures are the causal mechanisms responsible for the outcomes observed or that the measures supply clear indications about what policy initiatives should be employed, when or by whom.

Rather, the measures stand for a wide-ranging set of features of circumstance, development and chance, which provide the context within which further development takes place. This development is neither deterministic nor inexorable and the degree of predictability does not indicate that the processes that lead to particular outcomes are mechanistic or amenable to obvious, centrally determined interventions.

The particular interventions or supports that will make a difference to the pathways that lead from social background and early development to adolescent and adult outcomes must be applied at a local level and depend on there being skilled and well-resourced local practitioners who are able to make more informed assessments of need and risk than are possible in the national survey data used here.

Just as the Department of Health depends on general practitioners and other health practitioners to make decisions about diagnosis and treatment, so should those concerned with social policy have available to them a system of diagnosis and response that is informed by local-level experience and skill. In fact, equivalent if more advanced systems for health care are being developed in the NHS and internationally (see, for example, Billings *et al.*, 2006).

The ethics and legality of data matching

A set of very important caveats must in our view also be taken into account in any discussion of appropriate policy responses to the findings in these data, namely issues about the actual data that can or ought to be collected in administrative terms, about the ethics and legality of access to data and data-linking, and about the use of the data in the targeting of interventions. Importantly, the data used here are not available for use in policy-related exercises and are only for use in scientific research under strict ethical guidelines that ensure anonymity. In other words, no individual, family or other institution can be identified in any way.

However, information is regularly gathered in schools, doctors' surgeries and elsewhere that in fact might be considerably more predictive for adult outcomes than that collected in the datasets investigated in this research study. Moreover, teachers, social workers and other practitioners routinely form assessments and perceptions of children that can be remarkably accurate about their level of risk. Thus, there is no information barrier to the application of the findings of this study to policy. The barriers are rather in terms of ethical, legal and practical issues that require detailed consideration and debate.

Accuracy is far from total

There will always be individuals incorrectly identified. This means that early identification cannot be a final or absolute marker of risk and that any system of policy intervention must build in the capability to undertake closer monitoring of risk before intervention is determined and to change assessments of risk in the light of new information, chance events and developmental and contextual shifts. Children change considerably during childhood, as do family circumstances, and this needs to be allowed for.

Towards an intelligent system for preventive action

Our results indicate that it is possible to have a system of policy delivery based on accurate information about individual, family and community context and development. With the very rich data available in the UK birth cohort studies, it is possible to accurately identify children and families who would benefit from appropriate and effective intervention, were such interventions available.

In reality, the type of data and information available to policy-makers will be different from that of the cohort studies and so the information is presented as a guide to what might be possible rather than a definitive template. A great many other important longitudinal studies exist around the world and in the UK and each could also provide indications about the most useful topics of measurement. At local level, using administrative data, as well as local practitioner judgements such as those of teachers, medics, social workers and others, it would be possible to add to the forecast capability indicated here.

It would not be necessary to collect detailed data on all children. Rather, preventive action is based on a system of risk monitoring at which certain levels of risk would trigger greater monitoring and assessment, and ultimately, if judged appropriate, intervention. This is the same process as is followed in relation to medical practice.

The specific measures required

Our findings indicate that measurement of children's own achievements and teacher ratings, particularly from age seven and beyond, can be particularly predictive. Before this age, measurement of developmental health and social and family context will be more important.

The precise measures that are most relevant when it comes to the prediction of outcomes depend to a certain extent on the outcome of interest. Where these are related to mental health, for example, earlier measures of mental health will be particularly relevant. For other outcomes such as drug use, worklessness or violence in the home, for example, other measures may be more predictive. While there may be some commonality in the core measures required to identify individuals at risk, it is rarely possible to say that a particular risk factor will lead to a particular outcome. Important childhood risk factors may indicate that some degree of multiple adult deprivation is likely and that the individual may struggle with a number of features of adult life. However, it is often hard to gauge precisely which features of adult deprivation are most likely to be experienced.

It seems likely, therefore, that the most useful framework for developmental measurement and assessment would start from birth with indicators of childhood health and development, together with measurement of family income, education, parenting skill and social ties to the neighbourhood or in terms of wider social and familial networks. As children mature, teacher ratings will become relevant and should be built in. In cases where these forms of measurement indicate high levels of risk, then developmental knowledge of the children's own physical and mental health, behaviour, attitudes and aspirations might be added, together with more detailed information about the family and social context, in order to inform intervention and support.

Two issues that need much greater reflection and analysis are the questions of stigma and moral hazard. Both present problems for this form of policy system.

Stigma

It is very important that early tracking and early intervention do not work so as to reify the problems they are designed to remedy. This would happen if the response to early signals of risk was to create artificial, rigid and exclusive categories. Early prevention will not work if individuals and families simply become categorised as problems. This will exacerbate many of the issues of social exclusion and disengagement that are in part responsible for the outcomes observed.

However, neither can early intervention be fully effective at remedying the deepest problems of social exclusion if it is only ever voluntary. This has been a long-standing problem for those working in social services who have to make difficult judgements, for example, about when to take a child into care. What we are proposing here is that information be gathered and interpreted more effectively and earlier in the lives of children to make such dramatic and permanent choices less necessary rather than more so.

Moral hazard

It must also be a concern that where intervention is of a more positive kind, involving the extra expenditure of resources, then those at risk and others may experience or perceive a benefit from adding to risk rather than reducing it, in order to benefit from the additional resource. Related to this problem is the difficulty of ensuring that resources do indeed go to those most at risk. The inverse care law operates in all areas of social policy, as those with most resources of time, knowledge, social inclusion, income and ambition use those resources to ensure their access to public services at the cost of those with fewer of such resources.

Again, these challenges can only be met by a system in which informed and skilled professionals are able to make the important judgements. Moreover, many of the elements of risk that we are proposing be observed would not make rational choices for anyone seeking extra resources, and so the moral hazard problem may not be as great as sometimes supposed.

We already have in place a related system that may provide good evidence about what works in such terrain and about the risks and challenges of this type of identification and response. Existing systems of assessment and provision for special educational needs (SEN) are intended to determine the allocation of extra funding and intervention to support the learning of a relatively large proportion of the school population who have particular extra need. In this sense, the system rather mirrors the type of mechanism being proposed here in that there are many forms of SEN and many potential interventions to address these needs.

SEN is a particular risk indicator and the system for assessment and provision encounters its own challenges and difficulties. A broadening of the range of interventions that is triggered by a new set of risk indicators as proposed here would enable the formation of a system that first identifies; second, tracks and monitors; and third, supports and protects children and families identified as having levels of developmental risk that are likely to lead to subsequent problems and the further intergenerational and social transmission of the difficulties.

Summary

This chapter is about the identification of children at risk of high cost or high harm adult outcomes. It summarises findings from the UK birth cohort data about the extent to which information about children and their family environments is predictive of later outcomes. We find a potentially very high level of predictability in the extent to which we can identify those at risk using early childhood information about family context and child development. In our view, these findings are a challenge to which current central and local government should respond with appropriate and measured policy in the interests of social inclusion, personal welfare and the wider economic and social development of the UK.

However, the relationship between childhood risk and high cost or high harm outcomes in adolescence or adulthood is not always deterministic, mechanistic or inevitable. There are many steps on the pathway from risk to outcome. There are children at risk who do not experience harmful outcomes and there are children with low apparent or observable risk who do.

Therefore, policy responses must allow for flexibility and change. Administrative data should always be augmented by local-level, practitioner knowledge and the appropriate interventions should also be selected by local-level practitioners, who should work closely alongside local communities and agencies to avoid rigid tracking or excessive and unnecessary stigmatisation of vulnerable young people and their families.

9 Implications of the ecological model of home–school interaction for policy development

In this book, we have described a great number of interrelationships between factors that influence education and social outcomes for children. In particular, we described some of the most recent quantitative evidence suggesting that the education of the parents can have substantial effects on children's educational attainment. We proposed a theoretical framework based on the ecological model of developmental psychology to understand how children live in multiple and multi-layered contexts and how the education of their parents can impact upon parent–child interactions (proximal processes) and provision of wide-ranging resources (internal characteristics of the family environment), as well as other more distal factors such as family formation, income and employment. It is in this way that factors or circumstances associated with deprivation and disadvantage affect the way in which a child develops, and therefore reproduce inequalities across the generations.

Based on this ecological model, we carried out a review of empirical studies to assess the importance of each of the factors described by the model as key to improving children's educational outcomes and the role of education in the formation of these factors. In other words, we reviewed evidence on proximal family processes such as parenting styles, on internal characteristics of the family context such as parents' physical health, on distal family factors such as income and employment, and on other contexts such as neighbourhoods, schools and peers.

We also utilised the ecological model as a base for a quantitative study of the identification of children at risk of adult deprivation. In particular, we used a statistical model to determine the accuracy of early identification of children at risk from factors related to proximal and distal family variables, school and neighbourhood, as well as developmental characteristics of children themselves. In this concluding chapter we consider implications of the findings of our analysis and review for policy.

As we have shown in the preceding chapters, the intergenerational transmission of educational success plays a fundamental role in the persistence of social inequalities. Differences between children in terms of their parents' educational attainments and cognitive skills are an important reason for differences between children in terms of their own attainments and cognitive development. There are also substantial benefits of education that accrue to individuals (and society) in terms of what education enables parents to pass on to their children. The contribution of this book has been to assess the argument that these benefits are substantial, finding the argument to be strongly supported in theory and evidence.

We would also like to put the model presented here forward as a prism through which policy-makers might understand the multiple implications of government interventions. Understanding the way in which the features of the model interact can help in ensuring that policies run in synchronisation with developmental processes, rather than operating in opposition to these wider forces. We would invite those putting forward policies to consider how their proposed programme will interact with the features of the model described here. This book does not lead to firm conclusions about the benefits of specific interventions, but describes the contexts within which interventions must work.

There has been much discussion recently of the potential benefits of parenting programmes. These follow from the widespread finding that families are more important than schools as influences of children's development (Desforges, 2003). Analysis of this broader context suggests the limit on the ability of education systems to influence attainment and leads to the conclusion that engagement with parents will be very important. Yet parents themselves live in multiple contexts that constrain or enhance their interactions with their children. Therefore in going beyond the school to the home in the search for enhancement to educational attainment a range of actions must be involved. These include government ministries responsible for work, pensions, housing, crime, citizenship, health and social cohesion. Communities, the voluntary sector and most of all parents and young people themselves are also vital parties, whose own beliefs and perspectives must be integrated into policy development.

Summary: the key channels for education effects

Proximal family processes

Proximal family processes are very important as channels for the effects of parents' education on their children's outcomes. This is the direct mediated effect but there may also be important moderating effects. The benefits of proximal processes do not follow in a straightforward way directly from the appropriate behaviour of parents as recommended in the parenting literature without being accompanied by the understanding of parents about why they are doing what they are doing and how their child is responding. In enhancing these capabilities, education may also enhance the effectiveness of developmentally positive parenting behaviours.

Of course, much depends on the form of education. One cannot assume that post-sixteen study in and of itself necessarily guarantees that a person will be a better parent. The realisation of this benefit will depend both on the curricula and on the ethos of the learning experience. A year of studying mathematics, for example, may increase all kinds of cognitive functioning processes and bring substantial subsequent benefits in terms of income and employment but do little to enhance the understanding of parent–child relationships. Likewise, a short, unaccredited course in music that helps develop well-being, self-efficacy, creativity, communication and expressiveness may give considerable benefits in terms of parenting skill, even if leading to no labour-market advantage.

Therefore, we conclude that the available evidence suggests that education may enhance parenting. However, we would also emphasise that there is little evidence about which forms of education are most likely to achieve this effect. In fact, there is still a great deal of research work to be done to answer the crucial questions: for whom does education make a difference and when is education most effective?

Internal characteristics of the family environment

Both cognitions and parental mental health and well-being are important influences on children's attainments and both are likely to be influenced by parental education. In particular, cognitions such as aspirations and beliefs about self-efficacy are important mediators of the intergenerational education effect. In the context of poor parental mental health and well-being, education may have particularly important moderating effects in diminishing impacts of pre-school.

Distal family factors

Income and family size are important mediators of the effects of parental education. In some sense teenage motherhood also mediates education effects if one defines education in terms of early school attainment and engagement. Although family structure and maternal employment are not strong mediators of education effects, education does importantly moderate their effects. For example, education may provide protective capability for families dealing with income loss following parental break-up (see Blackwell and Bynner, 2002). It may also support parents in assessing maternal employment rights, good work–life balance or accessing good-quality pre-school education in order to moderate any effects of employment on child development. More research on these moderating benefits of education would be particularly valuable.

The importance of other developmental contexts

In addition to the family, the contexts of pre-schools, schools and neighbourhood are important for children's development and as channels for the intergenerational transmission of education. Education also has important protective capabilities in offsetting the negative effects of neighbourhoods, school and pre-school settings with poor characteristics.

Future research

From the evidence presented in this book, proximal family processes of warmth, discipline and educational behaviour in the home are important factors influencing child development. They are strongly influenced by family characteristics, which also play a substantial role in the transmission of educational advantage. Parents' cognitions, well-being and resources all have direct effects on proximal processes and so are major influences on children's attainments. These characteristics of the family are in turn influenced by distal factors, particularly parental education and income.

Education is also strongly related to each of these factors, all of which interact in important ways. Education can at its best not only enhance the developmentally supportive levels of each important, separate factor; it can also ease the relations between factors and provide resilience for families when other important elements are absent or where compound risk factors are excessive.

This perspective is supported by both the theory and evidence put forward here. However, the majority of this evidence has been mainly in terms of particular links in the chains of association rather than in the whole framework. In other words, there is evidence that education impacts on income, but not on *how* education can impact upon income, which can impact upon the availability of resources, and how education can enable parents to use these resources so that the development of their children reaches its full potential. Much of the evidence based on complex frameworks is fairly ambiguous and so could be interpreted in a number of ways. The interactions between the elements of the framework are complex and multi-layered, so sophisticated modelling techniques are required to test the theory empirically. Yet these techniques are better suited to establishing pathways of association than to proving the causal impact of factors.

There is a clear need, therefore, for research that uses large-sample longitudinal data and simple hypotheses to separate out particular aspects of the overall model and to use lifecourse information to identify elements of the overall causal picture with clarity. For example, it would be valuable to establish how changes in parents' aspirations for children respond to changes in children's actual attainments. This would help in clarifying how much of the association between child attainment and parent aspiration is due to aspirations being matched by parents to their children's apparent possibilities and how much to the effect of aspirations on attainment. Many other such relationships remain unexplored and with current longitudinal data available it is possible to investigate them.

Another way forward will be to make use of random allocation in interventions to establish causality with greater confidence. Through the generation of random variation in potentially causal factors it is possible to test the actual level of causal effect.

Also of value will be qualitative research that is integrated with the issues described in this book so as to shed light on the processes described. For example, it would be useful to explore issues raised in fieldwork research combined with data that are already available, such as the UK birth cohort studies. One can focus on cases that match or contradict the expected relationships, for example, using parenting, parental education and child's attainment or home resources, parental education, and child's well-being. Using biographical research techniques it is possible to explore the extent to which the cases selected from large-scale longitudinal surveys support or contradict the theoretical predictions made in this report about the relative importance of the different mediators of education. It is also possible to indicate which factors moderate the effects of education and/or to provide alternative perspectives on the role of education.

Themes for policy

Personalisation

There is momentum behind the notion of personalisation in education as in the rest of government provision (DfES, 2007). This is true of UK policy but also of the policies of the devolved administrations in Wales and Scotland and more broadly (OECD, 2006). It has been emphasised as a key element of policy for achieving the wider benefits of education, necessary for the achievement of an increase in social mobility. It harnesses a number of elements, explored below.

The idea of person–environment fit and the implications of this for the delivery of education and other government services

The ecological model that we have presented describes the complex set of aspects of the lives of individuals that may impact on their opportunities and/or life outcomes. Determining the most effective locus of intervention to enhance life chances is a difficult decision, often requiring detailed knowledge of the individual and her family, community and other contexts. Moreover, there is no single programme that will benefit all, at all points in life, in all contexts. Needs are heterogeneous and to meet these needs government provision must be aware of personal differences in needs and be able to respond to them.

The importance of inter-person interactions in the development of children and adults

Education theory emphasises the crucial role of pupil–teacher relations in the learning process, as well as of child–parent, parent–teacher and so on. These relationships must respond to the communication and needs of the individual child or adult if they are to support her learning. Learning theory emphasises the importance of scaffolding, and of recognising development and progress in learning. The essential principle is that children have different degrees of development and provision should be tailored accordingly. The realisation of this in the practice of teaching requires that, within reason, the teacher have good knowledge of the cognitive and affective development of each child or adult learner. One size does not fit all in the sense that one level or one speed of learning will not help all learners to progress and may have negative impacts on the learning of others.

Choice on the demand side of public services

Choice has come to be seen by some as one of the forces that drives up quality in provision since it creates a context in which clear signals can be sent to suppliers and in which they are responsive to those signals (LeGrand, 2006). It is argued that consumers in the private sector generally expect services to be tailored to their needs.

The application of this aspect of personalisation to the provision of public sector services is controversial because it assumes that the needs for consumption of services within the public sector are similar to those of consumption in the private sector. Yet, in the case of public service provision, the Government is providing goods and services in cases of market failure or credit and income constraints and at times of severe personal and community need. Therefore, it is questionable whether demand for the output of government expenditure can be adequately characterised as consumption and it is problematic, too, to label the originators of that demand as consumers.

Nonetheless, for these reasons and others, personalisation has become a major strand in current policy thinking. However, while recognising the potential value of personalisation, we must also recognise where it brings tensions in policy thinking and address some fundamental issues of policy provision. Not much is known yet about the mechanisms of personalisation or about its effectiveness relative to more universal forms of provision. There are questions about how much should be invested in encouraging one-to-one time with teachers, or small group time, and how this trade-off changes through the lifecycle. There is also a very important structural question of how to match pupils to schools in a way that recognises the particular needs, aspirations and capabilities of each child. It is also important to provide for children a context that, as much as is reasonable, is appropriate and developmentally positive for each child if the only mechanism is postal location.

The integration of services

The Government in Whitehall or Westminster cannot efficiently direct the flow of resources to support the education and development of individuals but is dependent on local-level agencies such as schools, communities, local authorities and other agencies to direct resource flows subject to negotiation and local directives. These agencies, in turn, are dependent on practitioners working in day-to-day interactions with learners and other recipients of public services to ensure that directives and objectives agreed at higher levels are met, that the appropriate services are provided at the point of need and at the time of need, and that interventions and interactions are of sufficient quality to enhance the development and learning of service recipients.

The model offered in this book is ecological in the sense that it recognises the importance of interactions between the contexts in which learners live and work, highlighting the role of the family as a context supporting or constraining learning, but also emphasising other contexts such as neighbourhoods, communities and workplaces as sources of influence and structure that impact on the formation of life chances and so constrain and/or enhance educational investments. These principles highlight the need for integrated services that recognise the many important interactions between contexts that impact on people's lives and that modulate the success or failure in the formation of life chances and the development of the benefits that flow from education and learning. There are five particular kinds of integration required.

Local integration

Local integration has been a key theme of much recent policy in England and the other UK nations. Particularly important elements of recent policy reform and investment in England include the following:

CHILDREN'S TRUSTS

Sure Start and Children's Centres have been major policy innovations for the early years designed to improve educational, developmental, health and other outcomes for children in the most deprived areas. Early evaluation suggests that the Sure Start programme has not been successful in some areas but the resources for childcare, post-natal support, parenting advice and links between agencies working with infants and pre-school children have proved very popular with parents and children's agencies (Wiggins *et al.*, 2005). The extension of Sure Start from 2004 onwards involved substantial reform, with management of the new Children's Centres returning to local authorities, which were required to develop universal, integrated 'children's plans' describing proposals for the integration of education and social work services as part of the ECM reform of services for children.

WORKFORCE PROFESSIONALISATION

Related to the changed funding and management of Children's Centres was the reform of the regulations, standards and training for those working with children, set out in the Children's Workforce Strategy (DfES, 2005a). This was intended to ease the integration of services, supporting professionals and agencies in joint working in the service of children's interests, in particular reducing to one the number of individuals and agencies involved in the management and monitoring of particular vulnerable children.

EXTENDED SCHOOLS

A third important arm of policy in this area is the extended schools programme, the offer (DfES, 2005b) that by 2010 all schools should be able to provide childcare and activities for children and young people from 8am to 6pm all year round; parenting support linked to other agencies and including family learning; swift and easy referral from schools to a wide range of specialised services for children; and widespread community use of schools facilities.

It was intended that these and related pressures to support the integration of local social, educational and health services will enable the development of local mechanisms. These mechanisms should provide early warning signs of developmental and behavioural difficulties that might eventually go beyond cases of severe abuse or neglect necessitating that the state intervene in often drastic and stressful circumstances. It is, however, important that local agencies act in integrated, effective and appropriate ways in such circumstances. The wider need of a broader group of children who may nonetheless experience elements of social exclusion, special educational needs or stressful and difficult family and personal circumstances is for interventions that can support resilience, engagement and development, through action with families, schools, communities and/or the children themselves. The selection of the appropriate intervention at the appropriate time requires developmental information to be centrally collated and analysed, and linked to those interventions by skilled professionals, alongside knowledge regarding their availability and effectiveness in different circumstances. These non-teaching, frontline professionals will need to have personal knowledge of the children, their families and communities, built up over a long period. It may also be appropriate that they hold budgets available for intervention as required. Their success, however, will depend on the level of integration of information flow, assessment and intervention at local level.

Vertical integration, accountability and communication

One of the most difficult features of policy development is determining the appropriate level of devolution of decision-making powers. In part, this relates to personalisation, as it is hard for central agencies to assess local need and policy appropriateness. The complexity and heterogeneity of personal and community circumstances call for the participation in decision-making of informed and responsible local agencies. Moreover, the more autonomy is allowed to local agencies and communities, the greater the opportunity for local engagement in the political process and for civic activity. At the same time, however, the natural diversity between communities in access to appropriate and stable resources of knowledge, skill and resilience mean that some degree of central participation is required to ensure equality and appropriateness of provision across areas. Moreover, since national government is held accountable for policy success, it is natural and inevitable that it maintains some degree of control and authority.

There is, therefore, an inevitable tension between objectives of centralisation and decentralisation, between central government accountability and local autonomy. The 2005 Schools White Paper (HM Government, 2005) was heralded by the Government as a major, if not *the* major, educational reform of the Blair years. Perhaps the central element of the proposed reforms was the independence of schools and the increases in autonomy for schools matched with increased opportunities for choice by parents. It was intended that these changes would enhance diversity and creativity and personalisation in learning. However, this White Paper was met with widespread concerns about how the changes would impact on school selection, on the mix of pupils across schools, on the interactions between schools in local communities and on how the increased diversity, autonomy and local independence would impact on the social class attainment gap and hence on social justice. This was a prime example of the tension between centralisation and decentralisation and the selection of the appropriate domain for decision-making. Excessive decentralisation, to the level of specific institutions such as schools, runs the risk of weakening the role of the local authority as an agency of local integration and social justice. We will see in the coming years how this tension between devolution and accountability is rebalanced.

What are the implications of this for joined-up government in supporting the achievement of greater educational equality? A key principle in policy development is that of subsidiarity, supporting local devolution except where there is good reason for higher-level involvement. Also of relevance is the importance of local-level processes, the engagement of teachers and other practitioners and also of families and communities in policy development and objective setting. This requires energisation of local democracy and community participation. That may be a difficult goal but any policy innovations that enhance local autonomy and increase the communication of objectives and challenges upwards and downwards between central government and local agencies and practitioners will support its achievement.

Integration and persistence through the lifecourse

Another crucial type of integration is the development of policy mechanisms and interventions that are not limited to specific narrow stages of the lifecourse. This applies equally to transitions within childhood as to transitions from childhood to adulthood and throughout life. Much recent policy discourse around the world has concerned the relative importance of funding and support for learning in different stages of the lifecourse, and the marginal effectiveness of expenditure in the early years or at other stages of childhood, post-sixteen or for adult education (Cunha *et al.*, 2006; Wößmann and Schütz, 2006). Yet, reductions in educational inequality are unlikely in our view to follow from specific expenditures limited to any particular life stage. In terms of social exclusion and the impact of family circumstances on child attainment, support in the early years is vital but if not followed up then the benefits are lost. As children move into adolescence they encounter a range of challenges, risks, outcomes and public services and the success of those services depends to a great extent on their integration with earlier intervention.

For example, there is evidence that youth clubs are an important mediator of life chances (Feinstein *et al.*, 2006). Beneficial contexts are those that provide autonomy and respect with some degree of adult facilitation and structure. Young people at risk of social exclusion are most likely to engage in such contexts if the process of engagement is built up through childhood, rather than left until adolescence. Involvement in out-of-school activities is commonly built up over a long period of time, during which relationships with other children and adults are formed, common understanding is developed and objectives and norms are discussed and set. Persistence and continuity in provision may be a vital element in its success.

Structural discontinuities in provision create artificial boundaries to policy and practice that limit the effectiveness of major systemic interventions. A good example of this is in relation to SEN, which are often undiagnosed and untreated until children start school, even though there may be early signs available to health visitors, childcare workers and other practitioners of earlier risks of developmental delay that, if responded to, may lead to more efficient and effective forms of intervention. Another example of an artificial age-structured boundary is in relation to the support provided for looked-after children, which ceases at age sixteen, leaving many vulnerable young people in considerable need and difficulty during the crucial transition into adulthood. This structural weakness may be responsible for widespread social and personal distress, social exclusion and the transmission across generations of social difficulties.

Policy mechanisms are required that can support the integration and persistence of support across life stages, so that the appropriate intervention is available at the time of need rather than at an arbitrarily pre-defined life stage. On the whole, the more that such support is persistent, the more effective it will be. This is not necessarily a question of continued intervention; more fundamentally it is a question of persistence in the monitoring and evaluation of need. Risk and contextual difficulties may become insurmountable at any stage of life and the more that knowledge of life-course development is maintained by skilled, local practitioners working in the system of education and social policy, the more effective the intervention will be.

The integration of policy domains: policy for the whole person

Perhaps the most fundamental form of integration that is called for by the ecological model is the recognition that, although policy targets may exist in relation to specific domains such as crime, health, or economic and educational achievement, success in each of these domains depends on the development of people, who are not structured in any way according to these behavioural outcomes. There are many sources of individual behaviour that are important for these outcomes. For example, emotional distress, cognitive impairment, poverty and social isolation may all in combination or in different ways lead to increases in the risk of socially costly outcomes such as poor mental health, criminality, social disengagement and/or unemployment; but there is no one-to-one relationship between each individual risk factor and each particular outcome. Thus, educational experiences at any stage of life may benefit the personal development of those who experience them but it is not possible to forecast with any accuracy which specific policy domain will receive the benefit.

Recognising and valuing this fundamental unity of the individual, within a social context, does not negate the great importance of wider social structures; but it does foreground the significance of the wider processes of human development that underpin success in relation to the very wide-ranging and diverse objectives of education and social policy. Affective and behavioural development is related to cognitive development, and educational practices will be most successful when they recognise the important continuities and complementarities between these different domains. Disengaged children and adults are harder to teach than those who are engaged. Misbehaviour and disorder in the classroom will create barriers to school success but may also stem from earlier difficulties in learning. We do not yet understand enough about the complementarities and substitution effects between these different features of development. The policy point emphasised here is that a narrow focus on outcomes in one specific domain of individual development, such as school achievement, may negate its own success if it fails to recognise the importance to those experiencing learning of wider features of development, for example behavioural and emotional.

A second point to highlight is that these wider features of development feed back into the lives of the next generation and into the effectiveness of policy now as these wider skills of empathy, warmth and social and communication skills are important both to parenting and in the enhancement of quality practice. An education system becomes too narrowly focused on cognitive skills if it is investing insufficient time and expenditure in support for these wider skills. As we have highlighted throughout this book, the key question is of the balance between supporting narrow cognitive achievement and success in qualifications on the one hand, and wider features of socialisation, psycho-social development and social interactivity and creativity on the other. Ultimately, the more that educational practice can see these as linked, each supporting the other as connected features of human development, the more effective it will be in supporting each domain. Choices have to be made about curriculum priorities, but the point being made here is more about the importance of the ethos and practice of teaching than its content. Although these are intimately linked we believe that teacher training and real opportunities for continued professional development can enhance practice and in so doing provide the most effective mechanism for policy impacts.

Nationally joined-up government

The final domain of integration is in relation to national government. Although there are great potential efficiency gains from integrating assessment and intervention strategies at the local level, there are potentially even greater efficiency gains to be realised through integration at the national level. This is exemplified in Figure 9.1, which describes some of the key inputs and outputs of the national-level education and health systems.

Standard outputs of the education system include qualifications and the development of skills. However, the education system is also a context in which other far-reaching features of development occur, with varying degrees of implicit and explicit agency. Key among these is the development of self-esteem, self-efficacy and other features of psycho-social identity. These are very important in the formation of health behaviours such as smoking, alcohol and drug misuse, sexual health, exercise and diet. Thus, outputs from the education system are often inputs to the health system. The mechanisms in policy delivery for the realisation of these

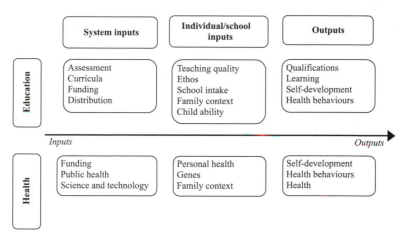

Figure 9.1 Inputs and outputs of the education and health systems

complementarities and common interests across departments are greatly underdeveloped. There are great potential cost savings and efficiency gains to be realised through the integration of services across these structural boundaries of government. Other examples could be given in relation to communities, housing, schools, transport, education and offending, among many others, where departmental boundaries create artificial rigidities that prevent the realisation of joint efficiency savings.

The importance of improving and maintaining quality of services

Yet we know from intervention evidence that only high-quality services and interventions can secure lasting improvements in the broad-ranging skills that matter for social mobility (Danziger and Waldfogel, 2000; Duncan *et al.*, 2007). Features of personal and social development such as self-regulation, engagement in learning and social and communications skills have social value (Jencks *et al.*, 1979; Bowles *et al.*, 2001; Carneiro and Heckman, 2003) that is insufficiently recognised in the education system. It is unrealistic, however, to build development of these attributes and skills into crowded curricula or to expect teachers and trainers to provide for these needs alongside those of league tables, exam results and other forms of assessment. Moreover, teachers may not have the skills required and, as should be apparent from the earlier section on the integration of services, teachers alone cannot provide the wide-ranging and highly personalised interventions required to redress problems of social immobility.

Development emerges from the interactions between individuals in families, schools, communities and workplaces. Good parenting reduces the risks of school failure of children and therefore has social benefits. Yet the skills and features of personal development and personality that underpin these interactions are not central to the school curriculum, much less to that common in vocational learning post-sixteen. This highlights the challenge of how the education system, broadly defined, is to support the development of the skills, capabilities, motivations and values that are the basis of these wide-ranging social interactions, which are important to so many domains of policy.

One difficult question that runs throughout is the challenge of how to improve the quality of learning experiences. In part this is a challenge for the training, professionalisation and continued professional development of practitioners. This question has been addressed through a focus on the structures imposed by central government in terms of targets and legislative frameworks. An agenda of choice and marketisation has also been put forward as a mechanism for improving the quality of provision. All of these mechanisms may have to play a role but it is incumbent on all proponents and opponents of each mechanism to explain how it will improve the quality of provision. This notion of quality is the central issue: that learning should be appropriate to the contextual and personal development of the learner. Learning should be personalised, assessed formatively, and entwined in local practices of social and community engagement. Learning should be linked to local government support to ensure that, as much as is practicable, the developmental needs of individuals of all ages are met. Learning should be recognised as having relevant wider social outcomes. Finally, the role of government is to ensure that interventions are preventive rather than reactive and punitive.

Making communities count: engaging local people in supporting their own children and young people

However, the ecological model stresses that, alongside the recognition of individual differences and the importance of personalisation in approach, development occurs in a social context, and neither should policy ignore this feature of the model. Community accountability for local services can make a vital contribution to the effective and sustainable delivery of im-proved outcomes for children and young people. The engagement of com-munities in the planning and delivery of services can be a valuable resource currently missing from the levers being employed to achieve better outcomes (Skidmore *et al.*, 2006). Government policies and initiatives tend to target the child, the family and the community in isolation from each other. Children who need public service interventions often have problems that relate to all three of these spheres, and mechanisms are therefore needed to ensure there is action at all three levels.

Concluding discussion and three key themes

We started this book with the recognition that the outcomes for one genera-tion create the opportunity structures for the next. In this sense, equality of opportunity and equality of outcome are inseparable and if we are con-cerned at all for one we must be equally concerned for the other.

Educational success is not just a matter of qualifications achieved but also of skills formed, personal development, impacts on identity and sense of self, and social networks gained or lost. These are outcomes of childhood and adolescence that will have long-lasting ramifications for the lives of those experiencing it. If and when they become parents, these outcomes and their consequences will have repercussions for their children. So *education is necessarily a substantial part of the process of the intergenerational transmission of opportunity and outcome.*

There are other substantial elements such as income, occupation, family dynamics, cognitions, housing, social networks, class, race, gender, ethnicity, place and era. It will often be the interactions between these elements of persons and contexts that will create the structural conditions within which real lives are lived. Therefore, *the search for a single magic element such as family structure, basic skills or housing is flawed.* We should be trying to understand how these different elements interact, which depends on a much more local-level analysis.

Neither should we forget the higher-level macro-social and macro-economic structures such as technology, climate change, cultural evolution and patterns of trade and employment that both limit and enable change at the level of the family in any specific time and place. In turn, the meaning and significance of educational experience and success will necessarily shift with these wider dynamic drivers. Particularly relevant for this book is the macro-social factor of education policy. We suggest that *the current policy debate has become overly fearful of innovation, creativity and individual and local freedom.* It is a sad reality that education in England remains regressive, rather than progressive, in the sense that on the whole we allow the best practice and the highest resourcing for those with the highest level of private advantages. This is an inefficient allocation of resources and means that government has a role to play in enhancing the quality of education for those dependent on its provision. However, central government concern for ensuring greater equity in terms of the quality of provision must go together with allowance of local diversity and local accountability if education is to ensure wide-ranging improvements in equity and quality.

Therefore, rather than asking senior civil servants or MPs to determine the appropriate range of options for those in education, we would prefer to see a greater range of providers offering a broader range of opportunities in a progressive system that genuinely enabled and empowered the agency of children, young people and adults. It is unfortunate and limiting that debates about choice focus so heavily on choice of school, which for most children then becomes a fixed reality for years on end, restricting diversity of experience and the possibility of social and learning interactions with people from other backgrounds, communities and of other ages. We would prefer to see more local-level flexibility in curriculum, educational pathways and time use, operating within broad learning communities that recognise the synergy within areas between work-based and community learning, HE, FE, schools and pre-schools. We would like to see more peer-to-peer learning, inter-school activity, local community engagement, adult learning and continued and meaningful professional development. These should be exciting, varied and dynamic so that more children, young people and families would choose to opt in because they see the value rather than because they can't afford an alternative.

This book offers a reflection on the state of theory and evidence on the role of education in intergenerational inequality. We have focused particularly on England, particularly on research from the last twenty years and particularly on research from development psychology and economics. These are all substantial limitations.

Despite this, we hope that readers will recognise glimpses of truth or accuracy in our attempted summary and build on, or challenge, our three key findings.

Notes

2 Understanding the importance of parents' education

1 Phineas P. Gage (1823–60) worked as a railroad construction foreman and suffered a traumatic brain injury when a tampering iron accidentally passed through his skull, damaging the frontal lobes of his brain. Reports suggest that, while leaving him perfectly functional, the resulting injury negatively affected his emotional, social and personality traits. Gage's condition led to changes in the scientific perception of the function and compartmentalisation of the brain with regard to emotion and personality.

4 The importance of what goes on in the family

1 Settings (N=141) were drawn from a range of providers: local authority day nursery, integrated centres, playgroups, private day nurseries, maintained nursery school and maintained nursery classes.

2 Similar to Head Start in the US, Sure Start aims to achieve better outcomes for children, parents and communities by bringing together early education, childcare, health and family support in a 'one-stop shop'. Originally targeted in the most deprived areas of England, its basic premise is to enhance children's intellectual, social and physical abilities, on the grounds that each domain contributes to a child's overall developmental competence and their readiness for school, thus to provide them with the best start in life.

5 Internal features of the family environment

1 Parents were asked to report which of the five qualities they thought was the most important quality for their child (under age thirteen) to learn: obedience, popularity, independence, hard work or helpfulness.

6 Distal family factors

1 The rate of return to education is defined as the extra income earned as a result of attaining one additional year or level of education and discounted to the time of entrance into the labour market.

7 The importance of other developmental contexts

1 Neighbourhoods may also impact on our distal factors, though we do not pursue this here.
2 In comparison with sample children who attended a pre-school centre, home children differ considerably in some of their socio-demographic characteristics. For example, home children are more likely to be from minority ethnic groups and larger families and have mothers with no formal qualifications.

8 A framework for supporting resilience in childhood

1 It is important to accurately specify the definition of true and false positives in any study as these terms are sometimes defined as here, conditional on the true state, but they can also be defined in terms of the probability of the true state conditional on the prediction. This alternative formulation of $P(TP)$ is as the proportion of predictions that are accurate. Which formulation is to be preferred depends on the use to which the information is to be put.

References

Acemoglu, D. and Pischke, J. S. (2001). Changes in the wage structure, family income and children's education. *European Economic Review*, 45, 890–904.

Ainsworth, M. D. S., Blehar, M. C., Waters, E. and Wall, S. (1978). *Patterns of Attachment: A Psychological Study of the Strange Situation*. Hillsdale, NJ: Erlbaum.

Alexander, K. L. and Entwisle, D. R. (1988). Achievement in the first two years of school: patterns and processes. *Monographs of the Society for Research in Child Development*, 53 (2), no. 218.

Alexander, K. L., Entwisle, D. R. and Bedinger, S. D. (1994). When expectations work: race and socioeconomic differences in school performance. *Social Psychology Quarterly*, 57 (4), 283–99.

Ammermueller, A. and Pischke, J. S. (2006). *Peer Effects in European Primary Schools: Evidence from PIRLS*, IZA, Discussion Paper, 2007.

Anderson, J. W., Johnstone, B. M. and Remley, D. T. (1999). Breast-feeding and cognitive development: a meta-analysis. *American Journal of Clinical Nutrition*, 70, 525–35.

Angrist, J. and Lang, K. (2004). Does school integration generate peer effects? Evidence from Boston's Metco Program. *American Economic Review*, 94 (5), 1613–34.

Antonovics, K. and Goldberger, A. (2003). *Do Education Mothers Make Bad Mothers? Twin Studies and the Intergenerational Transmission of Human Capital*. University of California at San Diego, Economics. Discussion Papers.

Arias, O., Hallock, K. and Sosa-Escudero, W. (2003). Individual heterogeneity in the returns to schooling: instrumental variables quantile regression using twins data. *Empirical Economics*, 26, 7–40.

Ashenfelter, O. and Krueger, A. (1994). Estimates of the economic return to schooling from a new sample of twins. *American Economic Review*, 84, 1157–74.

Asher, S. R. and Coie, J. D. (1990). *Peer Rejection in Childhood*. New York: Cambridge University Press.

Aughinbaugh, A., Pierret, C. R. and Rothstein, D. S. (2005). The impact of family structure transitions on youth achievement: evidence from the children of the NLSY79. *Demography*, 42 (3), 447–68.

Baker, L., Sonnenschein, S., Serpell, R., Fernandez-Fein, S. and Scher, D. (1994). *Contexts of Emergent Literacy: Everyday Home Experiences of Urban Pre-*

kindergarten Children. (Research Report No. 24). Athens, GA: National Reading Research Center, University of Georgia.

Ball, S. (1981). *Beachside Comprehensive.* Cambridge: Cambridge University Press.

Bandura, A. (1994). *Self-efficacy: The Exercise of Control.* New York: Freeman.

Bandura, A. and Walters, R. H. (1963). *Social Learning and Personality Development.* New York: Holt, Rinehart and Winston.

Barocas, R., Seifer, R., Sameroff, A. J., Andrews, T. A., Croft, R. T. and Ostrow, E. (1991). Social and interpersonal determinants of developmental risk. *Developmental Psychology,* 27, 479–88.

Baumrind, D. (1967). Child care practices anteceding three patterns of preschool behavior. *Genetic Psychology Monographs,* 75, 43–88.

Baumrind, D. (1971). Current patterns of parental authority. *Developmental Psychology Monographs,* 94, 132–42.

Baydar, N., Hyle, P. and Brooks-Gunn, J. (1997). A longitudinal study of the effects of the birth of a sibling during preschool and early grade school years. *Journal of Marriage and the Family,* 59, 957–67.

Becker, G. S. (1973). A theory of marriage: part I. *Journal of Political Economy,* 81, 813–46.

Becker, G. S. (1975). *Human Capital.* Washington, DC: National Bureau of Economic Research.

Becker, G. S. (1981). *A Treatise on the Family.* Cambridge, MA: Harvard University Press.

Becker, G. S. and Tomes, N. (1976). Child endowments and the quantity and quality of children. *Journal of Political Economy,* 84, S143–62.

Bee, H. L., Van Egeren, L. F., Streissguth, A. P., Nyman, B. A. and Leckie, M. S. (1969). Social class differences in maternal teaching strategies and speech patterns. *Developmental Psychology,* 1, 726–34.

Behrman, J. R. and Rosenzweig, M. R. (2002). Does increasing women's schooling raise the schooling of the next generation? *American Economic Review,* 92 (1), 323–34.

Behrman, J. R. and Taubman, P. (1986). Birth order, schooling and earnings. *Journal of Labor Economics,* 4, S121–45.

Bell, R. (1968). A reinterpretation of the direction of effects in studies of socialization. *Psychological Review,* 75, 81–95.

Bendell, D., Field, T., Yando, R., Lang, C., Martinez, A. and Pickens, J. (1994). 'Depressed' mothers' perceptions of their preschool children's vulnerability. *Child Psychiatry and Human Development,* 24, 3.

Berger, L. M., Hill, J. and Waldfogel, J. (2005). Maternity leave, early maternal employment and child health and development in the U.S. *The Economic Journal,* 115 (501), F29–47.

Berndt, T. J., Laychak, A. E. and Park, K. (1990). Friends' influence on adolescents' academic achievement motivation: an experimental study. *Journal of Educational Psychology,* 82 (4), 664–70.

Bernstein, B. (1977). Class and pedagogies: visible and invisible. In J. Karabel and A. H. Halsey (eds), *Power and Ideology in Education,* Oxford: Oxford University Press.

Bernstein, B. (1990). *The Structuring of Pedagogic Discourse: Class, Codes and Control.* Vol. 4. London: Routledge.

Bernstein, B. (1996). *Pedagogy, Symbolic Control and Identity: Theory, Research and Critique.* London: The Falmer Press.

Berthoud, R. (2000). *Family Formation in Multi-cultural Britain: Three Patterns of Diversity.* No. ISER Working Paper 34. University of Essex.

Bianchi, S. M. (2000). Maternal employment and time with children: dramatic change or surprising continuity? *Demography,* 37 (4), 401–14.

Billings, J., Dixon, J., Mijanovich, T. and Wennberg, D. (2006). Case finding for patients at risk of readmission to hospital: development of algorithm to identify high risk patients. *British Medical Journal,* 333, 327.

Bingley, P., Christensen, K. and Walker, I. (2005). *Twin-based Estimates of the Returns to Education: Evidence from the Population of Danish Twins.* Unpublished manuscript.

Björklund, A. and Sundström, M. (2002). *Parental Separation and Children's Educational Attainment: A Siblings Analysis on Swedish register Data.* Bonn, Germany: IZA Discussion Paper No. 643, Institute for the Study of Labor.

Black, S. E., Devereux, P. J. and Salvanes, K. (2004). *Fast Times at Ridgemont High? The Effects of Compulsory Schooling Laws on Teenage Births.* Working Paper 10911, National Bureau of Economic Research.

Blackwell, L. and Bynner, J. (2002). *Learning, Family Formation and Dissolution.* Research Report 4. Institute of Education: the Centre for Research on the Wider Benefits of Learning.

Blake, J. (1981). *Family Size and Achievement.* Berkeley, CA: University of California Press.

Blakely, T., Atkinson, J., Kiro, C. and Blaiklock, A. D. S. A. (2003). Child mortality, socioeconomic position, and one-parent families: independent associations and variation by age and cause of death. *International Journal of Epidemiology,* 32 (3), 410–18.

Blanden, J. and Gregg, P. (2004). *Family Income and Educational Attainment: A Review of Approaches and Evidence from the UK.* Working Paper 04/101. Centre for Research and Market Organisation.

Blanden, J., Goodman, A., Gregg, P. and Machin, S. (2002). *Changes in Inter-generational Mobility in Britain.* Centre for the Economics of Education Discussion Paper No. 026, 2002.

Blanden, J., Gregg, P. and Machin, S. (2005). Social mobility in Britain: low and falling. *CentrePiece,* 10 (1). London School of Economics.

Blau, F. D. and Kahn, L. M. (2006). *Changes in the Labour Supply Behaviour of Married Women: 1998–2000.* IZA Discussion Paper No. 2180, 1–64.

Bloom, B. (1964). *Stability and Change in Human Characteristics.* New York: John Wiley.

Blossfeld, H. P. and Huinink, J. (1991). Human capital investments or norms of role transitions? How women's schooling and career affect the process of family formation. *The American Journal of Sociology,* 97 (1), 143–68.

Blundell, R., Dearden, L., Meghir, C. and Sianesi, B. (1999). Human capital investment: the returns from education and training to the individual, the firm and the economy. *Fiscal Studies,* 20 (1), 1–3.

Blundell, R., Dearden, L., Goodman, A. and Reed, H. (2000). The returns to higher education in Britain: evidence from a British cohort. *Economic Journal*, 110, F82–99.

Blundell, R., Dearden, L., Meghir, C. and Sianesi, B. (2005). Evaluating the effect of education on earnings: models, methods and results from the National Child Development Survey. *Journal of Royal Statistical Society Series A*, 168 (3), 472–512.

Boggess, S. (1998). Family structure, economic status and educational attainment. *Journal of Population Economics*, 11, 205–22.

Bonell, C., Allen, E., Strange, V., Copas, A., Oakley, A., Stephenson, J. and Johnson, A. (2005). The effect of dislike of school on risk of teenage pregnancy: testing of hypothesis using longitudinal data from randomised trial of sex education. *Journal of Epidemiology and Community Health*, 59 (3), 223–30.

Bonjour, D., Cherkas, L., Haskel, J., Hawkes, D. and Spector, T. (2003). Returns to education: evidence from UK twins. *American Economic Review*, 93, 1799–812.

Bourdieu, P. (1973). Cultural reproduction and social reproduction. In R. Brown (ed.), *Knowledge, Education and Social Change*. London: Tavistock.

Bourdieu, P. (1984). *Distinction: A Social Critique of the Judgement of Taste*. Cambridge, MA: Harvard University Press.

Bowlby, J. (1969). *Attachment and Loss*, (vol. 1: *Attachment*). New York: Basic Books.

Bowlby, J. (1973). *Attachment and Loss*, (vol. 2: *Separation*). New York: Basic Books.

Bowles, S., Gintis, H. and Osborne, M. (2001). The determinants of individual earnings: a behavioral approach. *Journal of Economic Literature*, XXXIX, December, 1136–76.

Bradley, R. H. (1993). Children's home environments, health, behavior, and intervention efforts: a review using the HOME Inventory as a marker measure. *Genetic Psychology Monographs*, 119, 437–90.

Bradley, R. H. and Corwyn, R. F. (2003). Age and ethnic variations in family process mediators of SES. In M. H. Bornstein and R. H. Bradley (eds), *Socioeconomic Status, Parenting, and Child Development*. Mahwah, NJ: Lawrence Erlbaum Associates (pp. 161–88).

Bradley, R. H., Corwyn, R. F., Burchinal, M., Pipes McAdoo, H. and García Coll, C. (2001). The home environments of children in the United States part II: relations with behavioral development through age thirteen. *Child Development*, 72, 1868–86.

Brenner, V. and Fox, R. A. (1998). Parental discipline and behavior problems in young children. *The Journal of Genetic Psychology*, 159 (2), 251–6.

Bretherton, I. (1985). Attachment theory: retrospect and prospect. *Monographs of the Society for Research in Child Development*, 50 (1–2, serial no. 209).

Bronfenbrenner, U. (1979). *The Ecology of Human Development*. Cambridge, MA: Harvard University Press.

Bronfenbrenner, U. (1986). Ecology of the family as a context for human development: research perspectives. *Developmental Psychology*, 22, 723–42.

Bronfenbrenner, U. and Crouter, N. (1983). The evolution of environmental models in developmental research. In W. Kessen (ed.), *History, Theory, and Methods* (vol. 1, pp. 357–414). New York: Wiley.

Brooks-Gunn, J., Duncan, G. J., Klebanov, P. K. and Sealand, N. (1993). Do neighborhoods influence child and adolescent development? *American Journal of Sociology*, 99 (2), 353–95.

Brooks-Gunn, J., Klebanov, P. K. and Liaw, F. (1995). The learning, physical, and emotional environment of the home in the context of poverty: the Infant Health Development Program. *Children and Youth Services Review*, 17 (1/2), 251–76.

Brooks-Gunn, J., Klebanov, P. K. and Duncan, G. J. (1996). Ethnic differences in children's intelligence scores: roles of economic deprivation, home environment, and maternal characteristics. *Child Development*, 67, 396–408.

Brooks-Gunn, J., Duncan, G. J. and Maritato, N. (1997). Poor families, poor outcomes: the well-being of children and youth. In G. J. Duncan and J. Brooks-Gunn (eds), *Consequences of Growing Up Poor*. New York: Russell Sage Foundation (pp. 1–17).

Brown, B. B. (1990). Peer groups and peer culture. In S. S. Feldman and G. R. Elliott (eds), *At the Threshold: The Developing Adolescent*. Cambridge, MA: Harvard University Press (pp. 171–96).

Burns, E. (2001). Battling through the system: a working class teacher in an inner-city primary school. *International Journal of Inclusive Education*, 5 (1), 85–92.

Bus, A. G., van Ijzendoorn, M. H. and Pellegrini, A. D. (1995). Joint book reading makes for success in learning to read: a meta-analysis on intergenerational transmission of literacy. *Review of Educational Research*, 65 (1), 1–21.

Bynner, J. (2001). Childhood risks and protective factors in social exclusion. *Children and Society*, 15, 285–301.

Bynner, J. and Joshi, H. (2002). Equality and opportunity in education: evidence from the 1958 and 1970 birth cohort studies. *Oxford Review of Education*, 28 (4), 405–25.

Bynner, J. and Paxton, W. (2001). *The Asset Effect*. London: Institute for Public Policy Research.

Cairns, R. B. and Hood, K. E. (1983). Continuity and social development: a comparative perspective on individual difference prediction. In P. B. Baltes and O. G. Brim, Jr (eds), *Life-span Development and Behavior* (vol. 5). New York: Academic Press.

Caldwell, B. M. and Bradley, R. H. (1984). *Home Observation for Measurement of the Environment*. Little Rock, AR: University of Arkansas at Little Rock.

Campbell, K. E. and Lee, B. A. (1992). Sources of personal neighbor networks: social integration, need, or time? *Social Forces*, 70, 1077–100.

Card, D. (1999). The causal effects of education on earnings. In O. Ashenfelter and D. Card (eds), *Handbook of Labor Economics*. (vol. 3). Amsterdam: Elsevier (pp. 1801–63).

Carneiro, P. and Heckman, J. (2003). *Human Capital Policy*. National Bureau of Economic Research Working Paper 9495.

Case, A. C. and Katz, L. F. (1991). *The Company you Keep: The Effects of Family and Neighborhood on Disadvantaged Youths*. (Working Paper no. 3701). Cambridge, MA: National Bureau of Economic Research.

Chevalier, A. (2004). *Parental Education and Child's Education: A Natural Experiment*. IZA DP no. 1153. Bonn: The Institute for the Study of Labor (IZA).

Chevalier, A. and Feinstein, L. (2006). *Sheepskin or Prozac: The Causal Effect of Education on Mental Health* (Discussion Paper). London: Centre for Research on the Wider Benefits of Learning.

Chevalier, A., Harmon, C., O'Sullivan, V. and Walker, I. (2005). *The Impact of Parental Income and Education on the Schooling of their Children*. IFS Working Paper WP05/05: 1–30.

Child Trends (2002). *Charting Parenthood: A Statistical Portrait of Fathers and Mothers in America*. Washington, DC: Child Trends.

Choo, E. and Siow, A. (2006). Who marries whom and why. *Journal of Political Economy*, 114 (1), 175–201.

Christian, K., Morrison, F. J. and Bryant, F. B. (1998). Predicting kindergarten academic skills: interactions among child care, maternal education, and family literacy environments. *Early Childhood Research Quarterly*, 13, 501–21.

Clarke, A. D. B. and Clarke, A. M. (2000). Sleeper effects in development: fact or artefact. *Developmental Review*, 1, 344–60.

Clarke-Stewart, K. A. (1973). Interactions between mothers and their young children: characteristics and consequences. *Monographs of the Society for Research in Child Development*, 38 (6–7, Serial No. 153).

Cohn, T. F., Matias, R., Tronick, E. Z., Connell, D. and Lyons-Ruth, K. (1987). Face to face interactions of depressed mothers and their infants. In E. Z. Tronick and M. M. Field (eds), *New Directions for Child Development*. San Francisco, CA: Jossey-Bass.

Coie, J. D. and Dodge, K. A. (1998). Aggression and antisocial behaviour. In W. Damon (ed.), *Handbook of Child Psychology*, vol. 3: *Social, Emotional, and Personality Development* (5th edn). New York: Wiley (pp. 779–862).

Coleman, J. (1988). Social capital in the creation of human capital. *American Journal of Sociology*, 94, 95–120.

Coleman, J. S., Campbell, E. Q., Hobson, C. J., McPartland, J., Mood, A. M., Weinfeld, F. D. and York, R. L. (1966). *Equality of Educational Opportunity*. Washington: United States Office of Education.

Collins, W. A., Maccoby, E. E., Steinberg, L., Hetherington, E. M. and Bornstein, M. H. (2000). Contemporary research on parenting. *American Psychologist*, 55 (2), 218–32.

Conger, R. D., Conger, K. J. and Elder, G. H. (1997). Family economic hardship and adolescent adjustment: mediating and moderating processes. In G. J. Duncan and J. Brooks-Gunn (eds), *Consequences of Growing Up Poor*. New York: Russell Sage Foundation (pp. 288–310).

Conger, R. D., McCarty, J. A., Yang, R. K., Lahey, B. B. and Burgess, R. L. (1984). Mother's age as predictors of observed maternal behaviour in three independent samples of families. *Journal of Marriage and the Family*, 46 (2), 411–24.

Cook, T. D. and Murphy, R. F. (1999). *How Inner-city Children See their Family, School, Peers, and Neighbourhood: Developmental Change During the Transition to Adulthood*. (Working Paper). Evanston, IL: Institute for Policy Research, Northwestern University.

Cook, T. D., Herman, M. R., Phillips, M. and Settersten, J., R.A. (2002). Some ways in which neighbourhoods, nuclear families, friendship groups, and school jointly affect changes in early adolescent development. *Child Development*, 73 (4), 1283–1309.

Cooksey, E. C. (1997). Consequences of young mothers' marital histories for children's cognitive development. *Journal of Marriage and the Family*, 59, 245–62.

Corman, H. and Grossman, M. (1985). Determinants of neonatal mortality rates in the US. *Journal of Health Economics*, 4, 213–36.

Côté, J. E. and Levine, C. G. (2002). *Identity, Formation, Agency and Culture*. London: Lawrence Erlbaum.

Covington, M. V. (1992). *Making the Grade: A Self-worth Perspective on Motivation and School Reform*. New York: Cambridge University Press.

Crane, J. (1991). The epidemic theory of ghettos and neighborhood effects on dropping out and teenage childbearing. *American Journal of Sociology*, 96, 1126–59.

Cummings, E. M. and Davies, P. T. (1994). Maternal depression and child development. *Journal of Child Psychology and Psychiatry*, 35, 73–112.

Cunha, F., Heckman, J., Lochner L. and Masterov, D. (2006). Interpreting the evidence on life cycle skill formation. In E. Hanushek and F. Welch (eds), *Handbook of the Economics of Education*. Amsterdam: Elsevier.

Currie, J. and Moretti, E. (2002). *Mothers' Education and Intergenerational Transmission of Human Capital: Evidence from College Openings and Longitudinal Data*. (Working Paper 9360). National Bureau of Economic Research.

Dale, A. and Egerton, M. (1997). *Highly Educated Women: Evidence from the NCDS*. (Research Studies Series RS25). London: Department for Education and Employment.

D'Amico, R. J., Haurin, R. J. and Mott, F. L. (1983). The effects of mothers' employment on adolescent and early outcomes of young men and women. In C. D. Hayes and S. B. Kamerman (eds), *Children of Working Parents: Experiences and Outcomes*. Washington, DC: National Academy Press (pp. 130–219).

Danziger, S. and Waldfogel, J. (2000). *Securing the Future: Investing in Children from Birth to College*. New York: Russell Sage Foundation.

Davis, H., Peronaci, R. and Joshi, H. (1996). *Female Labour Force Participation in Britain, 1980 v 1994*. Paper presented at the ESPE tenth anniversary meeting (June 1996).

Davis-Kean, P. E. (2005). The influence of parent education and family income on child achievement: the indirect role of parental expectations and the home environment. *Journal of Family Psychology*, 19 (2), 294–304.

Davis-Kean, P. E. and Sexton, H. R. (2007). *Race Differences in Parental Influence on Child Achievement: Multiple Pathways to Success*. Paper presented at the Society for Research in Child Development. Boston, MA (March 2007).

Day, R., Peterson, G. and McCracken, C. (1998). Predicting spanking of younger and older children by mothers and fathers. *Journal of Marriage and the Family*, 60, 79–94.

Dearden, L. (1999). The effects of families and ability on men's education and earnings in Britain. *Labour Economics,* 6, 551–67.

Dearden, L., McIntosh, S., Vignoles, A. and Myck, M. (2002). The returns to academic and vocational qualifications in the UK. *Bulletin of Economic Research,* 54 (3), 249–74.

DeLeire, T. and Kalil, A. (2002). Good things come in threes: single parents, multigenerational family structure and adolescent adjustment. *Demography,* 39 (2), 393–412.

Dench, S. and Regan, J. (1999). *Learning in Later Life: Motivation and Impact.* The Institute for Employment Studies Report.

Department for Education and Skills (DfES). (2003). *21st Century Skills: Realising our Potential Individuals, Employers, Nation.* Cm. 5810. London: HMSO.

Department for Education and Skills (DfES). (2005). *Higher Standards, Better Schools for All – More Choice for Parents and Pupils.* London: HMSO.

Department for Education and Skills (DfES). (2005a). *Children's Workforce Strategy.* London: HMSO.

Department for Education and Skills (DfES). (2007). *2020 Vision.* Report of the Teaching and Learning in 2020 Review Group. London: HMSO.

Desforges, C. and Abouchaar, A. (2003). *The Impact of Parental Involvement, Parental Support and Family Education on Pupil Achievement and Adjustment: A Literature Review.* (Research Report 433). London: DfES.

De Tray, D. (1973). Child quality and the demand for children. *Journal of Political Economy,* 81 (2). S70–95.

Diaz, R., Neal, C. J. and Vachio, A. (1991). Maternal teaching in the zone of proximal development: a comparison of low and high risk dyads. *Merrill-Palmer Quarterly,* 37 (1), 83–108.

Dodge, K. A. (2006). Translational science in action: hostile attributional style and the development of aggressive behavior problems. *Development and Psychopathology,* 18, 791–814.

Douglas, J. W. B. (1964). *The Home and the School.* London: MacGibbon and Kee.

Downey, G. and Coyne, J. C. (1990). Children of depressed parents: an integrative review. *Psychological Bulletin,* 108, 150–76.

Duncan, G. J. (1994). Families and neighbors as sources of disadvantage in the schooling decisions of White and Black adolescents. *American Journal of Education,* 103, 20–53.

Duncan, G. J. and Brooks-Gunn, J. (1997). *Consequences of Growing Up Poor.* New York: Russell-Sage Foundation.

Duncan, G. J., Brooks-Gunn, J. and Klebanov, P. K. (1994). Economic deprivation and early-childhood development. *Child Development,* 65 (2), 296–318.

Duncan, G. J., Huston, A. and Weisner, T. (2007). *Higher Ground: New Hope for the Working Poor and their Children.* New York: Russell Sage Foundation.

Duncan, O. D. (1961). A socioeconomic index for all occupations. In A. J. Reiss (ed.), *Occupations and Social Status.* New York: The Free Press (pp. 109–61).

Dunn, J., Wooding, C. and Herman, J. (1977). Mothers' speech to young children: variation in context. *Developmental Medicine and Child Neurology,* 19, 629–38.

Eccles, J. S. (1993). School and family effects on the ontogeny of children's interests, self perceptions, and activity choices. In R. Dienstbier and J. E. Jacobs (eds), *Developmental Perspectives on Motivation* (vol. 40). Lincoln: University of Nebraska Press (pp. 145–208).

Eccles, J. S. (2005). Influences of parents' education on their children's educational attainments: the role of parent and child perceptions. *London Review of Education*, 3 (3), 191–204.

Eccles, J. S. and Gootman, J. (2002). *Communities and Youth: Investing In Our Future*. Washington, DC: National Academy Press.

Eccles, J. S. and Harold, R. D. (1996). Family involvement in children's and adolescents' schooling. In A. Booth and J. F. Dunn (eds), *Family School Links: How Do They Affect Educational Outcomes?* Mahwah, NJ: Erlbaum (pp. 3–34).

Eccles (Parsons), J. S., Adler, T. F., Futterman, R., Goff, S. B., Kaczala, C. M., Meece, J. L. and Midgley, C. (1983). Expectancies, values, and academic behaviours. In J. T. Spence (ed.), *Achievement and Achievement Motivation*. San Francisco, CA: Freeman (pp. 75–146).

Eccles, J. S., Jacobs, J., Harold-Goldsmith, R., Jayaratne, T. E. and Yee, D. (1989a). *The Relations Between Parents' Category-based and Target-based Beliefs: Gender Roles and Biological Influences*. Paper presented at the SRCD, Kansas City (April 1989).

Eccles, J. S., Wigfield, A., Flanagan, C., Miller, C., Reuman, D. and Yee, D. (1989b). Self-concepts, domain values, and self-esteem: relations and changes at early adolescence. *Journal of Personality*, 57, 283–310.

Eccles, J. S., Jacobs, J., Harold, R., Yoon, K. S., Aberton, A. and Freedman-Doan, C. (1991). Parents and gender-role socialisation. In S. Oshkamp (ed.), *Gender and Social Psychology*. Beverly Hills, CA: Sage.

Eccles, J. S., Furstenberg, F., McCarthy, K. A. and Lord, S. E. (1992). *How Parents Respond to Risk and Opportunity*. Paper presented at the Biennial Meeting of the Society for Research on Adolescences, Washington, DC.

Eccles, J. S., Jacobs, J. E., Harold, R. D, Yoon, K. S., Arbreton, A. and Freedman-Doan, C. (1993a). Parents and Gender-role Socialization during the Middle Childhood and Adolescent Years. *Gender issues in contemporary society*. Newbury Park: Sage.

Eccles, J. S., Wigfield, A., Harold, R. D. and Blumenfeld, P. (1993b). Ontogeny of children's self-perceptions and subjective task values across activity domains during the early elementary school years. *Child Development*, 64, 830–47.

Eccles, J. S., Wigfield, A. and Schiefele, U. (1997). Motivation to succeed. In N. Eisenberg (ed.), *Handbook of Child Psychology* (vol. 3, 5th edn). New York: Wiley (pp. 1077–95).

Edwards, L. N. and Grossman, M. (1982). Income and race differences in children's health in the mid 1960s. *Medical Care*, 20 (9), 915–30.

Egeland, B., Pianta, R. and O'Brien, M. A. (1993). Maternal intrusiveness in infancy and child maladaptation in early school years. *Development and Psychopathology*, 5, 359–70.

Elder, G. H. J. and Ardelt, M. (1992). *Families Adapting to Economic Pressure: Some Consequences for Parents and Adolescents*. Paper presented at the Biennial meeting of the Society for Research on Adolescence. Washington, DC (March 1992).

Elder, G. H. J., Pavalko, E. K. and Hasting, T. H. (1991). Talent, history and the fulfilment of promise. *Psychiatry*, 54, 251–67.

Elder, G. H. J., Eccles, J. S., Ardelt, M. and Lord, S. (1995). Inner-city parents under economic pressure: perspectives on the strategies of parenting. *Journal of Marriage and the Family*, 57, 771–84.

Entwisle, D. R. and Hayduk, L. A. (1978). *Too Great Expectations: The Academic Outlook of Young Children*. Baltimore, MD: John Hopkins University Press.

Epstein, J. L. and Sanders, M. G. (2002). Family, school, and community partnerships. In M. H. Bornstein (ed.), *Handbook of Parenting: Practical Issues in Parenting* (vol. 5). Mahwah, NJ: Erlbaum (pp. 407–37).

Ermisch, J. F. and Francesconi, M. (2000). The increasing complexity of family relations: lifetime experience of lone motherhood and stepfamilies in Great Britain. *European Journal of Population*, 16, 235–49.

Ermisch, J. F. and Francesconi, M. (2001). Family structure and children's achievements. *Journal of Population Economics*, 14, 249–70.

Ermisch, J. F. and Pevalin, D. J. (2003). *Who Has a Child as a Teenager?* ISER Working Paper 2003–30. Institute for Social and Economic Research, University of Essex.

Estrada, P., Arsenio, W. F., Hess, R. D. and Holloway, S. D. (1987). Affective quality of the mother–child relationship: longitudinal consequences for children's school relevant cognitive functioning. *Developmental Psychology*, 23, 210–15.

Evans, G. W. and English, K. (2002). The environment of poverty: multiple stressor exposure, psychophysical stress, and socioemotional adjustment. *Child Development*, 73 (4), 1238–48.

Evans, W. N., Oates, W. E. and Schwab, R. M. (1993). Measuring peer group effects: a study of teenage behavior. *Journal of Political Economy*, 100, 966–91.

Fagot, B. I. and Gauvain, M. (1997). Mother–child problem solving: continuity through the early childhood years. *Developmental Psychology*, 33, 480–8.

Fan, X. (2001). Parental involvement and students' academic achievement: a growth model analysis. *The Journal of Experimental Education*, 70 (1), 27–61.

Feinstein, L. (2002). Quantitative estimates of the social benefits of learning, 2: health (depression and obesity). Research Report, No. 6. London: Centre for Research on the Wider Benefits of Learning.

Feinstein, L. (2003). Inequality in the early cognitive development of British children in the 1970 Cohort. *Economica*, 73–98.

Feinstein, L. and Bynner, J. (2003). *The Benefits of Assets in Childhood as Protection Against Adult Social Exclusion: The Relative Effects of Financial, Human, Social and Psychological Assets*. Note to HM Treasury.

Feinstein, L. and Duckworth, K. (2006). *Are There Effects of Mothers' post-16 Education on the Next Generation? Effects on Children's Development and Mothers' Parenting*. Research Report, No. 19. London: Centre for Research on the Wider Benefits of Learning.

Feinstein, L. and Sabates, R. (2006). *Predicting Adult Life Outcomes from Earlier Signals: Identifying Those at Risk*. Report for the Prime Minister's Strategy Unit. WBL discussion paper, Institute of Education.

Feinstein, L. and Symons, J. (1999). Attainment in secondary school. *Oxford Economic Papers*, 51, 300–21.

Feinstein, L., Robertson, D. and Symons, J. (1999). Pre-school education and attainment in the NCDS and the BCS. *Education Economics*, 7 (3), 209–34.

Feinstein, L., Bynner, J. and Duckworth, K. (2006). Young people's leisure contexts and their relation to adult outcomes. *Journal of Youth Studies*, 9 (3), 305–27.

Ferri, E. and Smith, K. (2003). Family life. In E. Ferri, J. Bynner and M. Wadsworth (eds), *Changing Britain, Changing Lives: Three Generations at the Turn of the Century*. London: Institute of Education, University of London.

Ferri, E., Bynner, J. and Wadsworth, M. (eds) (2003). *Changing Britain, Changing Lives: Three Generations at the Turn of the Century*. London: Institute of Education, University of London.

Field, T., Morrow, C. and Adlestein, D. (1993). 'Depressed' mothers' perceptions of infant behaviour. *Infant Behaviour and Development*, 16, 99–108.

Finnas, F. (1996). Separations among Finnish women born between 1938–1967. *Yearbook of Population Research in Finland*, 33, 21–33.

Foster, P., Gomm, R. and Hammersley, M. (1996). *Constructing Educational Equality*. London: The Falmer Press.

Fox, R., Platz, D. and Bentley, K. (1995). Maternal factors related to parenting practices, developmental expectations, and perceptions of child behavior problems. *Journal of Genetic Psychology*, 156 (4), 431–41.

Fraser, B. J. and Fisher, D. L. (1982). Predicting students' outcomes from their perceptions of classroom psychosocial environment. *American Educational Research Journal*, 19, 498–518.

Fredricks, J. A. and Eccles, J. S. (2002). Children's competence and value beliefs from childhood through adolescence. *Developmental Psychology*, 38 (4), 519–33.

Frey, B. S. and Stutzer, A. (2002). *Happiness and Economics*. Princeton, NJ, and Oxford: Princeton University Press.

Furstenberg, F. F. (1992). *Adapting to Difficult Environments: Neighbourhood Characteristics and Family Strategies*. Paper presented at the Biennial Meeting of the Society for Research on Adolescences, Washington, DC.

Furstenburg, F. F., Brooks-Gunn, J. and Morgan, S. P. (1987). Adolescent mothers and their children in later life. *Family Planning Perspectives*, 19 (4), 142–51.

Furstenberg, F. F., Brooks-Gunn, J. and Chase-Lansdale, P. L. (1989). Teenage pregnancy and childbearing. *American Psychologist*, 44 (2), 313–20.

Furstenburg, F. F., Cook, T. D., Eccles, J. S., Elder, G. H. and Sameroff, A. (1999). *Managing to Make It: Urban Families and Adolescent Success*. Chicago, IL: University of Chicago Press.

Galindo-Rueda, F. (2003). *The Intergenerational Effect of Parental Schooling: Evidence from the 1947 School Leaving Age Reform*. Unpublished manuscript.

Ganzach, Y. (2000). Parents' education, cognitive ability, educational expectations and educational attainment: interactive effects. *British Journal of Educational Psychology*, 70, 419–41.

Garmezy, N. (1985). Risk and protective factors in the development of psycho pathology. In J. E. Stevenson (ed.), *Recent Research in Developmental Psychopathology*. Cambridge: Cambridge University Press.

Garmezy, N. (1991). Resiliency and vulnerability to adverse developmental outcomes associated with poverty. *American Behavioral Scientist*, 34, 416–60.

Garmezy, N. (1993). Developmental psychopathology: some historical and current perspectives. In D. Magnusson and P. Caeser (eds), *In Longitudinal Research on Individual Development: Present Status and Future Perspectives*. Cambridge: Cambridge University Press.

Garner, C. L. and Raudenbush, S. W. (1991). Neighbourhood effect on educational attainment: a multilevel analysis. *Sociology of Education*, 64, 251–62.

Gayle, V., Berridge, D. and Davis, R. (2002). Young people's entry into higher education: quantifying influential factors. *Oxford Review of Education*, 28 (1), 5–20.

Geronimus, A. T., Korenman, S. and Hillemeier, M. M. (1994). Does young maternal age adversely affect child development? Evidence from cousin comparisons in the United States. *Population and Development Review*, 20 (3), 585–609.

Gewirtz, S., Ball, S. and Bowe, R. (1995). *Markets, Choice and Equity in Education*. Buckingham: Open University Press.

Gibbons, S. A. (2002). *Empirical Essays in the Economics of Neighbourhoods and Education*. University College London, Ph.D. Dissertation.

Gibbons, S. A. and Machin, S. (2003). Valuing English primary schools. *Journal of Urban Economics*, 53 (2), 197–219.

Gibbons, S. A. and Telhaj, S. (2006). *Peer Effects and Pupil Attainment: Evidence from Secondary School Transition*. London: Centre for the Economics of Education.

Ginther, D. K. and Pollak, R. A. (2004). Family structure and children's educational outcomes: blended families, stylized facts, and descriptive regressions. *Demography*, 41 (4), 671–96.

Goldman, R. (2005). *Fathers' Involvement in their Children's Education: A Review of Research and Practice*. London: National Family and Parenting Institute.

Goldsmith, A., Veum, J. and Darity, W. (1997). The impact of psychological and human capital on wages. *Economic Inquiry*, 35 (4), 815–29.

Goodenow, C. (1993). Classroom belonging among early adolescents students: relationships to motivation and achievement. *Journal of Early Adolescence*, 13 (1), 21–43.

Goodman, S. H. and Brumley, H. E. (1990). Schizophrenic and depressed mothers: relational deficits in parenting. *Developmental Psychology*, 26, 31–9.

Goodnow, J. J. and Collins, W. A. (1990). *Development According to Parents: The Nature, Sources, and Consequences of Parents' Ideas*. London: Erlbaum.

Gottfried, A. E. (1990). Academic intrinsic motivation in young elementary school children. *Journal of Educational Psychology*, 82, 525–38.

Gottfried, A. E., Fleming, J. S. and Gottfried, A. W. (1998). Role of cognitively stimulating home environment in children's academic intrinsic motivation: a longitudinal study. *Child Development*, 69 (5), 1448–60.

Gottfried, A. W. and Gottfried, A. E. (1984). Home environment and cognitive development in young children of middle-socioeconomic-status families. In A. W. Gottfried (ed.), *Home Environment and Early Cognitive Development: Longitudinal Research*. New York: Academic Press (pp. 57–115).

Gottfried, A. W., Gottfried, A. E., Bathurst, K. and Guerin, D. W. (1994). *Gifted IQ: Early Developmental Aspects*. New York: Plenum.

Gottfried, A. W., Gottfried, A. E., Bathurst, K., Guerin, D. W. and Parramore, M. M. (2003). Socioeconomic status in children's development and family environment: infancy through adolescence. In M. H. Bornstein and R. H. Bradley (eds), *Socioeconomic Status, Parenting, and Child Development*. Mahwah, NJ: Lawrence Erlbaum Associates (pp. 189–208).

Gottlieb, G. (1983). The psychobiological approach to developmental issues. In M. M. Haith and J. J. Campos (eds), *Handbook of Child Psychology: Infancy and Biological Bases* (vol. 2). New York: Wiley (pp. 1–26).

Graham, S. (1991). A review of attribution theory in achievement contexts. *Educational Psychology Review*, 3, 5–39.

Gregg, P. and Machin, S. (2000). The relationship between childhood experiences, subsequent educational attainment and adult labour market performance. In K. Vleminckx and T. Smeeding (eds), *Child Well Being in Modern Nations: What Do We Know?* Bristol: Policy Press.

Gregg, P. and Washbrook, E. (2003). *The Effects of Early Maternal Employment on Child Development in the UK*. CMPO Working Paper, Series No. 03/070.

Gregg, P., Washbrook, E., Propper, C. and Burgess, S. (2005). The effects of a mother's return to work decision on child development in the UK. *The Economic Journal*, 115 (501), F48–80.

Grossman, M. and Joyce, T. (1990). Unobservables, pregnancy resolutions, and birth weight production functions in New York City. *Journal of Political Economy*, 98 (5), 983–1007.

Guo, G. and Harris, K. M. (2000). The mechanisms mediating the effects of poverty on children's intellectual development. *Demography*, 37 (4), 431–7.

Gutman, L. M., Sameroff, A. and Eccles, J. S. (2002). The academic achievement of African-American students during early adolescence: an examination of multiple risk, promotive and protective factors. *American Journal of Community Psychology*, 39, 367–99.

HM Government (2003). *Every Child Matters*. CM 5860. London: HMSO.

HM Government. (2005). *Higher Standards, Better Schools for All. More Choice for Parents and Pupils*. CM 6677. London: HMSO.

HM Government (2006). *Reaching Out: An Action Plan on Social Exclusion*. London: HMSO.

Halle, T. G., Kurtz-Costes, B. and Mahoney, J. L. (1997). Family influences on school achievement in low-income African-American children. *Journal of Educational Psychology*, 89, 527–37.

Hammond, C. (2002). 'Learning to be Healthy'. *The Wider Benefits of Learning Papers*, no. 3. London: Institute of Education.

Hammond, C. (2003). How education makes us healthy. *London Review of Education*, 1 (1), 61–78.

Han, W., Waldfogel, J. and Brooks-Gunn, J. (2001). The effects of early maternal employment on later cognitive and behavioural outcomes. *Journal of Marriage and the Family*, 63, 336–54.

Handler, J. F., Berlin, G. L., Cook, T. D., Crim, A. A., Dornbusch, S. M., Dryfoos, J. G., Fernandez, A. R. M., Freeman, R. M., Hagan, J., Irwin, C. E. Jnr, Jessor, R., Johnson-Powell, G., Shirley, A., Starfield, B. and Street, L. (1995). *Losing*

Generations: Adolescents in High-Risk Settings. Washington, DC: National Academy of Science Press.

Hanson, T. L., McLanahan, S. and Thomson, E. (1997). Economic resources, parental practices, and children's well-being. In G. J. Duncan and J. Brooks-Gunn (eds), *Consequences of Being Poor.* New York: Russell Sage Foundation (pp. 190–238).

Hanushek, E. A. (1992). Trade-off between child quantity and quality. *The Journal of Political Economy,* 100 (1), 84–117.

Harris, Y. R., Terrel, D. and Allen, G. (1999). The influence of education context and beliefs on the teaching behavior of African-American mothers. *Journal of Black Psychology,* 25, 490–503.

Harter, S. (1982). The perceived competence scale for children. *Child Development,* 53, 87–97.

Hartog, J. and Osterbeek, H. (1998). Health, wealth, and happiness: why pursue a higher education? *Economics of Education Review,* 17, 245–56.

Hauser, R. and Sewell, W. H. (1983). *Birth Order and Educational Attainment in Full Sibships.* Working paper no. 83–31. Madison, WI: University of Wisconsin-Madison.

Haveman, R. and Wolfe, B. (1995). The determinants of children's attainments: a review of methods and findings. *Journal of Economic Literature,* 23, 1829–78.

Haveman, R., Wolfe, B. and Wilson, K. (1997). Childhood poverty and adolescent schooling and fertility outcomes: reduced-form and structural estimates. In G. J. Duncan and J. Brooks-Gunn (eds), *Consequences of Growing Up Poor.* New York: Russell Sage Foundation (pp. 419–60).

Healy, T. and Côté. S. (2001). *The Well-Being of Nations: The Role of Human and Social Capital.* Paris: Organisation for Economic Cooperation and Development.

Heckman, J. (2005). *Lessons from the Technology of Skill Formation:* National Bureau of Economic Research. Working Papers 11142.

Heckman, J. and Rubinstein, Y., (2001). The Importance of Noncognitive Skills: Lessons from the GED Testing Program. *American Economic Review,* 91 (2).

Heckman, J. and Vytlacil, E. (2001). Identifying the role of cognitive ability in explaining the level of and change in the return to schooling. *The Review of Economics and Statistics,* 83 (1), 1–12.

Heider, F. (1958). *The Psychology of Interpersonal Relations.* New York: Academic Press.

Helliwell, J. F. (2002). *How's Life? Combining Individual and National Variables to Explain Subjective Well-being.* Working Paper 9065. National Bureau of Economic Research.

Hess, R. and Holloway, S. D. (1984). Family and school as educational institutions. In R. D. Parke (ed.), *Review of Child Development Research* (vol. 7: *The Family*). Chicago, IL: University of Chicago Press (pp. 179–222).

Hess, R. and Shipman, V. (1965). Early experiences and the socialization of cognitive models in children. *Child Development,* 34, 869–86.

Hiebert, E. H. and Adams, C. S. (1987). Fathers' and mothers' perceptions of their preschool children's emergent literacy. *Journal of Experimental Child Psychology,* 44, 25–37.

Hill, M. S., Yeung, W. and Duncan, G. J. (2001). Childhood family structure and young adult behaviours. *Journal of Population Economics*, 14, 271–99.

Hill, N. E. (2001). Parenting and academic socialization as they relate to school readiness: the roles of ethnicity and family income. *Journal of Educational Psychology*, 93, 686–97.

Hill, N. E., Castellino, D. R., Lansford, J. E., Nowlin, P., Dodge, K. A., Bates, J. E. and Pettit, G. S. (2004). Parent academic involvement as related to school behavior, achievement, and aspirations: demographic variations across adolescence. *Child Development*, 75 (5), 1491–509.

Hinshaw, S. P. (1992). Externalizing behavior problems and academic under-achievement in childhood and adolescence: causal relationships and underlying mechanisms. *Psychological Bulletin*, 111, 127–55.

Hipwell, A., Goossens, F., Melhuish, E. and Kumar, R. (2000). Severe maternal psychopathology and infant-mother attachment. *Development and Psychopathology*, 12, 157–75.

Hobcraft, J. (1998). *Intergenerational and Life-course Transmission of Social Exclusion: Influences of Childhood Poverty, Family Disruption, and Contact with the Police*. CASE Paper 15. London: Centre for Analysis of Social Exclusion, London School of Economics.

Hobcraft, J. (2000). *The Roles of Schooling and Educational Qualifications in the Emergence of Adult Social Exclusion*. CASE Paper 43. London: Centre for Analysis of Social Exclusion, London School of Economics.

Hobcraft, J. (2003). *Continuity and Change in Pathways to Young Adult Disadvantage: Results from a British Birth Cohort*. CASE Paper 66. London: Centre for Analysis of Social Exclusion, London School of Economics.

Hobcraft, J. and Kiernan, K. (1999). *Child Poverty, Early Motherhood and Adult Social Exclusion*. CASE Paper 28. London: Centre for Analysis of Social Exclusion, London School of Economics.

Hoem, J. M. (1997). Educational gradients in divorce and risks in Sweden in recent decades. *Population Studies*, 51 (1), 19–27.

Hoff, E. (2003a). Causes and consequences of SES-related differences in parent-to-child speech. In M. H. Bornstein and R. H. Bradley (eds), *Socioeconomic Status, Parenting, and Child Development*. Mahwah, NJ: Lawrence Erlbaum Associates.

Hoff, E. (2003b). The specificity of environmental influence: socioeconomic status affects early vocabulary development via maternal speech. *Child Development*, 74 (5), 1368–78.

Hofferth, S. L., Davis-Kean, P. E., Davis, J. and Finkelstein, J. (1998). *Child Development Supplement to the Panel Study of Income Dynamics: 1997 User Guide*. Ann Arbor, MI: University of Michigan, Institute of Social Research.

Hoff-Ginsberg, E. (1991). Mother–child conversation in different social classes and communicative settings. *Child Development*, 62, 782–96.

Hoff-Ginsberg, E. (1992). How should frequency input be measured? *First Language*, 12, 233–45.

Hoff-Ginsberg, E. (1998). The relation between birth order and socioeconomic status to children's language experience and language development. *Applied Psycholinguistics*, 19, 603–29.

Holden, G. W. and Miller, P. C. (1999). Enduring and different: a meta-analysis of the similarity in parents' child rearing. *Psychological Bulletin*, 125 (2), 223–54.

Holmlund, H., Lindahl, M. and Plug, E. (2006). *Estimating Intergenerational Schooling Effects: A Comparison of Methods*. Paper presented at the Second Network Workshop of the RTN 'Economics of Education and Education Policy in Europe', Uppsala (October 2005).

Hossain, Z., Field, T., Pickens, J. and Gonzalez, J. (1995). *Infants of 'depressed' mothers interact better with their nondepressed fathers*. Manuscript submitted for review.

Howes, C. (1990). Can the age of entry into child-care and the quality of child-care predict adjustment in kindergarten? *Developmental Psychology*, 26 (2), 292–303.

Hubbs-Tait, L., McDonald Culp, A., Culp, R. E. and Miller, C. E. (2002). Relation of maternal cognitive stimulation, emotional support, and intrusive behaviour during Head Start to children's kindergarten cognitive abilities. *Child Development*, 73 (1), 110–31.

Hungerford, T. and Solon, G. 1987. Sheepskin effects in the returns to education. *Review of Economics and Statistics*, 69 (1), 175–7.

Hunt, J. M. and Paraskevopoulos, J. (1980). Children's psychological development as a function of the inaccuracy of their mothers' knowledge of their abilities. *Journal of Genetic Psychology*, 136, 285–98.

Iacovou, M. (2001). *Family Composition and Children's Educational Outcomes*. Institute for Social and Economic Research Working Paper 01–12. Colchester: University of Essex.

Imbens, G. and Angrist, J. (1994). Identification and estimation of local average treatment effects. *Econometrica*, 62, 467–75.

Ireson, J. and Hallam, S. (2001). *Ability Grouping in Education*. London: Paul Chapman Publishing.

Isacsson, G. (2004). Estimating the economic returns to educational levels using data on twins. *Journal of Applied Econometrics*, 19, 99–119.

Jackson, A. P., Brooks-Gunn, J., Huang, C. and Glassman, M. (2000). Single mothers in low-wage jobs: financial strain, parenting, and preschoolers' outcomes. *Child Development*, 71, 1409–23.

Jacobs, J. and Eccles, J. S. (1992). The impact of mothers' gender-role stereotypic beliefs on mothers' and children's ability perceptions. *Journal of Personality and Social Psychology*, 63 (6), 932–44.

Jacobvitz, D. and Sroufe, L. A. (1987). The early caregiver–child relationship: attention-deficit disorder and hyperactivity in kindergarten: a prospective study. *Child Development*, 58, 1488–95.

Jalovaara, M. (2003). The joint effects of marriage partners' socioeconomic positions on the risk of divorce. *Demography*, 40 (1), 67–81.

Jencks, C. and Mayer, S. (1990). The social consequences of growing up in a poor neighbourhood. In M. G. H. McGeary and E. L. Lawrence (eds), *Inner City Poverty in the United States*. Washington, DC: National Academic Press (pp. 111–86).

Jencks, C., Bartlett, S., Corcoran, M., Crouse, J., Eaglesfield, D., Jackson, G. *Who Gets Ahead? The Determinants of Economic Success in America*. New York: Basic Books.

Jodl, K. M., Michael, A., Malanchuk, O., Eccles, J. S. and Sameroff, A. (2001). Parents' roles in shaping early adolescents' occupational aspirations. *Child Development*, 72 (4), 1247–65.

Joshi, H. (2000). *Production, Reproductions and Education: Women Children and Work in Contemporary Britain*. London: Institute of Education, University of London Press.

Joshi, H. and Verropoulou, G. (2000). *Maternal Employment and Child Outcomes*. Occasional Paper. London: The Smith Institute.

Joshi, H., Cooksey, E. C., Wiggins, R. D., McCulloch, A., Verropoulou, G. and Clarke, L. (1999). Diverse family living situations and child development: a multi-level analysis comparing longitudinal evidence from Britain and the United States. *International Journal of Law, Policy and the Family*, 13, 292–314.

Kiernan, K. (1997). *The Legacy of Parental Divorce: Social, Economic and Demographic Experiences in Adulthood*. London: London School of Economics.

Kiernan, K. and Mueller, G. (1998). *The Divorced and Who Divorces?* CASE Paper 7. London: Centre for Analysis of Social Exclusion, London School of Economics.

Kinderman, T. A. (1993). Natural peer groups as contexts for individual development: the case of children's motivation in school. *Developmental Psychology*, 29 (6), 970–7.

Klebanov, P. K., Brooks-Gunn, J. and Duncan, G. J. (1994). Does neighborhood and family poverty affect mothers' parenting, mental health, and social support? *Journal of Marriage and the Family*, 56 (2), 441–55.

Kohl, G. O., Lengua, L. J. and McMahon, R. J. (2000). Parent involvement in school conceptualizing multiple dimensions and their relations with family and demographic risk factors. *Journal of School Psychology*, 38, 501–23.

Kohn, M. L. (1977). *Class and Conformity: A Study in Values* (2nd edn). Chicago, IL: Chicago University Press.

Kubzansky, L. D., Kawachi, I. and Sparrow, D. (1999). Socioeconomic status, hostility, and risk factor clustering in the normative ageing study: any help from the concept of allostatic load? *The Society of Behavioural Medicine*, 21 (4), 330–8.

Ladd, G. W. (1990). Having friends, keeping friends, making friends, and being liked by peers in the classroom: predictors of children's early school adjustment? *Child Development*, 61, 1081–100.

Laosa, L. (1980). Maternal teaching strategies in Chicano and Anglo-American families: the influence of culture and education on maternal behavior. *Child Development*, 51, 759–65.

Le Grand, J. (2006). Equality and choice in public services. *Social Research: An International Quarterly of Social Sciences*, 73 (2), 695–710.

Lempers, J. D., Clark-Lempers, D. and Simons, R. L. (1989). Economic hardship, parenting, and distress in adolescence. *Child Development*, 60, 25–39.

Lerner, R. M. (1986). *Concept and Theories of Human Development* (2nd edn). New York: Random House.

Lerner, R. M. (1998). *Theories of Human Development: Contemporary Perspectives*. *Handbook of Child Psychology* (vol 1). New York: Wiley.

Leventhal, T. and Brooks-Gunn, J. (2000). The neighbourhoods they live in: the effects of neighbourhoods residence upon child and adolescent outcomes. *Psychological Bulletin*, 126 (2), 309–37.

Levy, D. M. (1943). *Maternal Overprotection*. New York: Columbia University Press.

Loeber, R. (1990). Development and risk factors of juvenile antisocial behavior and delinquency. *Clinical Psychology Review*, 10, 1–41.

Loury, L. D. (2006). All in the extended family: effects of grandparents, aunts and uncles on educational attainment. *The American Economic Review – Papers and Proceedings*, 96 (2), 275–9.

Luster, T. and Dubow, E. (1990). Predictors of the quality of the home environment that adolescent mothers provide for their school-aged children. *Journal of Youth and Adolescence*, 19 (5), 475–94.

Lyons-Ruth, K., Zoll, D., Connell, D. and Grunebaum, H. U. (1986). The depressed mother and her one-year-old infant: environment, interaction, attachment and infant development. In E. Z. Tronick and T. Field (eds), *Maternal Depression and Infant Disturbance: New Directions for Child Development* (vol. 34). San Francisco, CA: Jossey-Bass (pp. 61–82).

Ma, X. (2001). Participation in advanced mathematics: do expectation and influence of students, peers, teachers, and parents matter? *Contemporary Educational Psychology*, 26, 132–46.

Maccoby, E. E. and Martin, J. A. (1983). Socialization in the context of the family: parent–child interaction. In P. H. Mussen (ed.), *Handbook of Child Psychology*. New York: Wiley (pp. 1–101).

McCulloch, A. and Joshi, H. (1999). *Child Development and Family Resources: An Exploration of Evidence from the Second Generation of the 1958 Birth Cohort*. Institute for Social and Economic Research Working Paper 99–15. Colchester: University of Essex.

McGroder, S. M. (2000). Parenting among low-income, African-American single mothers with pre-school age children: patterns, predictors, and developmental correlates. *Child Development*, 71 (3), 752–71.

McLanahan, S. (1997). Parent absence or poverty: which matters more? In G. J. Duncan and J. Brooks-Gunn (eds), *Consequences of Growing Up Poor*. New York: Russell Sage Foundation (pp. 35–48).

McLanahan, S. and Bumpass, L. (1988). Intergenerational consequences of marital disruption. *American Journal of Sociology*, 94 (1), 130–52.

McLoyd, V. (1990). The impact of economic hardship on black families and development: psychological distress, parenting, and socioemotional development. *Child Development*, 61 (2), 311–46.

McLoyd, V. and Wilson, L. (1991). The strain of living poor: parenting, social support, and child mental health. In A. C. Huston (ed.), *Children in Poverty*. Canada: Cambridge University Press (pp. 105–35).

McLoyd, V., Jayaratne, T. E., Ceballo, R. and Borquez, J. (1994). Unemployment and work interruption among African-American single mothers: effects on parenting and adolescent socioemotional functioning. *Child Development*, 65, 562–89.

Magnuson, K. (2003). *The Effect of Increases in Welfare Mothers' Education on their Young Children's Academic and Behavioral Outcomes: Evidence from the National Evaluation of Welfare-to-Work Strategies Child Outcomes Study*. Institute for Research on Poverty. Discussion Paper No. 1274–03. Madison, WI: University of Wisconsin.

Magnuson, K. and Duncan, G. J. (2004). Parent- vs. child-based intervention strategies for promoting children's wellbeing. In A. Kalil and T. DeLeire (eds), *Family Investments in Children's Potential: Resources and Parenting Behaviors that Promote Success.* Mahwah, NJ: Lawrence Erlbaum Associates.

Magnusson, D. and Stattin, H. (1998). Person-context interaction theories. In W. Damon and R. M. Lerner (eds), *Handbook of Child Psychology* (vol. 1: *Theoretical Models of Human Development*, 5th edn). New York: Wiley (pp. 685–759).

Majumder, A. K., May, M. and Pant, P. D. (1997). Infant and child mortality determinants in Bangladesh: are they changing? *Journal of Biosocial Science*, 29, 385–99.

Makosky, V. P. (1982). Sources of stress: events or conditions? In D. Belle (ed.), *Lives in Stress: Women and Depression.* Beverly Hills, CA: Sage.

Manlove, J. (1997). Early motherhood in an intergenerational perspective: the experiences of a British cohort. *Journal of Marriage and the Family*, 59, 263–79.

Manski, C. F., Sandefur, G. D., McLanahan, S. and Powers, D. (1992). Alternative estimates of the effects of family structure during adolescence on high school graduation. *Journal of American Statistical Association*, 87 (417), 25–37.

Margo, J. and Dixon, M. (2006). *Freedom's Orphans: Raising Youth in a Changing World.* London: Institute of Public Policy Research.

Marjoribanks, K. (1988). Perceptions of family environments, educational and occupational outcomes: social-status differences. *Perceptual and Motor Skills*, 66, 3–9.

Marmot, M., Smith, G., Stansfeld, S., Patel, C., North, F., Head, J., White, I., Brunner, E. and Feeney, A. (1991). Health inequalities among British civil servants: The Whitehall II study. *Lancet*, 337 (8754), 1387–93.

Martin, S. P. and Parashar, S. (2006). Women's changing attitudes towards divorce, 1974–2002: evidence from an educational cross-over. *Journal of Marriage and the Family*, 68 (1), 29–40.

Massey, D. S. and Denton, N. A. (1993). *American Apartheid: Segregation and the Making of the Underclass.* Cambridge, MA: Harvard University Press.

Mastekaasa, A. (2006). Is marriage/cohabitation beneficial for young people? Some evidence on psychological distress among Norwegian college students. *Journal of Community and Applied Social Psychology*, 16 (2), 149–65.

Masten, A. S. and Coatsworth, J. D. (1998). The development of competence in favorable and unfavorable environments: lessons from research on successful children. *American Psychologist*, 53 (2), 205–20.

Maurin, E. and McNally, S. (2005). *Vive la Revolution! Long Term Returns of 1968 and the Angry Students.* Centre for the Economics of Education Discussion Paper, CEEDP0049, London.

Melhuish, E., Sylva, K., Sammons, P., Siraj-Blatchford, I., Taggart, B., Dobson, A. and Jeavons, M. (1999). *Technical Paper 4 – The Effective Provision of Pre-school Education (EPPE) Project: Parent, Family and Child Characteristics in Relation to Type of Pre-school and Socio-economic Differences.* London: DfEE/Institute of Education, University of London.

Michael J. B., Lillard, L. A. and Stern, S. (2006). Cohabitation, marriage, and divorce in a model of match quality. *International Economic Review*, 47 (2), 451–94.

Miech, R. A. and Shanahan, M. J. (2000). Socioeconomic status and depression over the lifecourse. *Health and Social Behavior*, 41 (2), 162–76.

Miller, P., Mulvey, C. and Martin, N. (1997). Family characteristics and the returns to schooling: evidence on gender differences from a sample of Australian twins. *Economica*, 64, 137–54.

Miller, S. A. (1988). Parents' beliefs about children's cognitive development. *Child Development*, 59, 259–85.

Miller, S. A. and Davis, T. L. (1992). Beliefs about children: a comparative study of mothers, teachers, peers, and self. *Child Development*, 63, 1251–65.

Miller, S. A., Manhal, M. and Mee, L. L. (1991). Parental beliefs, parental accuracy, and children's cognitive performance: a search for causal relations. *Developmental Psychology*, 27 (2), 267–76.

Mirowsky, J. and Ross, C. (2002). Depression, parenthood and age at first birth. *Social Science & Medicine*, 54, 1281–98.

Mistry, R. S., Vandewater, E. A., Huston, A. C. and McLoyd, V. (2002). Economic well-being and children's social adjustment: the role of family process in an ethnically diverse low-income sample. *Child Development*, 73 (3), 935–51.

Mooney, M. (1984). Women's educational attainment and the timing of entering into parenthood. *American Sociological Review*, 49 (4), 491–511.

Moos, R. H. (1979). *Evaluating Educational Environments*. San Francisco, CA: Jossey-Bass.

Mortimore, J., Mortimore, P. and Thomas, H. (1994). *Managing Associate Staff: Innovation in Primary and Secondary Schools*. London: Paul Chapman Associates.

Mortimore, P. and Blackstone, T. (1982). *Disadvantage in Education*. London: Heineman.

Mortimore, P., Sammons, P., Jacob, R., Stoll, L. and Lewis, D. (1988). *School Matters: The Junior Years*. Salisbury: Open Books.

Murphey, D. A. (1992). Constructing the child: relations between parents' beliefs and child outcomes. *Developmental Review*, 12, 199–232.

Murray, L. (1992). The impact of postnatal depression on infant development. *Journal of Child Psychology and Psychiatry*, 33, 543–61.

Murray, L., Fiori-Cowley, A., Hooper, R. and Cooper, P. (1996). The impact of postnatal depression and associated adversity on early mother–infant interactions and later infant outcome. *Child Development*, 67, 2512–26.

Nagy, W. E., Herman, P. A. and Anderson, R. C. (1985). Learning words from context. *Reading Research Quarterly*, 20, 233–53.

National Institute of Child Health and Human Development (NICHD) Early Child Care Research Network (1997). The effects of infant child care on infant–mother attachment security: results of the NICHD study of early child care. *Child Development*, 68, 860–79.

National Institute of Child Health and Human Development (NICHD) Early Child Care Research Network (1998). Early child care and self-control, compliance, and problem behaviour at 24 and 36 months. *Child Development*, 69, 1145–70.

Neuman, S. B. and Celano, D. (2001). Access to print in low-income and middle-income communities: an ecological study of four neighbourhoods. *Reading Research Quarterly*, 36 (1), 8–26.

Nicholls, J. G. (1978). The development of the concepts of effort and ability, perceptions of academic attainment, and the understanding that difficult tasks require more ability. *Child Development*, 49, 800–14.

Ogbu, J. U. (1988). Class stratification, racial stratification, and schooling. In L. Weis (ed.), *Class, Race, and Gender in American Education*. Albany, NY: SUNY (pp. 63–82).

Oreopoulos, P. (2006). The compelling effects of compulsory education schooling: evidence from Canada. *Canadian Journal of Economics*, 39 (1), 22–52.

Oreopoulos, P., Page, M. E. and Stevens, A. (2003). *Does Human Capital Transfer from Parent to Child? The Intergenerational Effects of Compulsory Schooling*. No. 10164. Cambridge, MA: National Bureau of Economic Research.

Organisation for Economic Cooperation and Development (OECD) (2005). *Education at a Glance*. Paris: OECD.

Organisation for Economic Co-operation and Development (OECD) (2006). *Personalising Education*. Paris: OECD.

Osborn, A. F. and Milbank, J. E. (1987). *The Effects of Early Education: A Report from the Child Health and Education Study*. Oxford: Clarendon Press.

O'Toole, J. and Wright, R. E. (1991). Parental education and child mortality in Burundi. *Journal of Biosocial Science*, 23 (3), 255–62.

Pagani, L. S., Boulerice, B. and Tremblay, R. E. (1997). The influence of poverty on children's classroom placement and behavior problems. In G. J. Duncan and J. Brooks-Gunn (eds), *Consequences of Growing Up Poor*. New York: Russell Sage Foundation (pp. 311–39).

Pallas, A. M., Entwisle, D. R., Alexander, K. L. and Stluka, M. F. (1994). Ability-group effects: instructional, social, or institutional? *Sociology of Education*, 67, 27–46.

Parsons, S. and Bynner, J. (1998). *Influences on Adult Basic Skills: Factors Affecting the Development of Literacy and Numeracy from Birth to 37*. London: The Basic Skills Agency.

Patterson, G. R. (1986). Performance models for antisocial boys. *American Psychologist*, 41 (4), 432–44.

Patterson, G. R., DeBaryshe, B. D. and Ramsey, E. (1989). A developmental perspective on antisocial behavior. *American Psychologist*, 44 (2), 329–35.

Peters, H. E. and Mullis, N. C. (1997). The role of family income and sources of income in adolescent achievement. In G. J. Duncan and J. Brooks-Gunn (eds), *Consequences of Growing Up Poor*. New York: Russell Sage Foundation (pp. 340–81).

Phinney, J. S. and Feshbach, N. D. (1980). Non-directive and intrusive teaching styles of middle- and working-class English mothers. *British Journal of Educational Psychology*, 50, 2–9.

Pleck, E. H. and Pleck, J. H. (1997). Fatherhood ideals in the United States: historical dimensions. In M. E. Lamb (ed.), *The Role of the Father in Child Development* (3rd edn). New York: Wiley (pp. 33–48).

Plowden, B. H. (1967). *The Plowden Report: Children and their Primary schools: A Report of the Central Advisory Council of Education, England*. London: Central Advisory Council for Education, HMSO.

Plug, E. (2004). Estimating the effect of mother's schooling on children's schooling using a sample of adoptees. *American Economic Review*, 94 (1), 358–68.

Plug, E. and Vijverberg, W. (2005). Does family income matter for schooling outcomes? Using adoptees as a natural experiment. *The Economic Journal*, 115 (506), 879–906.

Ramey, C. T. and Ramey, S. L. (1992). Early education intervention with disadvantaged children: to what effect? *Applied and Preventative Psychology*, 1, 131–40.

Ramey, C. T. and Ramey, S. L. (1998). Prevention of intellectual disabilities: Early interventions to improve cognitive development. *Preventive Medicine*, 27, 1–9.

Ramey, C. T., Campbell, F. A., Burchinal, M., Skinner, M. L., Gardner, D. M. and Ramey, S. L. (2000). Persistent effects of early childhood education on high-risk children and their mothers. *Applied Developmental Science*, 4 (1), 2–14.

Ramey, S. L. and Ramey, C. T. (2000). Early childhood experiences and developmental competence. In J. Waldfogel and S. Danziger (eds), *Securing the Future: Investigating in Children from Birth to College*. New York: Russell Sage Foundation (pp. 122–50).

Raymo, J. M. (2003). Educational attainment and the transition to first marriage among Japanese women. *Demography*, 40 (1), 83–103.

Reiss, D., Plomin, R. and Hetherington, E. M. (1991). Genetics and psychiatry: an unheralded window on the environment. *The American Journal of Psychiatry*, 148, 283–91.

Reynolds, A. J. (1992). Comparing measures of parental involvement and their effects on academic achievement. *Early Childhood Research Quarterly*, 7, 441–62.

Robertson, D. and Symons, J. (2003). Do peer groups matter? Peer group versus schooling effects on academic attainment. *Economica*, 70, 31–53.

Rogoff, B. (1990). *Apprenticeship in Thinking: Cognitive Development in Social Context*. New York: Oxford Press.

Rose, M. R. (2001). Review of a means to an end: the biological basis of aging and death. *Quarterly Review of Biology*, 76, 342–3.

Rosenzweig, M. R. and Schutlz, P. T. (1989). Schooling, information and non-market productivity: contraceptive use and its effectiveness. *International Economic Review*, 30 (2), 457–77.

Ross, C. and van Willigen, M. (1997). Education and the subjective quality of life. *Journal of Health and Social Behavior*, 38, 275–97.

Rowe, K. J. (1991). The influence of reading activity at home on students' attitudes towards reading, classroom attentiveness and reading achievement: an application of structural equation modelling. *British Journal of Educational Psychology*, 61, 19–35.

Rowlingson, K., and McKay, S. (1998). *The Growth of Lone Parenthood: Diversity and Dynamics*. London: PSI.

Rubin, K. H., Burgess, K. B. and Hastings, P. D. (2002). Stability and social-behavioural consequences of toddlers' inhibited temperament and parenting behaviours. *Child Development*, 73 (2), 483–95.

Rutter, M. (1990). Psychosocial resilience and protective mechanisms. In J. Rolf, A. S. Masten, D. Chichetti, K. H. Nuechterlin and S. Weintraub (eds), *Risk and*

Protective Factors in the Development of Psychopathology. New York: Cambridge University Press (pp. 181–214).

Rutter, M. (1997). Nature–nurture integration: the example of anti-social behaviour. *American Psychologist*, 52, 390–8.

Sabates, R. and Feinstein, L. (forthcoming). Effects of government initiatives on youth crime. Oxford: Oxford Economic Papers.

Sacerdote, B. (2000). *The Nature and Nurture of Economic Outcomes.* NBER Working Paper 7949.

Sacerdote, B. (2004). *What Happens When We Randomly Assign Children to Families?* Unpublished manuscript.

Sacker, A., Schoon, I. and Bartley, M. (2002). Social inequality in educational achievement and psychosocial adjustment throughout childhood: magnitude and mechanisms. *Social Science & Medicine*, 55, 863–80.

Saint-Paul, G. (1996). Unemployment and increasing returns to human capital. *Journal of Public Economics*, 61, 1–20.

Sameroff, A. (1983). Developmental systems: contexts and evolution. In W. Kessen (ed.), *Handbook of Child Psychology* (vol. 1: *History, Theory, and Methods*). New York: Wiley (pp. 237–94).

Sameroff, A. and Chandler, M. J. (1975). Reproductive risk and the continuum of caretaker casualty. In F. D. Horowitz (ed.), *Review of Child Development Research* (vol. 4). Chicago, IL: University of Chicago Press.

Sameroff, A., Bartko, W. T., Baldwin, A., Baldwin, C. and Seifer, R. (1998). Family and social influences on the development of child competence. In M. Lewis and C. Feiring (eds), *Families, Risk, and Competence.* Mahwah, NJ: Lawrence Erlbaum Associates (pp. 161–86).

Sammons, P. (1999). *School Effectiveness: Coming of Age in the Twenty-first Century.* London: Lisse, Swets and Zeitlinger.

Sammons, P., Sylva, K., Melhuish, E., Siraj-Blatchford, I., Taggart, B. and Elliot, K. (2002). *Technical Paper 8a: Measuring the Impact of Pre-school on Children's Cognitive Progress over the Pre-school Period.* London: Institute of Education.

Sammons, P., Sylva, K., Melhuish, E., Siraj-Blatchford, I., Taggart, B., Elliot, K. and Marsh, A. (2004). *The Effective Provision of Pre-school Education (EPPE) Project: Technical Paper 11. Report on the Continuing Effects of Pre-school Education at Age 7.* London: DfES/Institute of Education.

Sammons, P., Sylva, K., Melhuish, E., Siraj-Blatchford, I., Taggart, B., Grabbe, Y. and Barreau, S. (2007). *Summary Report. Influences on Children's Attainment and Progress in Key Stage 2: Cognitive Outcomes in Year 5.* London: DfES, Research Report No. 828.

Sampson, R. J., Raudenbush, S. W. and Earls, F. (1997). Neighborhoods and violent crime: a multilevel study of collective efficacy. *Science*, 277, 918–24.

Sandgren, S. and Strom, B. (2006). *Peer Effects in Primary Schools: Evidence from Age Variation.* Unpublished paper. Dragvoll, Norway.

Schaefer, E. (1959). A circumplex model for maternal behavior. *Journal of Abnormal and Social Psychology*, 59, 226–35.

Schneider, B. and Coleman, J. (1993). *Parents, Their Children, and Schools.* Boulder, CO: Westview Press.

Schoon, I., Bynner, J., Joshi, H., Parson, S., Wiggins, R. D. and Sacker, A. (2002). The influence of context, timing, and duration of risk experiences for the passage from childhood to mid-adulthood. *Child Development*, 73, 1486–504.

Schulenberg, J., Vondracek, F. W. and Crouter, A. C. (1984). The influence of the family on vocational development. *Journal of Marriage and the Family*, 10, 129–43.

Schultz, P. T. (1981). *Economics of Population*. Reading, MA.: Addison-Wesley.

Schultz, T. W. (1961). Investment in human capital. *American Economic Review*, L1 (1–17).

Schwartz, C. R. and Mare, R. D. (2005). Trends in educational assortative marriage from 1940 to 2003. *Demography*, 42 (4), 621–46.

Schweinhart, L., Weikart, C. and Larner, M. (1986). Consequences of three pre-school curriculum models through age fifteen. *Early Education Research Quarterly*, 15–45.

Seefeldt, C., Denton, K., Galper, A. and Younoszai, T. (1999). The relation between Head Start parents' participation in a transition demonstration, education, efficacy and their children's academic abilities. *Early Childhood Research Quarterly*, 14 (1), 99–109.

Seginer, R. (1983). Parents' educational expectations and children's academic achievements: a literature review. *Merrill-Palmer Quarterly*, 29, 1–23.

Sénéchal, M. and LeFevre, J. (2002). Parental involvement in the development of children's reading skill: a five-year longitudinal study. *Child Development*, 73 (2), 445–60.

Sénéchal, M., LeFevre, J., Thomas, E. and Daley, K. (1998). Differential effects of home literacy experiences on the development of oral and written language. *Reading Research Quarterly*, 32, 96–116.

Shea, J. (2000). Does parents' money matter? *Journal of Public Economics*, 77 (2), 155–84.

Sianesi, B. and Van Reenen, J. (2003). The returns to education: macroeconomics. *Journal of Economic Surveys*, 17 (2), 157–200.

Sigle-Rushton, W. and McLanahan, S. S. (2002). The living arrangements of new unmarried mothers. *Demography*, 39 (3), 415–33.

Singh, K., Bickley, P. G., Keith, T. Z., Keith, P. B., Trivette, P. and Anderson, E. (1995). The effects of four components of parental involvement on eight-grade student achievement: structural analysis of NELS-88 data. *School Psychology Review*, 24 (2), 299–317.

Skidmore, P., Bound, K. and Lownsbrough, H. (2006). *Community Participation: Who Benefits?* York: Joseph Rowntree Foundation.

Slaughter, D. T. and Epps, E. G. (1987). The home environment and academic achievement of black American children: an overview. *Journal of Negro Education*, 56, 3–20.

Slavin, R. E. (1990). Achievement effects of ability grouping in secondary schools: a best-evidence synthesis. *Review of Educational Research*, 60, 471–99.

Smith, J. R., Brooks-Gunn, J. and Klebanov, P. K. (1997). The consequences of living in poverty for young children's cognitive and verbal ability and early school achievement. In G. J. Duncan and J. Brooks-Gunn (eds), *Consequences of Growing Up Poor*. New York: Russell Sage Foundation (pp. 132–89).

Smith, T. E. (1989). Mother–father difficulties in parental influence on school grades and educational goals. *Sociological Inquiry*, 59, 88–91.

Sorhaindo, A. and Feinstein, L. (2006). *What Is the Relationship Between Child Nutrition and School Outcomes?* Research Report No. 18. London: Centre for Research on the Wider Benefits of Learning, Institute of Education.

Stein, A., Gath, D. H., Butcher, J., Bond, A., Day, A. and Cooper, P. (1991). The relationship between post-natal depression and mother-child interaction. *British Journal of Psychiatry*, 158, 46–52.

Steinberg, L. (1990). Challenges in studying minority youth. In S. Feldman and G. Elliot (eds), *At the Threshold: The Developing Adolescent*. Cambridge, MA: Harvard University Press.

Steinberg, L., Elmen, J. D. and Mounts, N. S. (1989). Authoritative parenting, psychosocial maturity, and academic success among adolescents. *Child Development*, 60, 1424–36.

Steinberg, L., Lamborn, S. D., Dornbusch, S. M. and Darling, N. (1992). Impact of parenting practices on adolescent achievement: authoritative parenting, school involvement and encouragement to succeed. *Child Development*, 63 (5), 1266–81.

Steinberg, L., Lamborn, S. D., Darling, N., Mounts, N. and Dornbusch, S. M. (1994). Over-time changes in adjustment and competence among adolescents from authoritative, authoritarian, indulgent, and neglectful families. *Child Development*, 65, 754–70.

Sternberg, A. and Wikstrom, M. (2004). Higher education and the determination of aggregate male employment by age. *Education Economics*, 12 (1), 87–101.

Stevens, J. H. Jnr (1982). *Child Development Knowledge and Parenting skills*. Paper presented at the Annual Meeting of the American Educational Research Association, New York.

Stevens, J. H. Jnr (1984). Child development knowledge and parenting skill. *Family Relations*, 33, 237–44.

Stevens, R. J. and Slavin, R. E. (1995). The cooperative elementary school: effects on students' achievement, attitudes, and social relations. *American Educational Research Journal*, 32, 321–51.

Strand, S. (1997). Pupil progress during Key Stage 1: a value added analysis of school effects. *British Educational Research Journal*, 23 (4), 471–88.

Sullivan, A. (2001). Cultural capital and educational attainment. *The Journal of the British Sociological Association*, 35 (4), 893–912.

Sylva, K., Siraj-Blatchford, I., Melhuish, E., Sammons, P., Taggart, B., Evans, E. Dobson, A. (1999). *Technical Paper 6 – the Effective Provision of Pre-school Education (EPPE) Project: Characteristics of the Centres in the EPPE Sample: Observational Profiles*. London: DfEE/Institute of Education, University of London.

Taylor, R. D., Casten, R. and Flickinger, S. (1993). The influence of kinship social support on the parenting experiences and psychosocial adjustment of African-American adolescents. *Developmental Psychology*, 29, 382–8.

Teti, D. D., Gelfand, C. M., Messinger, D. S. and Isabella, R. (1995). Maternal depression and the quality of early attachment: an examination of infants, preschoolers, and their mothers. *Developmental Psychology*, 31, 364–76.

Tzeng, M. S. (1992). The effects of socioeconomic heterogamy and changes on marital stability. *Journal of Marriage and the Family*, 54, 609–19.

UNICEF. (2002). *A League Table of Educational Disadvantage in Rich Nations.* Innocenti Report Card No. 4, November 2002. Florence: UNICEF Innocenti Research Centre.

Uribe, F. M. T., Levine, R. A. and Levine, S. E. (1993). Maternal education and maternal behavior in Mexico: implications for the changing characteristics of Mexican Immigrants to the United States. *International Journal of Behavioral Development*, 16, 395–408.

van Bakel, H. J. A. and Riksen-Walraven, J. M. (2002). Parenting and development of one-year-olds: links with parental, contextual and child outcomes. *Child Development*, 73 (1), 256–73.

Wachs, T. D. (2000). *Necessary But Not Sufficient*. Washington, DC: American Psychological Association.

Wagner, B. M. and Phillips, D. A. (1992). Beyond beliefs: parent and child behaviors and children's perceived academic competence. *Child Development*, 63, 1380–91.

Webster-Stratton, C. (1990). Long-term follow-up of families with young conduct-problem children: from preschool to grade school. *Journal of Clinical Child Psychology*, 19 (2), 144–9.

Webster-Stratton, C. and Hammond, M. A. (1997). Treating children with early-onset conduct problems: a comparison of child and parent training interventions. *Journal of Consulting and Clinical Psychology*, 65 (1), 93–109.

Weiner, B. (1985). An attributional theory of achievement motivation and emotion. *Psychological Review*, 92, 548–73.

Wentzel, K. R. (1993). Does being good make the grade? Social behavior and academic competence in middle school. *Journal of Educational Psychology*, 85, 357–64.

Werner, E. E. (1989). Vulnerability and resiliency: a longitudinal perspective. In M. Brambring, F. Lösel and H. Skowronek (eds), *Children at Risk: Assessment, Longitudinal Research and Intervention*. Berlin: Walter de Gruyter.

Werner, E. E. and Smith, R. S. (1992). *Overcoming the Odds. High Risk Children from Birth to Adulthood*. Ithaca, NY: Cornell University Press.

West, J., Wright, D. and Hausken, E. G. (1995). *Child Care and Early Education Program Participation of Infants, Toddlers, and Preschoolers*. Washington, DC: US Department of Education.

Wigfield, A. (1994). Expectancy-value theory of achievement motivation: a developmental perspective. *Educational Psychology Review*, 6, 49–78.

Wigfield, A. and Asher, S. R. (1984). Social and motivational influences on reading. In P. D. Pearson, R. Barr, M. L. Kamil and P. Mosenthal (eds), *Handbook of Reading Research* (vol. 1). White Plains, NY: Longman (pp. 423–52).

Wigfield, A. and Eccles, J. S. (1992). The developmental of achievement task values: a theoretical analysis. *Developmental Review*, 12, 265–310.

Wigfield, A., Eccles, J. S., MacIver, D., Reuman, D. and Midgley, C. (1991). Transitions at early adolescence: changes in children's domain-specific self-perceptions and general self-esteem across the transition to junior high school. *Developmental Psychology*, 27, 552–65.

Wiggins M., Rosato M., Austerberry H., Sawtell M. and Oliver S. (2005). *Sure Start Plus National Evaluation: Final Report 2005*. London: Social Science Research Unit, Institute of Education, University of London.

Wilson, W. J. (1997). *When Work Disappears*. New York: Knopf.

Wolfe, B. (1980). Childbearing and/or labour force participation: the education connection. *Research in Population Economics*, 2, 365–86.

Wolfe, B. and Haveman, R. (2002). *Social and Non-market Benefits from Education in an Advanced Economy*. Paper presented at Education in the 21st Century: Meeting the Challenges of a Changing World. Federal Reserve Bank of Boston (Conference Series 47). Boston, MA.

Wooldridge, J. M. (2002). *Econometric Analysis of Cross Section and Panel Data*. Cambridge, MA: MIT Press.

Wößmann, L. and Schütz, G. (2006). *Efficiency and Equity in European Education and Training Systems*. Analytical Report for the European Commission prepared by the European Expert Network on Economics of Education (EENEE).

Young, R. A. and Friesen, J. D. (1992). The intentions of parents in influencing the career development of their children. *Career Development Quarterly*, 40, 198–207.

Index